A HISTORY OF BRITAIN AND THE WORLD

A Five-year Course for Grammar Schools

by

C. F. STRONG, O.B.E., M.A., Ph.D.

BOOK FIVE

THE TWENTIETH CENTURY AND THE CONTEMPORARY WORLD

THE HEADQUARTERS OF THE UNITED NATIONS IN NEW YORK

This group of three buildings, standing on the banks of the Hudson against a background
of skyscrapers, was designed under the direction of an international architectural committee.
The foundation stone was laid in 1949, and the General Assembly met there first in 1952.
The tall vertical block houses the Secretariat; the stone building (with dome), beside it, is
the meeting-place of the General Assembly; the low building in front, on the water's edge,
contains halls for the meetings of U.N. Councils

THE
TWENTIETH CENTURY
AND THE
CONTEMPORARY
WORLD

C. F. STRONG
O.B.E., M.A., Ph.D.

*Formerly Director of Education for Tottenham.
Sometime History Master at Sloane School,
Chelsea. Author of "Modern Political Constitu-
tions," "The Story of the American People,"
"Dynamic Europe," etc.*

UNIVERSITY OF LONDON PRESS LTD
WARWICK SQUARE, LONDON E.C.4

A History of Britain and the World

BOOK ONE	THE ANCIENT AND EARLY MEDIEVAL WORLD
BOOK TWO	THE WORLD OF THE MIDDLE AGES
BOOK THREE	THE EARLY MODERN WORLD
BOOK FOUR	THE LATER MODERN WORLD
BOOK FIVE	THE TWENTIETH CENTURY AND THE CONTEMPORARY WORLD

First printed 1956
Second Edition 1959
Third Edition *Copyright* © *1961* by C. F Strong

Printed and bound in England for the UNIVERSITY OF LONDON PRESS, LTD.,
by HAZELL WATSON & VINEY LTD., Aylesbury and Slough

PREFACE

THIS book recounts the history of the twentieth century so far as it has gone, and presents a picture of the contemporary world; the world, that is to say, as it is in the age in which we live. This is, perhaps, the most difficult of all periods to write or to read about, because, during the twentieth century, social, economic and political life has become much more complicated than in any earlier epoch, and the sources of information about it have grown correspondingly more numerous and varied. Yet no period is of greater interest and importance. Moreover, the study of the contemporary world is a proper part of the study of history, since, as has been truly said, "although history did not happen in order to produce the present, it has in fact done so".

This book thus concludes our History of Britain and the World. It is, nevertheless, complete in itself and may be read independently of the four previous volumes in the series. This, of course, does not mean that the twentieth century can be understoood apart from its background in earlier periods. Hence, before proceeding to the main story, I have tried in the Introduction briefly to place the twentieth century in the setting of the living past from which it has emerged.

The story of this half-century seems to fall naturally into the three parts into which I have divided it, taking the First World War as the central topic of Part One, the Second World War as the pivotal point of Part Two, and the continuing problem of world peace as the main theme of Part Three. But here, perhaps, a word of warning is advisable. A book dealing with the history of the contemporary world is bound to suffer from the apparent arbitrariness of its stopping-place, and readers may look in vain for references to very recent events. Technically, this difficulty is imposed by the nature of book production and the unavoidable time-lag between the final stages of preparing a book for the press and the moment of its actual publication. Besides, although a contemporary historian may hope to encourage an intelligent reading of newspapers, it is no part of his business to produce " stop-press news". Hence, in the later chapters of this book I am concerned not to announce the latest events but rather to prepare the ground for a discerning view of current affairs. Therefore, in revising the subject-matter for this new edition, I have tried to bring it up to date with the least possible disturbance of the text, confining myself to cases where vital changes have since occurred or where the later sequence of events seemed to require emphasis. For the rest, I have extended the chronological table on page 345.

The book is thus designed not only for those preparing for an examination on the period but also for students wishing to be acquainted with this vital story as the indispensable background to science and other modern studies.

I gratefully acknowledge the encouragement which I have received from friends and colleagues in the planning of this series, and I wish specially to thank Mr. H. Raymond King, M.A., Headmaster of Wandsworth School, London; Mr. E. W. Edwards, M.A., Lecturer in the University College of South Wales and Monmouthshire; and Mrs. Eve Edwards, B.A., for their constant help and advice at the various stages of the preparation of this book. My thanks are also due to Mr. W. R. Hecker, M.A., B.Sc., Headmaster of St. Dunstan's College, Catford, for his expert aid with the chapter on Science and Civilisation, and to Mr. W. E. Payne, M.A., Senior History Master at Wandsworth School, for his valuable suggestions about books for further study.

London, 1961   C. F. STRONG

CONTENTS

CONTENTS

PART THREE

THE UNITED NATIONS AND THE
PROBLEM OF WORLD PEACE

ILLUSTRATIONS

The pictures in this book are on separate pages facing the text. The reader will find each picture referred to under its subject in the Index, where, whenever a topic is so illustrated, the number of the page which the picture faces is printed in heavy type.

LIST OF MAPS

LIST OF CHARTS AND DIAGRAMS

ACKNOWLEDGMENTS

ACKNOWLEDGMENTS are due to the following for permission to reproduce illustrations in this book:

The Associated Press, Camera Press, Ltd., Central Press Photos, Ltd., William Collins Sons & Co., Ltd., the Exclusive News Agency, Fox Photos, Ltd., the Imperial War Museum, International News Photos, the Kemsley Picture Service, the Keystone Press Agency, the Mansell Collection, Marconi's Wireless and Telegraph Co., Ltd., Mirrorpic, the Northern Nigerian Information Service, the *Nursing Mirror*, the *Pakistan News*, the Hulton Picture Library, the Portuguese State Information and Tourist Office, the Royal Society, the *Soviet Weekly*, Topical Press, Ltd., the Turkish Embassy, the United Nations, the United States Information Service, and the Wright-Fleming Institute.

INTRODUCTION

BACKGROUND OF THE TWENTIETH CENTURY

THE twentieth century, so far as it has gone, has been a time of unprecedented ferment and change. But, although the changes of our epoch are in many respects peculiar to the twentieth century, the significance of this half-century cannot be appreciated except in the light of the past from which it has emerged. The crucial fact of this period is that it has been dominated by two world wars more universal in their range, more devastating in their action, and more revolutionary in their consequences than any previous wars. Yet the ultimate causes of those wars are not to be found in the century in which they occurred. For the twentieth century alone did not create the political divisions which encouraged the wars, or the social and economic conditions which aggravated them, or the technological advances which made them so deadly, or the diplomatic methods which failed to prevent them.

It is true that, when the new century dawned, the darkest portents of disturbance and disaster were scarcely visible on the international horizon. On January 1, 1901, Adolf Hitler was still a schoolboy in Austria; Benito Mussolini was just about to become a schoolmaster in Italy; and Joseph Stalin had only recently been expelled, for his political views, from a theological college in Georgia. But the roots of the theories and systems which those men of action were later to vitalise lay in the past, and, from some points of view, even in the remote past. It is that living past which has shaped the contemporary world in its political, social, economic, cultural and spiritual aspects. A brief survey of that past is therefore necessary to get the twentieth century in proper perspective.

The modern world owes much to the ancient past, for it was then that the foundations of Western civilisation were laid. The Greeks bequeathed to us their many-sided culture, the Romans their conception of law and order, and the founders of the Christian Church their spiritual way of life. These origins of our common inheritance, however, were greatly indebted to Eastern civilisations. In fact, Western and Eastern cultures constantly impinged upon each other long before modern European empires were established in Asia, and certainly many centuries before the West bestowed on the East the dubious gift of modern technological civilisation. The Greek civilisation, thus reinforced by Eastern influences, was carried by the Romans to Western Europe, and through this Græco-Roman world the Romans also made possible the spread of Christianity, which in the fourth century became the sole official religion of the Empire.

The decline of the Roman Empire in the West was hastened by the invasions of the Teutonic peoples, who broke across the imperial frontiers in the fourth and fifth centuries. The Roman government was finally overthrown and replaced by kingdoms established by the Visigoths in Spain, the Franks in Gaul, the Lombards in Italy, and the Anglo-Saxons in Britain. This infusion of German blood transformed the Romanised West. The principal survivor from the wreck of the old Roman order was the Christian Church, with its centre at Rome. It succeeded in converting the conquerors, and through its alliance with the Franks created a new Empire in the West when in 800 the Pope crowned the Frankish King Charlemagne as Emperor. This act gave a new significance to the Catholic Church, which through the remaining centuries of the Middle Ages dominated the religious and educational life of Western and Central Europe. The old Græco-Roman culture thus lost much of its original character and became dimmed by the interpretations of ecclesiastical scholars. And not until after the passage of several centuries was the eclipse dispelled by the enlightenment of the great movement known as the Revival of Learning.

In theory the medieval Empire was united and universal, but in practice Europe was constantly moving towards the division into separate states which we know to-day. At first the disintegrating forces were mainly three: the break-up of Charlemagne's Empire, the attacks of the Norsemen, and the spread of Islam. In 843 Charlemagne's dominions were divided between his three grandsons, and in 962 the Pope crowned as Emperor a Saxon king of Germany, Otto the Great. Thus was established the Holy Roman Empire of the German Nation, which continued as a German institution, with a special interest in Italy as the home of the Pope, until it faded out of existence in 1806. Its persistence long after it could serve any useful political purpose had the effect of delaying the national unification of Germany and Italy until the second half of the nineteenth century.

The raids of the Norsemen, which began at the end of the eighth century, affected most of the countries of Europe. The Swedes, otherwise called Ruotsi or Rus, crossed the Baltic, and, penetrating the lands of the Slavs as far south as the Black Sea, mingled with the northern Slavs, to whom they gave the name Russians. The Danes, together with some Norwegians, made permanent settlements in Western Europe, gradually mixing with the Anglo-Saxons in eastern England and with the French in northern France. From their Duchy of Normandy the French Norsemen, or Normans, conquered England in the eleventh century. They thus added fresh blood to the existing Anglo-Saxon-Danish stock, and from this fusion of peoples the English nation finally emerged.

Meanwhile, the old Roman Empire in the East continued to exist under the name of Byzantine Empire, which, with its capital, Constantinople, forming a bridge between the Western and Eastern worlds, developed an important medieval civilisation of its own. Yet, although it survived the fall of the Roman Empire in the West by a thousand years, during most of that time its existence was threatened by the rising tide of Islam, which finally overwhelmed it. Within a century of the death of

Mohammed, the founder, in 632, Islam held sway under his successors (Caliphs) over an empire extending from Spain in the west to the borders of India in the east, which finally broke up into three Caliphates based on Baghdad in Mesopotamia, Cairo in Egypt, and Cordova in Spain. Each of these cities became the centre of a rich culture which greatly influenced medieval life and learning and thus contributed to the growth of Western, as well as Eastern, civilisation.

The Mohammedan attack on Christendom in the southeast of Europe, which failed under the Arabs in the eighth century, succeeded under the Turks in the fourteenth century. The Seljuk Turks, in their westward movement from inner Asia, conquered the Empire of the Arabs and were converted to their faith, and it was against them that the Crusades were fought in the twelfth and thirteenth centuries. In their turn the Seljuks gave way to the Ottoman Turks, who systematically prepared an attack on Europe. They crossed the Dardanelles in 1355, captured Constantinople in 1453, and during the two succeeding centuries swept through the Balkans, conquered Hungary, and were not held until they reached the very gates of Vienna. So originated the tangled Balkan problem which continued into the present century.

While the lands of the eastern Mediterranean were thus falling a prey to the Mohammedan Turks, in Italy there developed out of the medieval learning of the West, which in its later days was strongly influenced by Arabic scholarship, a movement destined to reawaken Europe to the forgotten origins of its culture. Beginning in the fourteenth century with the revival of the study of classical languages, the Renaissance became a revolution in art and science, which, with the aid of the newly introduced craft of printing, spread rapidly from Italy to the rest of Western Europe. The Renaissance was one of the great formative movements in world history. It not only opened the minds of Europeans to the grandeur of their ancient heritage but gave a secular emphasis to education, hitherto dominated by the Church. By undermining that

14

domination, the Renaissance brought the Middle Ages to a close and heralded the dawn of modern times.

The new age fully opened with the voyages of exploration which, towards the close of the fifteenth century, resulted in the charting of a direct sea route, via the Cape of Good Hope, to India and the Far East, and in the discovery of America. These explorations were encouraged by the new horizons disclosed by the Renaissance and assisted by the science of astronomy, the invention of the mariner's compass, and the creative study of geography, for which Marco Polo, through his travels in the Far East during the last quarter of the thirteenth century and his book about them, was largely responsible. The importance of this Age of Discovery in helping to shape the modern world cannot be exaggerated. It brought about an Oceanic Revolution which ended the great days of the Mediterranean as a maritime highway and gave to the western states of Europe a new position in the middle of the known world, whereas they had hitherto been on its edge. These were the states thus destined to found overseas empires, to Europeanise America, and to carry Western civilisation to the lands of the more ancient civilisations in the East.

The disintegration of the medieval world caused by the effects of the Renaissance and the voyages of discovery was completed by the Protestant Reformation in the Church, which began in 1517 when Martin Luther attacked the sale of indulgences by the Pope. Luther's revolt brought about the most extraordinary upheavals. It split Europe into two armed camps, and led to years of warfare and persecution. It created Protestant Churches in countries hitherto Catholic, and so led the way to the growth of Established Churches and of new sects outside the control of the State; in this sense it opened the road which ultimately led to the modern practice of religious toleration. Moreover, it prompted the movement for reform in the Catholic Church itself, known as the Counter-Reformation.

The religious wars resulting from the Reformation led to

the revolt of the Netherlands from Spain and the foundation of the Dutch Republic, and to a series of civil wars in France which ended in the establishment of the Bourbon dynasty. England, where the Anglican Church had been definitively established on the accession of Elizabeth I in 1558, played a vital part in these struggles, particularly through her defeat of the Spanish Armada in 1588. The ultimate results were disastrous for Germany, where the Thirty Years' War (1618–48) ended in the recognition of no fewer than 343 separate states. Finally, the religious wars brought about the decline of Spain, and hence of Portugal, as the leading imperial Powers, and left the road clear for the eighteenth-century struggle for empire between Britain and France. But they still left the Catholic Church the great international society which it remains to-day.

While Germany was being thus atomised and the imperial sun of Spain was setting, France was moving towards her most brilliant epoch under Louis XIV. At that time, when continental states were governed by absolute monarchs, a constitutional struggle between King and Parliament was going on in England. The final settlement in 1689 established the principle of government by King in Parliament. In the following century the British evolved the Cabinet system, a method of responsible government later adopted by British Self-governing Dominions and, indeed, by most states in Europe and others in various parts of the world, which thus acknowledged their indebtedness to the British legislature as the "Mother of Parliaments". The eighteenth century, too, saw the emergence of Prussia under the Hohenzollerns as a rival to Austria under the Hapsburgs for the ultimate hegemony of Germany, and the rise of Russia as a Power on the European scene through the policies of Peter the Great and his successors. At that time also the imperial struggle between Britain and France led to the destruction of the French political power in America and India and left Britain supreme overseas.

During the second half of the eighteenth century occurred three revolutions—the Industrial, the American, and the

French—which certainly rank among the most formative factors in the background of the twentieth century. Out of the Industrial Revolution, which began in Britain and later spread not only through Europe but to all the other continents, developed the Machine Age in which we live to-day. The simple spinning and weaving inventions with which it began were succeeded by the application of steam-power to industrial machines, by steam navigation, and by the locomotive. The mechanical revolution was thus followed by a revolution in transport, which, again starting in England in the second quarter of the nineteenth century, gradually spread all over the world. The revolt of the American Colonies and the War of Independence (1775–83) resulted in the establishment of the United States and the ultimate growth of a new world Power across the Atlantic. The French Revolution, which broke out in 1789, destroyed the Old Régime and, through the military victories of Napoleon, disseminated the democratic seed through the European continent, and aroused a sense of nationalism which became militant in the nineteenth century.

After the fall of Napoleon in 1815, there was a period of reaction, against which the oppressed peoples revolted in 1830 and 1848. Although at the time these revolutions were suppressed, they were followed in the second half of the century by the unification of Italy (1859–71) and Germany (1864–71), the creation of the Third Republic in France (1871–5), and the recognition of the sovereign independence of Serbia, Rumania and Montenegro (1878). National unity was also behind the struggle of the North against the South in the American Civil War (1861–5), for, although the question of Negro slavery caused it and slavery was abolished as a result of it, the main issue was the fate of the American Union, which was ultimately preserved by the victory of the North.

Militant nationalism having created unified states in continental Europe, the Industrial Revolution, which each of them experienced, drove them first to the protection of their new industries by tariff walls and next to the search for world

N.B.

markets. Hence there followed an outburst of imperialism, which arose from a combination of the political force of nationalism and the economic force of the Industrial Revolution. Moreover, the Industrial Revolution was producing, in its turn, a scientific and technological revolution, which intensified the growth of methods of transport and communication, speeding up travel, annihilating distance, and facilitating the process of emigration from Europe to other parts of the world. It also led to the production of armaments of unprecedented power and deadliness, which placed the under-developed peoples of the world at the white man's mercy. The result was a scramble for colonies, as well as for markets, which, towards the close of the nineteenth century, brought about the partition of Africa, the dismemberment of China, and the awakening of Japan.

Thus the modern world was imposing on the ancient classical and Christian foundations of Western civilisation an increasingly heavy technological superstructure. But at the end of the nineteenth century the risks attending this process of social architecture were only dimly and fitfully appreciated. The danger lay in the fact that, while the scientific genius of Western man was producing techniques of world scope and significance, his political development was still confined within the limits of the nation-state. So far, that is to say, he had invented no effective diplomatic machinery for the international control of the forces which his technical skill was letting loose on the world. That was the hidden peril of the general situation as the nineteenth century closed. The crucial problem of the twentieth century, which became progressively acute as the century advanced, was therefore how to save the whole top-heavy structure of civilised society from toppling in ruins.

PART ONE

DEMOCRACY AND THE FIRST WORLD WAR

Chapter 1

THE WORLD AT THE OPENING OF THE TWENTIETH CENTURY

MACHINES AND A SHRINKING WORLD

IN Europe the twentieth century opened in an atmosphere of optimism. From the standpoint of material progress, Western civilisation had undoubtedly reached its highest point of development so far. Generally speaking, the conditions of life for most people were more comfortable and secure than at any time since the dawn of the Machine Age. The internal organisation of most states, based on national unity, seemed to promise an increasing enjoyment of liberty. The international situation, superficially at least, also encouraged a hopeful outlook. Britons and Boers, it is true, were engaged in a bitter struggle in South Africa, but, apart from local conflicts in the Balkans, there had been general peace in Europe for almost thirty years, since the end of the Franco-German War in 1871. That general peace, however, was not to continue far into the twentieth century, and the outbreak of the First World War in 1914 quickly proved how false was the optimism with which the century had dawned.

The world at the opening of the twentieth century was shrinking, not, of course, in an absolute physical sense but in a relative social sense. The advance of science and technology was bringing the different parts of the world into closer touch with one another than ever before. Transcontinental railways already linked Europe and the Far East of Asia, and the Atlantic and Pacific coasts of North America, while the locomotive was beginning to appear in remote places up to then

19

barely explored by Europeans. The internal-combustion engine had arrived as a means of locomotion, and in the early years of the century motor transport was already supplementing the railways in many different parts of the world.

Steamships were crossing the oceans at unprecedented speeds, already covering the journey from Europe to America, for example, in six days. The telegraph and telephone set up communications between places hitherto unconnected except by post, while nearly half a million miles of submarine cable joined the continents. In 1899 Marconi had succeeded in sending a message by wireless telegraphy across the English Channel, and was carrying out further experiments which resulted two years later in his sending one across the Atlantic. That amazing achievement, moreover, was only the precursor of the still greater marvel of wireless telephony, which was not far off. Meanwhile, aeronautical engineers in various countries were hopefully experimenting with what were then called "flying machines". In that vast potential sphere of mechanical transport the first solid success was accomplished by the American brothers, Orville and Wilbur Wright. In 1903, by attaching a petrol engine to a glider, they made a series of short flights in a heavier-than-air machine and thus inaugurated the era of the aeroplane.

An important development associated with the progress of the internal-combustion engine, in both automobiles and aeroplanes, was a rapid expansion of the mining of petroleum for power and the production of rubber for tyres. Petroleum was discovered in parts of America, in Russia, Rumania, Persia, and the Dutch East Indies, while rubber plantations began to be intensively cultivated in Brazil, Africa, Ceylon, Malaya, French Indo-China, and tropical Africa. The exploitation of these areas for such technical purposes helped to break down their isolation and so supplemented the work of mechanical transport in annihilating the distances which had divided the regions of an older world.

WORLD POPULATION AND ECONOMIC
INTERDEPENDENCE

Thus European man, with the aid of his machines, was, in effect, causing the world to shrink, and yet, by that same means, enlarging it by bringing hitherto little-known areas within the ambit of his economic activities. But, even more significantly, this technological advance was accompanied by progress in the application of medical science which had the effect of lengthening human life and reducing the death-rate, first among the more highly developed communities and later in the more backward areas of the world. The consequent expansion of the world, in human terms, was already evident in the nineteenth century, for during that century the total population of the world had almost doubled, from about 900 millions in the year 1800 to nearly 1,600 millions in 1900.

During the first fourteen years of the twentieth century the rate of population increase accelerated to an annual average of 15 millions, or twice the average of the previous century, so that by the time of the outbreak of the First World War it was about 1,800 millions. Of these numbers Europe accounted for 180 millions in 1800, 400 millions in 1900, and 460 millions in 1914; and Great Britain for 10 millions in 1800, 38 millions in 1900, and 43 millions in 1914. This world trend of increase has not only continued but quickened in more recent years, and the total population of the world is now estimated to be rising at the rate of more than 50 millions a year, or more than treble the average of the earlier years of the century. As, proportionately, this increase is much heavier in Asia than elsewhere, the consequent change in the balance of human forces presents the contemporary world with a profound social and political problem, which we must discuss in a later chapter.

This remarkable growth of population was accompanied by the migration of people from some parts of the world to others. In the nineteenth century 40 millions emigrated from Europe, and, what is more striking, 9 million Chinese left their native

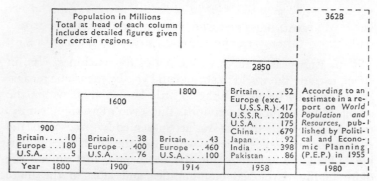

Population in Millions. Total at head of each column includes detailed figures given for certain regions.				
				3628
			2850	
		1800	Britain......52 Europe (exc. U.S.S.R.).417 U.S.S.R. ...206 U.S.A......175 China......679 Japan.......92 India ......398 Pakistan 86	According to an estimate in a report on *World Population and Resources*, published by Political and Economic Planning (P.E.P.) in 1955
	1600			
900 Britain.....10 Europe ...180 U.S.A. 5	Britain.....38 Europe . .400 U.S.A. 76	Britain.....43 Europe ...460 U.S.A.....100		
Year 1800	1900	1914	1958	1980

GROWTH OF WORLD POPULATION IN THE NINETEENTH AND
TWENTIETH CENTURIES

land. The Europeans went chiefly to America and Australia, but the Chinese went not only to America but also to parts of tropical Asia. At the opening of the twentieth century these movements were reaching their height. Between 1906 and 1910 the annual average from Europe was nearly 1½ millions, and the entry into the U.S.A. alone for the decade 1900–10 was the highest ever—namely 8,795,386. Equally remarkable was the movement from European to Asiatic Russia. More than 3½ millions went in the nineteenth century and almost as many in the first dozen years of the twentieth century. Yet these migrations did not stop the rise of population in Europe, which continued to grow in spite of these drains upon its stock.

When the twentieth century opened, Europe, despite the rapid growth of the United States, was still the economic centre of the world. It was from Europe, and especially from Britain, that most of the money flowed to finance the great commercial and industrial undertakings following in the wake of the New Imperialism which had led to the partition of Africa among the European Powers and the dismemberment of China. In fact, the steamship, the railway, the telegraph, the telephone and the cable had made the world one market based on Europe. For example, Britain imported four-fifths of her wheat, France a third of her coal, and Germany most of her wool. Moreover, this world-wide interchange of goods carried with it an interchange of capital and the organisation of national companies with international affiliations. Thus, in spite of the fact that most states adopted a policy of protection, there was a world-wide economic interdependence.

THE POLITICAL SITUATION IN EUROPE

In the field of politics the world of the twentieth century inherited from the nineteenth century the ideal of national democracy, and at the opening of the century most European states were applying it as a principle of government. That is to say, there was a general spread of liberalism in government which, while securing the national cohesion of the state, aimed at ensuring for its members a widening enjoyment of democratic rights and liberties through the instrumentality of an elected legislature. This system had, of course, originated in Britain, where, by the beginning of the twentieth century, although the ideal of universal adult suffrage had not yet been realised, political democracy was more advanced than in any other country except, perhaps, Switzerland.

The essence of the British system in its modern form is not merely that it postulates an elected legislature, or Parliament, but that it involves the principle of responsible government; that is to say, the executive power in the government is exercised by a body of Ministers, called the Cabinet, which is responsible to Parliament. It was the presence or absence of this principle of responsibility which differentiated the states of Europe at the opening of the twentieth century. Generally speaking, the line of cleavage was between the states in the west of Europe which enjoyed Cabinet government, and the imperial states of Germany, Austria-Hungary, Russia and Turkey which retained an element of autocracy.

France remained loyal to the Third Republic, which had been finally established in 1875 after her defeat in the war with Germany. At the head of the Third Republic was the President, elected for a seven-year term by the Senate and Chamber of Deputies sitting together as the National Assembly. The President acted through the Prime Minister and Cabinet, who were responsible to the Chambers. Italy, which had achieved its unification through stages culminating in the occupation of Rome in 1871, was under the constitutional monarchy of the House of Savoy. For that royal house the century opened with tragedy. In 1900 King Humbert, who in 1878 had succeeded his father, Victor Emmanuel II, the first King of United Italy, was assassinated by an anarchist, and was succeeded by his son, Victor Emmanuel III. The King of Italy, like the monarch in Britain, acted politically through a Cabinet responsible to Parliament, a system which continued until the Fascists undermined it after the First World War. Spain and Portugal, too, were constitutional monarchies each with a Parliament and Cabinet, although neither worked smoothly and both were later abolished.

The Low Countries—that is, Belgium and the Netherlands —were each monarchies working through Cabinets responsible to Parliament. Both countries enjoyed great economic prosperity round about the opening of the century, although Belgium was much more industrialised. The three Scandinavian kingdoms—Denmark, Norway and Sweden—were all monarchical constitutional states. Norway, which had been joined to Sweden since 1814, established herself as an independent state in 1905, and, like Denmark, moved rapidly along the democratic road, using Parliament for the passing of much social legislation. But the most democratic state in continental Europe was Switzerland. Like the United States of America, it was a federal republic, comprising a number of districts, or cantons, and known as the Swiss Confederation.

The constitutional situation in the Empires of Germany, Austria-Hungary, Russia and Turkey was different from that in Western Europe. The German Empire, which Bismarck had created in 1871, had a legislature with two Houses, of which the lower, called the *Reichstag*, was a representative assembly. But, although it was elected on a broad franchise, it had little effective power, because the chief Minister, called the Imperial Chancellor, was responsible not to the *Reichstag* but to the Emperor (*Kaiser*). Imperial Germany, however, had been founded on military success, and nothing short of defeat in war could destroy it.

The Dual Monarchy of Austria-Hungary was organised in accordance with a compromise, known as the *Ausgleich*, reached in 1867, under which Austria and Hungary were each recognised as autonomous under the Emperor of Austria, who was also King of Hungary. The constitution established in each part a separate Parliament, which was elected by the people and to which the Ministers were largely responsible. The presence of groups of dissatisfied Slavs in each part of the dual state complicated the problem of representative government. A constitutional revision in 1907 attempted to satisfy the claims of the Slavs in the Austrian part by granting them separate racial constituencies, but, as we shall see, such political contrivances could not save the "Ramshackle Empire" of Austria-Hungary from disintegration eleven years later at the end of the First World War.

In Russia no real attempt was made before the twentieth century to satisfy the demands of moderate reformers who wished to establish a Parliament on the Western model as a means of limiting the Czarist autocracy. Only the Russian disasters in the war with Japan (1904–5) forced the hands of the Czar, who agreed to the establishment of a Parliament, or *Duma*, which was inaugurated in 1906. But, as you will read later, the parliamentary experiment failed and was finally overwhelmed in 1917 by the Bolshevik Revolution.

In Turkey a parliamentary constitution had been proclaimed in 1876, but, in spite of the efforts of reformers to make it work, it remained a dead letter, and the autocratic government of the Sultan was not finally overthrown until after the First World War.

AMERICA, ASIA AND AFRICA

By the opening of the twentieth century the various peoples of European origin who occupied the American continent had successfully struggled through the main formative phase of their national development, and the political map of America was, broadly speaking, as we know it to-day. The Dominion of Canada, Newfoundland (which did not become a province of the Dominion until 1949) and the United States filled most of the northern continent, the frontier between them running, for the western half of its length, along the 49th parallel. The rest of the mainland, stretching from the southern border of the United States along the Rio Grande to the southernmost point at Cape Horn and known as Latin America, was occupied, almost exclusively, by seventeen independent republics, all Spanish-speaking except Brazil which was of Portuguese origin. Between North and South America lay the many Caribbean islands, including Haiti and the Dominican Republic.

By this time the United States had carried the westward-moving frontier to the Pacific Ocean and had opened up the former Wild West, although Oklahoma, Arizona and New Mexico, besides Alaska and Hawaii, had yet to be admitted to complete the Union of fifty states. Shortly before the century opened, the United States had defeated Spain in the war of 1898, and as a result of it occupied the West Indian island of Cuba, which the Spanish agreed to evacuate, and had gained also the Spanish island of Puerto Rico in the Caribbean, and the island of Guam and the Philippine archipelago in the Pacific. Thus the United States passed beyond its continental frontiers and became an imperial Power. The spirit of this New Imperialism was personified in Theodore Roosevelt, who in 1901 became President of the "United States and its Insular Possessions", and who carried through the negotiations for the cutting of the Panama Canal, which in 1915 was to be finally opened to world traffic.

American merchants had long had commercial interests in

the Pacific, but the United States now assumed heavy political responsibilities there, at the very time when the European Powers, urged on by the New Imperialism, were feverishly engaged in dismembering China and unwittingly encouraging the emergence of Japan as a first-class Power. This European process of "sewing a modern hem along the edge of an ancient garment", which had been going on since the middle of the nineteenth century, reached its climax in the last two years of the century with the arrival of Germany on the Far Eastern scene. This led to the final scramble among the European Powers for spheres of influence in China with which the century closed. This, then, was the position in the Far East at the opening of the twentieth century. First, the ancient Chinese Empire was in a state of rapid decay. Secondly, Britain, Russia, France and Germany had each been granted a lease of a vital port and base of power on the coasts of China proper. Thirdly, Japan was undergoing a political and technological revolution, which at length enabled her not only to dominate China but to challenge the European Powers themselves in the Pacific.

A similar scramble for "places in the sun" occurred in Africa towards the close of the nineteenth century. There, at the opening of the twentieth century, the position was that tropical Africa, hitherto called the "Dark Continent", was carved up among the Powers of Europe, each of whom thus acquired colonies which they could exploit as they wished. In the north, while the destination of Morocco and Tripoli had still to be settled, Egypt was governed under the guidance of a British Consul-General (Lord Cromer) and the Sudan under an Anglo-Egyptian Condominium. In South Africa the war between the British and the Boers, which had broken out in 1899, continued its course, and with this unhappy burden Imperial Britain entered the twentieth century.

Chapter 2

THE UNITED KINGDOM AND THE EMPIRE
(1900–14)

THE SOUTH AFRICAN WAR

AT the opening of the twentieth century the United Kingdom of Great Britain and Ireland was still the centre of a far-flung Empire which then constituted the most powerful, wealthy and heterogeneous group of communities in the history of the world. It was spread across all the oceans, which were commanded by British sea-power, and it occupied large spaces, in both temperate and tropical zones, in every continent of the globe. It included great Self-governing Dominions like Canada, vast dependencies like India, Crown Colonies like Hong Kong, Protectorates like Bechuanaland, occupied areas like Egypt, besides the Condominium of the Anglo-Egyptian Sudan, and regions where its suzerainty was in force, such as the princely states of India. Its various parts ranged in size from the Crown Colony of Gibraltar, with an area of $2\frac{1}{4}$ square miles, to the Dominion of Canada, with an area of over 3 million square miles.

As the twentieth century dawned the present pattern of the British Commonwealth of Nations was clearly emerging. That the people of Canada, Australia and New Zealand were conscious of their identity as separate nations was proved by their political organisation, which in Canada and Australia took the form of a federation, the Dominion of Canada having been founded in 1867 and the Commonwealth of Australia being inaugurated on January 1, 1901. The standing of these new overseas nations under the British Crown was already recognised in the meetings known as Imperial Conferences, which were well established by the close of the nineteenth century. In India, too, and in certain of the colonies, local opinion was beginning to be consulted through native representatives on councils, whose function was to advise the government on the spot.

In the course of the growth of this vast Empire wars had been frequent, but at the beginning of the twentieth century there was general peace except in one part of it, namely South Africa. At that time a Conservative Government was in power under Lord Salisbury, who was then serving his third period as Prime Minister. This Conservative Government had come into power as the result of the election of 1895. It was Salisbury's third Cabinet, but his first to be formed from both Conservatives and Unionists. The Unionists were the former Liberals who had broken with William Gladstone over Irish Home Rule in 1886. The revolt was led by Joseph Chamberlain, who was now one of Salisbury's most vigorous and powerful colleagues. He held the office of Secretary of State for the Colonies, and in this position had to bear the brunt of the difficulties which led in 1899 to the outbreak of war in South Africa between the British and the Dutch settlers (or Boers, a Dutch word meaning farmers).

This South African War was the culmination of a long period of Boer discontent, which had been seething ever since the Great Trek in 1836 when the Boers had left British South Africa and founded the independent republics of the Transvaal (afterwards called the South African Republic) and the Orange Free State. There had, in fact, been an earlier war in 1880–1, when the Boers demanded the restoration of the independence which they had lost through their inability to cope with the hostility of the Zulus. The first Boer War, in which the British had suffered serious military defeat, led to the regranting of independence to the Boer republics. Anglo-Boer relations became embittered once more after the discovery of gold in the Transvaal in 1886, which led to a gold rush and the growth of a large non-Boer community, mainly British, in Johannesburg. These *Uitlanders* (or outsiders), as the Boers called them, pressed for a share in social and political rights, which Paul Kruger, the President of the South African Republic, denied them.

After the failure of the Jameson Raid, which was an attempt on the part of the Uitlanders to force the issue by the illegal use of arms in 1895, relations between the two sides further deteriorated. Several attempts were made to find a peaceful settlement, but they all failed, and in 1899, when Britain refused to withdraw her troops from the Transvaal borders, Kruger declared war. Thus Britain was involved in what proved to be her first serious armed conflict since the Crimean War nearly fifty years before. The war was fought with great bitterness on both sides. At home it split the Liberal Party into three: the Liberal Imperialists, who fully approved it; the "pro-Boers", who wanted to stop it; and a middle group who reluctantly agreed that, once started, it must be fought out. Abroad it brought on Britain the criticism and odium of most of the Powers, including France and Germany.

At first the British suffered serious reverses, which aroused the patriotic feelings of the nation. Thousands of men, not only in Britain but in the overseas Dominions, volunteered for service in South Africa. Generals Roberts and Kitchener, famous for their services in India and Egypt, were sent out to retrieve the situation. In the first six months of 1900 Roberts captured Bloemfontein and Pretoria, the Boer capitals, and the two republics were annexed to the Empire. Kruger escaped to Holland and Roberts returned home, leaving Kitchener to round up the remaining guerrilla Boer commandos, who maintained the unequal struggle for another eighteen months. Not until May 1902 did the Boers sue for peace, which was finally made by the Treaty of Vereeniging. The British made a large grant to help to restore the neglected farms of the demobilised Boers, permitted the Afrikaans (South African Dutch) language to be taught in schools, and promised self-government, which was

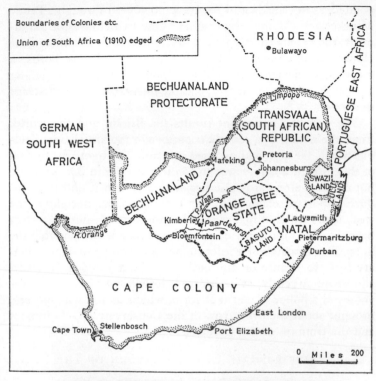

SCENE OF THE SOUTH AFRICAN WAR, 1899-1902
Showing also the boundaries of the Union of South Africa (1910).

granted to the Transvaal in 1906 and to the Orange Free State in 1907.

Soon afterwards the first steps were taken towards the union of the four colonies (Cape of Good Hope, Natal, Transvaal and the Orange Free State). In 1908 a convention of representatives from all four met, and in 1909 agreed to form the Union of South Africa, which was inaugurated in 1910. Under this constitution powers were granted to a central government, leaving local powers to each of the four parts, which were called provinces. A Governor-General, representing the King, was ap-

31

pointed, as in Canada and Australia, to govern through a Prime Minister and Cabinet responsible to the two Houses of Parliament: the Senate (partly nominated and partly elected) and the House of Assembly, elected by the people. Louis Botha, a great Boer statesman as well as a noble military commander against the British in the war, became the first Prime Minister of the Union.

The war had important results for Britain and the world. First, the nation was acutely conscious of the anti-British feeling which the war had aroused abroad. The immediate effect of this foreign hostility was to confirm Britain in her isolation, but not long afterwards she began to abandon it and to introduce important changes in her foreign policy. Secondly, the weaknesses which it had revealed in the British military system brought about a reform of the army, which made possible the immediate dispatch of a fully trained and equipped expeditionary force to France on the outbreak of war in 1914. Thirdly, and more urgently, it reinforced Joseph Chamberlain's advocacy of a policy of Tariff Reform, which, as you will now see, brought about the overthrow of the Conservative Government and the triumph of the Liberals.

TARIFF REFORM AND THE RETURN OF THE
LIBERALS

In January 1901, in the middle of the South African War, Queen Victoria died after a remarkable reign of sixty-four years, and was succeeded by her son, Edward VII, a monarch of a very different stamp, who was already sixty on his accession. He was very popular both at home and abroad, where he was known as the "Uncle of Europe". He played very little part in politics, but his love for France undoubtedly eased the growth of improved Anglo-French relations which marked his reign. Meanwhile, in 1900 Parliament had been dissolved, and the Conservatives under Lord Salisbury had been again returned as a result of the "Khaki Election", so called from the colour of the British soldier's war-service uniform and the fact that the election made a special appeal to the war-time patriotism of the people. In 1902 Lord Salisbury resigned and was succeeded as Prime Minister by his nephew, Arthur Balfour, who, however, retained most of his uncle's ministers, including Joseph Chamberlain as Colonial Secretary.

As soon as the war was over, the Conservative Government turned to peace measures, which, although some of them were excellent in intention and effect, aroused the hostility of large sections of the nation. First, in 1902, Parliament passed an important Education Act, which is a landmark in the history of education in England. The Act abolished the School Boards, established in 1870, and transferred their powers to the County and County Borough Councils, which were given the duty of developing secondary as well as elementary education. It also empowered the council of any borough or district with a certain minimum population to administer elementary schools. A further provision of the Act brought the Church schools within the public system by arranging for the cost of education in those schools to be defrayed by public funds while leaving with their managers the control of religious teaching, the appointment of teachers, and the duty of maintaining the buildings. This part of the Act aroused the passionate resentment of the Nonconformists, who organised a movement of "passive resistance" to the payment of rates. Although this opposition died down and the Act was made to work, the cry of financing sectarian teaching was used with great effect against the Conservatives at the next election.

Next, in 1904 Parliament passed a Licensing Act whose object was to reduce the number of public-houses in certain districts. The Act proposed that where a publican's licence was withdrawn for reasons of redundancy, he should receive compensation to be met by a levy on the brewery trade. This aroused the anger of the temperance movement, largely composed of Nonconformists, who denounced the measure as a "Brewers' Bill" and accused Balfour of "endowing the trade". The Act, in fact, proved to be socially beneficial, but it provided the ground for another powerful anti-Conservative cry at the polls. A third Conservative measure sanctioned the importation of Chinese unskilled labourers, or Coolies, into South Africa, where labour was short in the gold-mines. Tens of thousands of Coolies thus came to South Africa, where they lived in compounds in the most degrading conditions. The trade unionists and others in Britain naturally denounced what they called this "Chinese slavery", which caused a great revulsion of feeling against the government.

The issue which finally settled the fate of Balfour's government was Joseph Chamberlain's campaign for Tariff Reform, which its originator called Fair Trade. His aim was to knit the Mother Country and her Colonies more closely through mutual economic benefits. He therefore proposed to put a tax on certain imported articles and then to reduce it for such articles imported from the various parts of the Empire. This scheme of Imperial Preference, as it was called, implied the end of Free Trade on which for half a century the bounding prosperity of Britain had been built. Moreover, since the only considerable commodities which the Colonies had to export were agricultural and pastoral products, Chamberlain's plan inevitably involved taxes on food, which meant a rise in the cost of living. Hence the working people were solidly against it. To be free to devote himself to his new crusade, Chamberlain resigned from the Colonial Office, and to strengthen his campaign formed the Tariff Reform League.

The effect of Chamberlain's insistence on Tariff Reform was to split the Conservative Party and to heal the rupture caused by the Boer War among the Liberals. Balfour, unable to close the Conservative ranks, resigned in 1905, and was replaced by Campbell-Bannerman at the head of a Liberal Cabinet. Parliament was then dissolved, and in January 1906 there was a General Election in which all the accumulated grievances of Nonconformists, temperance supporters, working men and Free Traders were concentrated against the Conservatives. The result was that the Liberals were returned with a majority of no less than 84 over all other parties and groups combined. The Liberals won 377 seats against only 157 gained by the Conservatives and Unionists, of whom about 100 were Chamberlainites. Even more significant was the election of no fewer than 53 Labour members. Of these, 29 sat as an independent party; the remaining 24 sat with the Liberals and were hence called "Lib-Labs". One of them, John Burns, the foremost leader in the great dock strike of 1889, joined Campbell-Bannerman's Ministry, and thus became the first Cabinet Minister drawn from the ranks of Labour. The election was indeed a triumph for the Liberals, who did not fail to make the most of their new opportunities.

THE LIBERAL REFORMS

The opening years of the twentieth century in Britain showed the effect of the great social changes which had taken place in the second half of the nineteenth century. The vastly increased population, concentrated in rapidly growing towns and their suburbs, the extension of the franchise and the spread of popular education had created a new society more conscious of its rights and more clamant for its liberties. A trade depression at the beginning of the century caused unemployment and discontent, which resulted in a number of strikes. The Conservative Government had attempted to regulate the problem of unemployment by the Unemployed Workmen Act, which empowered the Local Government Board to keep a register of the unemployed, a plan out of which later grew the general provision of Labour Exchanges. But the only long-term policy which they could suggest was the protection of industry against the free importation of foreign goods in the hope of encouraging employment at home, a policy decisively rejected in the election of 1906.

The Liberals, on the other hand, offered a policy of social reform which would give to the workers at the same time greater security and a larger share of the national wealth. To carry out such a programme, the Liberals had not only an absolute majority in the House of Commons and a strong Labour backing, but also a number of talented Cabinet Ministers. Besides Herbert Asquith and David Lloyd George, these included Edward Grey, a great Foreign Secretary, John Morley, an enlightened Secretary for India, and Richard Haldane, who, as Secretary for War, reformed the military system and founded the Territorial Army.

Several Acts were passed to improve conditions of employment in mines and factories. A Workmen's Compensation Act of 1906 greatly extended the benefits provided by the first Act of the kind passed during the Conservative administration in 1897. In 1909 another Act established Trade Boards, composed of employers and employees, to secure minimum wages in certain "sweated industries". In the same year Labour Exchanges were established to help the unemployed to find work. In 1912, following a miners' strike, new legislation enforced a minimum wage for all mine workers. Meanwhile, in 1906 a new law permitted local authorities to provide free meals for necessitous school-children. In 1908 a more comprehensive Act provided for the care of children in need of protection and for the treatment of juvenile offenders. It also ensured the free medical examination and care of children and free medical attention for mothers at the birth of their children. In the same year Parliament also passed the first Old Age Pensions Act. Besides all this, a housing and town planning Act of 1909 authorised local authorities to condemn and demolish insanitary houses and tenements and to put up model dwellings in their place.

At length came the great National Insurance Act of 1911. Part I of the Act laid down a broad scheme of insurance for many categories of workers against sickness. To build up the necessary funds for the financing of the scheme, employers, employees and the Treasury were all to contribute. The already existing friendly societies, as well as the trade unions, were brought in to help to administer the scheme and ensure its smooth working. The medical profession, which at first raised several objections to the scheme, finally agreed to co-operate. The plan, which has been much extended since, undoubtedly raised the standard of national health. Part II of the Act provided for unemployment insurance in certain trades on the same contributory basis.

The same liberal spirit informed the Royal Commission which had been appointed in 1905 to inquire into the working of the Poor Law as it had operated since the last major amendment of it in 1834, and which reported in 1909. While all its members agreed on certain measures, such as the suppression of the then existing system of workhouse and relief administration by Guardians, there were, in fact, two reports, the majority report and the minority report. The minority report became the more influential in succeeding years, for it, in fact, suggested the prevention of destitution by an extension of social insurance.

THE BUDGET OF 1909 AND THE PARLIAMENT
ACT OF 1911

In 1908, on the retirement of Campbell-Bannerman, Herbert Asquith became Prime Minister and Lloyd George Chancellor of the Exchequer. These two statesmen were very different from each other in origin and background, although they both ended their political careers as earls in the House of Lords. Asquith, a member of a Yorkshire family of Congregationalists, was a brilliant scholar who had carried off all the classical prizes at Oxford and became a barrister before he entered Parliament in 1886. Lloyd George, the son of a poor Baptist schoolmaster, was educated at a Welsh elementary school but managed later to qualify as a solicitor. In 1890, at the age of 27, he was elected M.P. for Caernarvon Boroughs, a seat which he held without a break for the next fifty-five years. Yet they were both ardent Liberals and, as such, shared the responsibility for the introduction of the new social legislation.

Of the political storms caused by the new Liberal policy, none was more violent than that aroused by Lloyd George's Budget of 1909. The Budget was designed primarily to meet the cost of the new social services, of the increased naval estimates, and of government plans for the development of motor transport. Apart from new indirect taxes on tobacco, beer, spirits, motor-cars and petrol, the direct taxes proposed included higher death duties, a slightly increased income-tax, and the introduction for the first time of super-tax on high incomes. But what caused the heaviest storm was the proposal to introduce duties on land values, or what was called "unearned increment" on the growing value of land, as well as a duty on the capital value of undeveloped land and on mineral resources. The landlords called this a "doctrine of confiscation". As their interests were mainly represented in the House of Lords, the Conservative leaders decided on a fatal step. When the Budget, having passed the Commons by a huge majority, came up to the Lords for their formal approval, they refused to pass it.

Now, although there was no actual law which said so, it had been a recognised convention of the Constitution for at least two and a half centuries that Money Bills were the sole concern of the Commons and that their submission to the Lords was merely a matter of form. When, therefore, the Lords vetoed the Budget of 1909, the Commons resolved that the Lords' action was a breach of the Constitution. The government decided to seek the support of the electorate. Parliament was, therefore, dissolved, and in January 1910 there was a General Election in which the Conservatives were again heavily defeated, for, although the Liberals actually had a majority of only two over the Conservatives, with the addition of Labour and Irish votes they could muster a majority of 124 on the issue of the Lords' Veto. The Budget was immediately passed by the Commons, and the Lords then approved it without a division.

The government next proceeded to prepare a Bill, called the Parliament Bill, to restrict the Lords' powers by statute law; but party disputes were silenced for a time by the death of King Edward VII, who was succeeded by his son, George V.

When the controversy was resumed, an all-party conference was held, but it failed, and in December 1910 a second election produced almost exactly the same balance of parties as in the previous January. In 1911 Asquith reintroduced the Parliament Bill, which passed the Commons and went to the Lords, who tried to amend it. Thereupon Asquith advised the King to create sufficient Liberal peers to secure the passage of the Bill. This threat was sufficient to force most of the Lords to give way, although some, called "Die-Hards", determined to fight "in the last ditch", and in August 1911 the Bill passed the Lords and became law.

The main provisions of the Act were three: (1) that any Bill, certified by the Speaker as a Money Bill, becomes law one month after being passed by the Commons, whatever the Lords may do; (2) that any non-money Bill, if passed by the Commons in three successive sessions, even though rejected each time by the Lords, becomes law two years after its original introduction in the Commons; (3) that the maximum life of a Parliament is five years. The Bill foreshadowed the ultimate reform of the composition and functions of the Lords, but nothing has since been done to give effect to that proposal. All that has happened is that in 1949 the period of the Lords' suspensive veto was reduced to one year and in 1958, by an Act permitting the creation of Life-Peers, women were for the first time admitted to the House of Lords.

INDUSTRIAL UNREST AND THE IRISH HOME RULE QUESTION

During the first fourteen years of the twentieth century there was much industrial unrest leading to frequent strikes, which became even more intense after 1910. In 1901 the trade unions had had a serious set-back by a legal decision in what was known as the Taff Vale Case. The Taff Vale Railway Company won an action for damages against the Amalgamated Society of Railway Servants for losses caused by a trade dispute. The Union appealed against the judgment, and in the end the case went to the House of Lords, as the final Court of Appeal, but the Lords upheld the decision of the lower court. The decision seemed to deprive the unions of most of their hard-won rights. In 1906, however, the Trade Disputes Act made it illegal for any court in future to consider such actions for damages against trade unions.

Another case arose in 1909 when a branch secretary of the Amalgamated Society of Railwaymen, named Osborne, challenged the right of a union to demand from all its members a contribution to a political fund, whether a member wished to pay it or not. This case, too, went finally to the House of Lords, which delivered what was called the Osborne Judgment declaring the enforced levy illegal. This was a body-blow to the unions, but their right to make a compulsory political levy was restored by the Trade Union Act of 1913, although, as you will see, the question arose again after the General Strike of 1926.

Such decisions as these tended to make some trade unionists despair of constitutional methods, and they turned away from the hope of building up an effective Parliamentary Labour Party to the intensive use of the strike weapon. Hence between 1910 and 1912 there was a positive epidemic of strikes, especially on the railways and in the mines. Nevertheless, many responsible trade union leaders remained loyal to the parliamentary ideal, and there was a gradual reaction in favour of political action, particularly after the introduction of payment of members in 1911, which relieved the unions of the previous financial burden of maintaining their parliamentary representatives by grants from their funds.

Strife was not confined to the industrial field: it was also employed as a weapon by a large body of women who demanded the vote. From about 1907 the militant movement for woman suffrage organised by the women's Social and Political Union, under such leaders as Mrs. Pankhurst and Mrs. Pethick Lawrence, grew in violence. Outrages, such as window-breaking and the burning down of pillar-boxes, were of frequent occurrence, and when the women were imprisoned they went on hunger-strike. The movement continued until 1914, when internal dissensions were stilled by the external peril, and not until the last year of the First World War was the first Act passed to give women the vote.

Finally, violence was used in Ireland to prevent the implementation of the Home Rule Act, which was passed in 1912 and, since the Lords vetoed it, would become effective in 1914 under the provisions of the Parliament Act. The Act, by which the Liberals redeemed a pledge to their Irish supporters then under the leadership of John Redmond, proposed a separate Parliament in Dublin for the internal affairs of the whole of Ireland, while the Parliament at Westminster was to remain the Parliament of the United Kingdom, to which Ireland was to continue to send representatives. The plan was opposed both by Republican groups in the Catholic south and by the majority in the Protestant north. In the north the Ulster Volunteers were recruited to fight for the right to remain part of the United Kingdom. They were organised by an Irish barrister and M.P. named Edward Carson, supported by many Conservatives, and were actually helped in their training by British army officers stationed in that part of Ireland.

Thus by the spring of 1914 the British Government was faced with a civil war in Ireland which it would be bound to suppress by armed force. But, just when civil war seemed unavoidable, it was averted by the European crisis, in face of which the parties pledged their support of the government in the war. In September 1914, therefore, the third Home Rule Bill became law, but with the proviso that the Act should rest in abeyance until after the war, when an amending Bill was to be considered. Events in Ireland during and after the war, however, sealed the fate of Home Rule as conceived before it, and in the end a much more radical solution of the Irish question had to be found.

Chapter 3

THE APPROACH OF THE FIRST WORLD WAR

THE BALANCE OF POWER

AT the opening of the twentieth century the peace of Europe
was maintained through a balance of power based on two
opposing alliances: the Triple Alliance of Germany, Austria
and Italy, completed in 1882; and the Dual Alliance of France
and Russia, formed in 1894. They were defensive alliances,
only to become effective if any member of the one attacked
any member of the other, with a special proviso in the case of
the Triple Alliance that in no circumstances should Italy be
required to fight against Great Britain. Britain, following her
traditional policy of avoiding entanglement in the diplomatic
complications of continental Europe, had remained outside
these alliances. But after the Boer War and in the face of
German naval rivalry, she began to feel acutely the dangers of
her isolation. Yet, as things turned out, her first move away
from her isolation was not towards a European Power but
towards one in the Far East, namely Japan.

The extraordinary political and technological revolution
through which Japan had passed in the later years of the
nineteenth century drove her to seek expansion at China's
expense. The obvious areas for her to exploit were Manchuria
and Korea. Here, however, the danger for Japan was a clash
with Russia, who was pursuing an equally aggressive expansionist policy in the Far East, and who, if war should ensue,
might be joined in arms by her ally France. The surest way to
counteract such a threat was for Japan to find a European ally.
In these circumstances, Japan approached Britain, who was

naturally anxious to discourage Russia from further encroach-
ment on Chinese territory. Consequently, in 1902 the Anglo-
Japanese Alliance was formed. Its main condition was that, if
either party were attacked by two Powers in combination, the
alliance should come into armed effect.

Russia, who underestimated Japanese strength, continued
her active policy in the Far East, and in 1904 this led to the
outbreak of war with Japan. France and Britain remained
interested spectators of this war in which a newly-risen Asiatic
force overwhelmingly defeated one of the Great Powers of
Europe by Western weapons and methods. When peace was
made by the Treaty of Portsmouth in 1905, Russia had to
surrender to Japan her lease of Port Arthur and to abandon her
projects of expansion in Manchuria, although she retained
control of the Chinese Eastern Railway to Vladivostok. The
general effect of the war was to leave both Manchuria and Korea
without defence against Japanese exploitation.

Besides thus establishing Japan as the dominant Power in
the Far East, the Russo-Japanese War had two other effects
of world importance. First, the growing weakness of China
led in 1911 to a revolution which overthrew the Manchu
dynasty and established a republic in its place. Secondly, in
Russia the disasters of the war caused a popular revolt which
not only forced the Czar to establish the *Duma*, or Parliament,
but revealed the growing strength of disruptive forces which
were eventually to establish the Communist régime.

THE TRIPLE ENTENTE AND ANGLO-GERMAN
RIVALRY

Meanwhile, in Europe the diplomatic situation was changing
through the growth of better relations between Britain and
France. In 1904 the two countries entered into a series of
agreements which came to be known as the *Entente Cordiale*,
or cordial understanding. These agreements, which settled
outstanding colonial differences, chiefly in Africa, helped to
dispel Britain's sense of isolation in Europe and gave France

a greater feeling of confidence about the future, especially in view of the growing threat of Germany's hostility. There was a disturbing example of this danger in 1905 when the Kaiser, William II, visited Morocco, which was then generally recognised as being under the influence of France, who had reached agreements on the subject with Britain and Spain. At Tangier the Kaiser made a speech declaring that Germany did not recognise these agreements and that she stood for the independence of Morocco. This utterance led to what was called the first Moroccan crisis, which was followed in 1906 by a conference of the Powers concerned at Algeciras. The principal effect of the conference was to tighten the bonds of Anglo-French friendship. In fact, the two countries held secret discussions about possible military arrangements in the event of war, although they did not make a formal alliance.

Russia, greatly weakened through her humiliating defeat by Japan, also felt the need of a further counterpoise to German strength. Consequently, in 1907 Britain and Russia started discussions by which they reached agreement over Asian affairs, as Britain and France had already done over Africa. The agreements covered policies with regard to Tibet and Afghanistan, as well as Persia which the parties agreed to divide into British and Russian "spheres of influence". In this way the *Entente Cordiale* between Britain and France was broadened into a larger understanding known as the Triple Entente. Germany chose to regard this understanding as an encirclement of herself by hostile forces, at a time when she was seeking what the Kaiser called "a place in the sun" worthy of her military greatness and economic growth. That growth was, indeed, remarkable, for in the second half of the nineteenth century the population of Germany rose by 50 per cent., her foreign trade trebled itself, and her mercantile marine grew at a tremendous pace. Hence the Germans needed more markets for the increasing manufactures which their resources made possible and their industry produced.

This urge explains the three main lines of German policy

up to 1914. First, Germany determined to play a more decisive role in colonial affairs and particularly in Africa. This accounted for the three Moroccan crises which German conduct precipitated: the first in 1905, already referred to; the second at Casablanca in 1908; and the third at Agadir in 1911. The last was so serious that it nearly caused a European war. Germany, in fact, sent a gunboat to the port of Agadir in an attempt to prevent the establishment of a French Protectorate over Morocco. For the moment the question was amicably settled, but the Agadir Incident was regarded as a danger-signal to the world. Secondly, Germany sought a sphere of influence in the eastern Mediterranean (Levant), which implied a drive through the Balkans to the East (*Drang nach Osten*). Here Germany envisaged a continuous chain of power, linked by a railway from Berlin to Baghdad.

Thirdly, Germany developed a naval policy which was perhaps the gravest menace to the balance of power, since that balance depended largely on British sea supremacy. The basis of British practice in naval ship production had long been what was called the two-Power standard, meaning that Britain's navy should be equal to the navies of any two other Powers combined. In 1906 Britain built the first "all-big-gun turbine-driven battleship", which she called *Dreadnought*. The battle power of this ship was so great that it tended to render all pre-Dreadnought warships obsolete, and soon other countries, and especially Germany, were copying her design. As Germany planned to build more warships, she also proposed to widen the Kiel (or Kaiser Wilhelm) Canal, which was too small to carry warships of the Dreadnought type. The Kaiser prompted the naval programmes which were in the hands of his naval commander-in-chief, Admiral von Tirpitz, and backed by a powerfully interested body called the Navy League. It was evident, from these activities, that Germany was bent not only on building many more warships but also on using them in the North Sea, and Britain could not fail to realise the peril in which she might be placed by this naval policy of a Power with whose military might she could not hope to compete. Between 1909 and 1911, therefore, she entered into negotiations with Germany in an attempt to limit shipbuilding programmes. But Germany refused to agree to any limitation of naval armament unless it was accompanied by a treaty, which would have weakened Britain's links with France and Russia. Hence the negotiations broke down and the armaments race went on.

The dangerous atmosphere generated by the growing Anglo-German rivalry was made more tense by the race in land armaments in which all the Great Powers were indulging. These armaments, moreover, became more and more deadly as technological improvements were constantly applied to them, and it seemed that the mounting load might at any moment set the Continent ablaze.

INTERNATIONAL PEACE MOVEMENT

The great question was whether the international agencies working for peace could operate in time to forestall the disaster of war. There were a great number of such agencies all over the world. First, there were the technological advances, to which we have referred earlier. The more these developments drew the different parts of the world together into close co-operation and interdependence, the more they made war a manifest absurdity. Banking and insurance, too, had followed trade in binding nations together. Thirty states belonged to the Universal Telegraph Union formed in 1875, and sixty to the Universal Postal Union founded in 1875, with its headquarters at Berne in Switzerland. A convention for the standardisation of Patent Laws, first proposed in 1883, had been ratified by nineteen states, while copyright laws, as proposed in 1887, were made uniform in fifteen countries.

The Christian Churches (Protestant, Catholic and Orthodox) each formed a vast international society overstepping state boundaries. Other religious associations with international affiliations included Missionary Societies, the Evangelical Alliance, the Salvation Army, the Y.M.C.A. and Y.W.C.A., the

World's Student Christian Federation, and the World Alliance for Promoting International Friendship. But such societies were by no means confined to religious organisations. There were, for example, an International Parliamentary Union and also an International Agricultural Institute. There was the Red Cross Society, founded in 1864, to which all civilised nations belonged. There were, besides, international federations of trade unions and co-operative societies, while congresses were frequently held by such political bodies as socialist leagues and women suffrage organisations. Amateur sportsmen revived the Olympic Games in 1896 and business-men formed an international association of Rotary Clubs in 1912, while innumerable pacifist organisations held annual meetings to demand the limitation of armaments. Moreover, great industrialists, like Andrew Carnegie and Alfred Nobel, devoted a large part of their fortunes to the endowment of peace propaganda.

It was evident that the people did not want war. But governments, too, took a hand in the movement for peace. In America in 1881 the United States had invited the Latin American Republics to participate in a Pan-American Conference "for the purpose of considering and discussing the methods of preventing war between the nations of America", and further such conferences were held in later years in Washington and in various capitals of Latin America. Meanwhile, in Europe, on the initiative of the Czar of Russia, a conference was held at The Hague in 1899. The envoys of twenty-six states attended and discussed such questions as the limitation of armaments and the humanising of the methods of warfare. One lasting outcome of the Conference was the establishment at The Hague of a Permanent Court of International Arbitration for the peaceful settlement of disputes between nations. A second Hague Conference was held in 1907 and was attended by envoys of fifty-four states. It elaborated the conclusions of the earlier conference, and produced a great mass of memoranda on various international questions. It was agreed to call future meetings, but the Conference never met again.

The Czar, in his invitation to the first Hague Conference, had referred to the "horrors of war", which, he said, "make every thinking being shudder in anticipation". The matter, however, was less affected by ideals than by material forces which rapidly got beyond control. International societies and Hague Conferences could do no more than touch the fringe of the problem. The forces of political and economic nationalism, of capitalist imperialism, and of militarism, supported by armament interests, were too firmly entrenched in the soil of twentieth-century Europe to be dispersed by conference resolutions. So it appeared that all that the peoples of the world could do was to sit on the edge of the volcano until they were overwhelmed by the eruption. And when the eruption at length occurred, it was in the Balkans that it began.

THE BALKAN TANGLE

The last general settlement in the Balkans had been made at the Congress of Berlin in 1878, when, as we have seen, Serbia was made an independent state, Austria was granted a protectorate over Bosnia and Herzegovina, and Turkey was left with a continuous stretch of European territory running across the peninsula from Constantinople to the Adriatic. In the years that followed, the Balkan states, Rumania, Serbia, Montenegro and Bulgaria, each adopted a constitution on the Western model. But what was even more remarkable was the political revolution in Turkey. Although in 1876 a parliamentary constitution had been promulgated in Turkey, no Parliament had met for thirty years. In July 1908 a party known as the Young Turks organised a revolt at Salonika, demanding the implementation of the 1876 Constitution. To this the Sultan, Abdul Hamid II, at first agreed but afterwards recanted. In 1909, therefore, the rebels deposed him, and he was succeeded by his brother. Meanwhile, taking advantage of this disturbance, Austria had, in October 1908, annexed Bosnia and Herzegovina outright, while Bulgaria declared the independence of all her territories.

The professed object of the Young Turks in their revolution

HERBERT ASQUITH (1858-1928)
(afterwards Earl of Oxford) Liberal Prime Minister
(1908-16).

LOUIS BOTHA (1862-1919)
First Prime Minister of the Transvaal (1906-1910)
and of the Union of South Africa (1910-19)

THE FIRST DREADNOUGHT

The first all-big-gun turbine-driven battleship, built for the British Navy, passing out of harbour in 1906.

COUNT VON SCHLIEFFEN
(1833–1913)
Chief of the German General Staff (1891–1907).

THEOBALD VON BETHMANN
HOLLWEG (1856–1921)
German Imperial Chancellor (1909–17).

SARAJEVO
A general view of the Bosnian town where the Austrian Archduke Ferdinand was assassinated on June 28, 1914.

was to maintain their hold on their European territory and to "Ottomanise" it; that is to say, to impose the Turkish language, to control education, and to disarm the subject-peoples. This was an intolerable prospect to the Christian peoples of the Balkans, particularly in Macedonia, with its Bulgars, Greeks and Serbs all hoping to be joined to their brethren outside. Moreover, Austria's annexation of Bosnia and Herzegovina seemed to shut out Serbia from any hope of westward expansion to the Adriatic. These two facts led the Balkan states in 1912 to sink their differences and to form the Balkan League, which in the same year declared war on Turkey.

The First Balkan War which broke out in the autumn of 1912 was disastrous for the Turks, who were defeated at all points. The Greeks and Serbs overran Macedonia and captured Salonika, while the Bulgarians besieged Adrianople and drove the Turks back on Constantinople. The war ended with the Treaty of London, which deprived Turkey of all her European territory except Constantinople and its immediate environs. The Turks having been expelled, the victors now had to find a way of dividing the spoils. The London Conference decided to make Albania an independent state, thus depriving Serbia of her only outlet to the Adriatic. Serbia, therefore, refused to accept the findings of the Conference, and this caused the outbreak of the Second Balkan War in 1913.

Bulgaria, egged on by Austria, declared war on Serbia and Greece, who were later joined by Rumania, and even by Turkey who saw here her chance to recover some of her losses. The war was disastrous for Bulgaria. She was defeated in a few weeks, and by the Treaty of Bucharest, which ended the war, lost almost everything, including a million of the people she had gained from the first war. A strip to the north-east of Bulgaria (the Dobrudja) went to Rumania, Turkey recovered Adrianople, and Greece gained a small part of Macedonia and western Thrace. But Serbia was the greatest beneficiary, acquiring most of Macedonia at the expense of Bulgaria, who was left with one small outlet to the Ægean Sea.

AUSTRIA-HUNGARY AND THE BALKAN LANDS IN 1914
Showing the different nationalities within the Dual Monarchy.

Nothing could have been less auspicious for Austria's dream of expanding her influence to the Ægean than the Treaty of Bucharest. It set in her southern path a Serbia greatly increased in size, strength and prestige. The Serbs were now undoubtedly the strongest nation in the Balkans. Patriotic Serbs looked forward to the day when a great united Yugoslavia would emerge from the incorporation in one state of those Serbs, Croats and Slovenes who were still subjects of the Dual Monarchy of Austria-Hungary. Serbia was the natural nucleus of such an enlarged national state, as Piedmont had been of Italy and Prussia of Germany. But it was obvious that this meant the break-up of the multi-national Austro-Hungarian Empire, and Austria naturally determined to resist

50

it. In fact, from the moment of the making of the Treaty of Bucharest Austria set to work to undo it. Indeed, on the day before it was signed she actually invited Italy to join her in a war against Serbia; but Italy refused.

From then on relations between Austria-Hungary and Serbia became increasingly hostile. Some fiery South Slav patriots dreamed of achieving their ends by conspiratorial short-cuts, while Austria determined to prevent their dreams coming true. A certain body of opinion in Austria-Hungary thought that one solution would be to establish a triune kingdom, in which Austrian Germans, Magyars and Slavs should enjoy equal rights. The Archduke Ferdinand, the heir-apparent to the Austrian throne, was believed to favour such a solution, which was known as Trialism. It was, however, opposed both by the Magyars and by those Slavs who wished to see a Greater Serbia. The Powers meanwhile prepared for any eventuality. Germany increased her standing army by nearly a quarter of a million men and imposed a special tax for war purposes. France, having no more men to enlist, lengthened the period of compulsory military service from two to three years. Russia, too, expanded her army; while Britain went ahead with her enlarged naval programme and completed her preparations for an expeditionary force.

Here, then, as the year 1914 dawned, was a situation full of peril which only required a spark to start the blaze, and it is not surprising that the match was applied in the Balkans. There, on June 28, 1914, the Archduke Ferdinand and his wife, while on a visit to Bosnia, were murdered in the streets of Sarajevo, the capital.

Chapter 4

THE FIRST WORLD WAR

THE OUTBREAK OF WAR

THE causes of the assassination of the heir-apparent to the Austrian throne are still obscure. The actual perpetrator was a Serb named Princep, but there is no evidence to show that the Serbian Government had any previous knowledge of it. The news of the murder sent a thrill of horror through Europe, and the deed was naturally condemned by every government. To Austria it was a heaven-sent opportunity to settle accounts with Serbia, which, the Austrian Foreign Minister said, must now be "eliminated as a political factor in the Balkans". Accordingly, on July 23, 1914, Austria sent an ultimatum to Serbia. It contained ten points, eight of which Serbia accepted. The remaining two, which, if accepted as they stood, would have destroyed her independence, Serbia offered to submit to the Hague Court for arbitration. Austria declared Serbia's answer evasive and unacceptable, and began to mobilise. Serbia made the only possible reply and similarly mobilised.

While most of the Powers supported Serbia's arbitration proposal, Germany insisted that Austria and Serbia be left alone to fight the matter out, which, as Germany well knew, was tantamount to allowing Austria to annihilate Serbia. The German Government, apparently, thought that the three Entente Powers were so preoccupied with domestic difficulties —violent strikes in Russia, resistance to the new three-year military service law in France, and the Irish Home Rule controversy in Britain—that they would be unable to interfere. In this Germany entirely misjudged the situation, for the machinery of the alliances now came into operation, and events moved inexorably on to a general war. Thus when, on July 28, Austria declared war on Serbia, Russia immediately mobilised in Serbia's defence. Germany called on Russia to demobilise and, when she refused, declared war. This involved France under the Dual Alliance, and, when she began to mobilise, Germany declared war on her also.

Germany's strategy was to avoid war simultaneously on two fronts, by first making a rapid and overwhelming assault on France, before the slow-mobilising Russians could get into their stride, and then, turning east, to crush Russia in detail. To ensure a speedy victory over France, Germany had a plan, already long worked out and known from the name of its deviser as the Schlieffen Plan. Under this plan, in order to avoid the loss of time involved in reducing the French frontier fortresses, the Germans were to attack France by a circling movement through Luxemburg and Belgium. Accordingly, on August 2, the Germans invaded Luxemburg and delivered to Belgium a twelve-hour ultimatum demanding free passage for German troops. This was in direct defiance of the long-standing treaty, signed by the European Powers, including Britain and Germany, which guaranteed Belgian neutrality but which Bethmann-Hollweg, the German Chancellor, now called "a scrap of paper". Britain, however, kept her pledge, and, on August 4, declared war on Germany.

Probably Britain must sooner or later have entered the war in sheer self-defence against Germany's threat to control the southern littoral of the English Channel, a threat made more serious by the growing strength of the German navy. But the fact is that the German invasion of Belgium gave Britain's declaration of war a moral sanction and brought the nation solidly behind the government. The Self-governing Dominions, too, unanimously decided to fight on Britain's side, which was also joined by Japan under the terms of the Anglo-Japanese alliance. But before long the war involved other states. Italy, who at first declared her neutrality on the ground that her allies (the Central Powers) were not fighting a defensive war, in 1915 entered on the side of the Entente Powers (the Allies). The Central Powers were strengthened by the adhesion of Turkey, in November 1914, and Bulgaria, in October 1915, while the Allies were afterwards joined by Rumania, Portugal and China, and ultimately by the United States and some of the Latin American Republics.

So a local quarrel became a European conflict and then a world war. It was a new kind of war, not so much in its geographical extent—for there had been earlier wars fought simultaneously in four continents—as in its intensity, in the man-power and armaments involved, in the scale of its casualties and in the absorption of the people in its service. It was a war not of governments and armed forces merely, but of nations and, to some extent, of political ideas and systems. Moreover, it was the first war to disrupt the economy of the whole world, because, as we have seen, the various national economies had become so interdependent.

The course of the war confounded all the prophets. It was anticipated that the war would be short, and the Germans were confident that they would be "home by Christmas". Strategists held that there could be no effective reply to a series of rapid offensives made possible by the new engines of war. Economists contended that the cost would be so enormous that no nation would be able to bear the financial strain. All these forecasts were belied. The war lasted more than four years, and the cost, astronomical though the figures were, was met by improvisations of war finance undreamed-of by pre-war economic science. The offensive was met by the defensive device of deep trenches protected by aprons of barbed wire and the use of machine-guns, against which the infantry could not advance except after long preparatory artillery barrages, later assisted by the spraying of poison gas. What was expected to be a war of rapid manœuvre, therefore, became a war of fixed positions, a war not of dashing open movements but of attrition, or wearing down, in which victory went finally to

54

the side whose reserves of man-power, resources in materials, food supplies and fighting morale held out longest.

GERMANY IN THE ASCENDANT

The Germans very nearly brought off their western *coup* "before Christmas". They were in Brussels by August 20, after a gallant resistance by the Belgians who retreated to Antwerp. The British Expeditionary Force under Sir John French took up a position on the left of the French at Mons on the Belgian border, but both armies were forced to retreat. It seemed that nothing could save Paris, when, between September 4 and 9, the French right, under Marshal Joffre, turned on the invaders in the valley of the Marne. The Germans in the west had been momentarily weakened by an unexpected Russian invasion of East Prussia, which forced the German command to send two army corps post-haste from west to east. This slight easing of the pressure in the west gave Joffre his chance to drive the Germans back from the Marne to the Aisne. Although he could not dislodge them further, Joffre's "Miracle of the Marne" immediately preserved Paris and ultimately saved France and the Western world.

The British then raced towards the coast to save the Channel ports, and encountered the Germans at Ypres, near the Belgian border. The Germans failed, after two desperate battles, to take the town, which was reduced almost to rubble, but remained an Allied salient, or bulge, for the rest of the war. The British Expeditionary Force was destroyed at the two battles of Ypres, but those battles saved Calais and Boulogne and thus kept open the shortest route for men and supplies from Britain to France. The original British Army was rapidly replaced by volunteer armies built up by Lord Kitchener until his tragic death by drowning in 1916, when conscription was introduced for the first time in British history. So the Germans were forced to abandon their hope of finishing the war quickly. Both sides dug themselves in, and for the next three years the Western Front remained fixed in a continuous line of trenches from the North Sea to the Alps.

On the Eastern Front manœuvre was still possible. Although the Russians were heavily defeated in East Prussia at the battles of Tannenberg and the Masurian Lakes in 1914, they carried out a successful campaign against the Austrians in Galicia, until the Germans arrived to stiffen the Austrian resistance. By August 1915 the Germans had driven the Russians out of Poland, Lithuania and Courland, but the Russians retreated in good order and managed to hold their own soil. The Russian defeat was fortunate for the Austrians, who had to face a new war on their south-western borders through the decision of Italy to join the Allies. But this Allied advantage hardly offset the one the Central Powers enjoyed by the fact that Turkey had already thrown in her lot with them. The danger to Russia of Turkey's moves against her in the Caucasus led the British in 1915 to undertake the disastrous Gallipoli campaign. This assault on the Dardanelles, whose object was to make contact with Russia, met well-led Turkish opposition, which ultimately forced the Allies to withdraw.

In 1916 the Germans planned to deliver a knock-out blow to France at Verdun. But the French under Pétain, who was later to belie his glorious past, put up an unbreakable defence with the slogan: "They shall not pass!" (*Ils ne passeront pas!*), so that the Germans at last had to abandon the campaign. There followed an attempted break-through by the British, under Sir Douglas (afterwards Earl) Haig, on the River Somme, which resulted in the most gigantic battle in history to that date. This battle was a ghastly illustration of the futility of the frontal attack on the Western Front. On the first day the British lost 60,000 men and after a month's fighting they had advanced about two miles. In three months' fighting the flower of Europe's youth perished on that fateful field in the summer of 1916, for the British lost 400,000 men, the French 200,000, and the Germans half a million.

Early in 1917 the Germans carried out a voluntary retirement to shorten their Western line. This unexpected move disrupted the plans of the French command, which, nevertheless, decided to attack. But so utter a failure was it that the French troops mutinied, and this obliged the British to undertake a prolonged offensive in order to give the French Government time to restore the morale of the army and the nation. Hence was fought the battle of Passchendaele in the mud of Flanders. It lasted from July to November 1917, and ended with the capture of Passchendaele village, but at the cost of 300,000 British casualties. Yet it achieved its purpose of enabling the French to stay in the war. In October of the same year was fought the battle of Cambrai, noteworthy for the first use to any extent of the tank, a British invention, which was to play a decisive part in the final victory.

THE WAR AT SEA AND THE ENTRY OF AMERICA

In 1916 an important change took place in the British Government. Lloyd George, who had taken over the War Office on Kitchener's death, felt that the war was not being waged with sufficient vigour from London. On this issue he quarrelled with Asquith, still the Prime Minister in a Coalition Ministry of all parties which he had formed in 1915. In December 1916 Asquith resigned and Lloyd George became Prime Minister in a Cabinet representing all parties. In this position Lloyd George led the nation to final victory.

Although in no previous war had Britain ever taken so large a part in land fighting, her greatest strength was still on the sea, where she remained supreme. There were few actual sea battles in the war. In December 1914 a British fleet sank some German cruisers off the Falkland Islands in South America, and after this no German fleet ventured again on to the high seas until May 1916, when the battle of Jutland was fought. This time the British lost twice as many ships as the Germans, but the German fleet returned to Kiel Harbour, where it stayed until the end of the war, when a serious mutiny there played some part in persuading Germany to sue for peace. In spite of the lack of spectacular victories, however, Britain's control of the sea ultimately proved the decisive factor in the war. Central Europe became, in fact, a beleaguered fortress, from which all attempts of the besieged to break out failed.

In her attempts to break the stranglehold of the British blockade, Germany developed two weapons: aircraft and submarines. Small aeroplanes and airships (*Zeppelins*) did a certain amount of bomb damage, but in the First World War, unlike the Second, air-raids constituted little more than an occasional nuisance. A much graver menace were the German submarines, or U-boats, which established a serious counter-blockade of the British Isles. Early in 1915 the Germans began to attack not only Allied shipping but neutral vessels. In May 1915 they sank the British Cunard liner, the *Lusitania*, with the loss of nearly 1,200 lives, including 128 Americans. When the American President, Woodrow Wilson, protested, the Germans promised not to attack civilian or neutral vessels in future. This pledge rendered Germany's counter-blockade largely ineffective, while leaving the British blockade of Germany absolute. The German people meanwhile were reduced to a very low diet through lack of imports. In desperation the German Government was at last driven, in January 1917, to announce that any ship, enemy or neutral, would be destroyed on sight and sunk without a trace.

This decision, carried into ruthless effect, caused the Americans, in April 1917, to declare war on Germany, followed by a similar declaration against Austria at the end of the year. Thus this German folly not only turned a European into a truly world war but made an ultimate Allied victory certain. The Germans, who had hundreds of U-boats ready for this unrestricted submarine warfare, calculated that it would enable them to starve Britain into surrender before the Americans could be ready for active participation in the war in Europe. And they very nearly succeeded. By the spring of 1917, one ship in four was being sunk. The menace, however, was gradually checked, and finally dispelled, by the development of the convoy system, whereby merchant vessels sailed in company, under the protection of warships. The Americans assured the success of the plan by the energy and speed with which they enlarged their navy and produced new merchant ships and vast quantities of war materials. But even more important was the effect on the morale of the Allies, who were thus encouraged in their determination to continue the dire struggle by the certainty of ultimate victory.

Moreover, as the year 1917 proceeded, brighter news came from the Near East, where the British and Imperial forces had begun at last to make successful moves against the Turks. Advancing from Egypt under the command of General Allenby, these forces drove the Turks out of Palestine, and before the end of the year entered Jerusalem. The tide also turned against the Turks in Mesopotamia, where an Anglo-Indian army expelled the Turks from Kut in February 1917 and from Baghdad in March. By the autumn they had overrun the whole country. In that season, too, the Italians held the Austrian advance at the river Piave, where in 1918 they opened the offensive which finally drove the invaders out of Italy.

Unrestricted U-boat warfare was a desperate measure. If the Germans could have foreseen what was to happen on the Eastern Front later in the year 1917, they might have resisted this gambler's throw. For before the end of the year Russia was out of the war. During the first weeks of 1917 discontent, through starvation, war reverses and colossal losses, was rampant in Russia. Bread riots, strikes and popular demonstrations against the war and the autocratic government of the Czar grew in number and bitterness. Troops called out to quell the rioters refused to fire on them. By March the situation had become so ugly that, only a fortnight before America's declaration of war, the Czar was persuaded to abdicate and a Provisional Government was set up. But, as you will read in a later chapter, this parliamentary régime was overthrown by the Bolsheviks, who established a Soviet Republic in its place. The new Russian leaders, having failed to persuade the nations at war to make peace, entered into separate negotiations with the Germans who, in March 1918, imposed upon them the humiliating Treaty of Brest-Litovsk.

THE VICTORY OF THE ALLIES

Thus Russia finally deserted the Allied cause, and Germany not only gained much territory but got rid of the incubus of a war on two fronts. With forty divisions thus freed from the east, General Ludendorff, now the real master of Germany, prepared his last grand bid for victory in the west. His plan was to strike with overwhelming force at the junction of the British and French lines, and then to make for Paris and the Channel ports. The plan only just failed.

There were, in fact, four separate German offensives. The first, in March 1918, won back the British gains on the Somme but did not quite divide the French from the British. It was then that the Allies decided on a unified command, and appointed the French Marshal Foch as commander-in-chief of all forces. The second offensive came in April at Ypres, but the British, "with their backs to the wall", as Haig said in his orders, just managed to hold their ground and so saved the Channel ports. The third was at the end of May against the French, who were driven back across the Marne but prevented the Germans from reaching Paris. The fourth offensive came in July, but Foch held the Germans, and then counter-attacked, driving the Germans again across the Marne.

While the Americans were arriving in France at the rate of a quarter of a million a month and the Germans were showing increasing signs of exhaustion, the Allies carried out a succession of attacks which gave the enemy no breathing space. By September 1918 Foch was through the vast network of fortifications known as the Hindenburg and Siegfried Lines, and Ludendorff realised that the game was up. He persuaded his government to sue for peace at any price. During the six weeks which it took to arrange an armistice, Germany's allies fell away, each asking for a truce—Bulgaria in September,

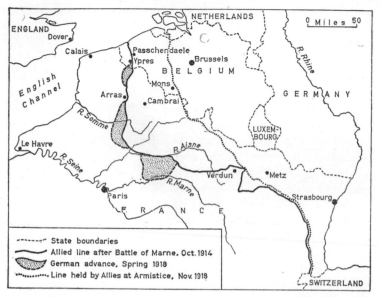

THE WESTERN FRONT IN THE FIRST WORLD WAR

Turkey in October, and Austria-Hungary at the beginning of November.

Meanwhile, strange things were happening in Germany, where the people, weakened by lack of food, disheartened by grief and demoralised by Allied propaganda, wanted only peace. The Allies refused to treat with the government of the Kaiser who, after a naval mutiny at Kiel and a general strike, abdicated on November 9, and fled, with the Crown Prince, to Holland. The Imperial régime was replaced by a provisional republican government, whose representatives signed the Armistice on November 11, 1918, as the British re-entered the shattered town of Mons, from which they had retreated in the first month of the war. The armistice with Germany arranged for the immediate evacuation of all invaded territories and the Allied occupation of the Rhineland, with the three Rhine bridgeheads at Cologne, Mainz and Coblenz. Germany also had

61

to surrender vast quantities of war material: guns, aeroplanes, locomotives, submarines and warships.

In the Far East of Asia, too, the events culminating in the armistice of 1918 were scarcely less significant in the growth of the contemporary world than those in Europe. What happened, in fact, was nothing less than the transfer of power in China from the European Powers to Japan. In the first few months of the war Japan, as an armed ally of the Western Powers, took possession of the lands in China and the Pacific which had been conceded to Germany at the end of the previous century. In 1915 the Japanese forced China to comply with demands which made them the virtual masters of Manchuria. They captured markets formerly monopolised by European Powers not only in Asia but even in South America, while their mercantile marine and their carrying trade grew enormously. Japan certainly made hay while, for her, the sun shone in the later months of the war. China was enfeebled, Russia in the throes of civil war, Britain, America, France and Germany completely occupied elsewhere. Japan simply stepped in to fill the vacancy thus created, and she did so with great efficiency and utter ruthlessness. By the end of the First World War she stood on equal terms with the Western Powers. Twenty years later, as you will see, she was to use her new-found strength with deadly effect against them.

So ended the First World War, a war in which eight million men had been killed and twenty million wounded. It ended as strangely as it had begun. The immediate occasion of this world conflagration was the assassination of a Hapsburg prince in an obscure Balkan town. At the time of the armistice which concluded it, large tracts of the victors' territory were still occupied by the forces of the vanquished, while the neighbouring soil of the chief loser was untrod by enemy foot. In this situation the Allied statesmen hoped to make a settlement which should establish a new world of peace and security. How vain that hope was you will gather as our story proceeds.

Chapter 5

THE TREATIES AND THE LEAGUE OF NATIONS

THE PEACE CONFERENCE

THE Peace Conference, which opened in Paris in January 1919, differed in several respects from any previous gathering of its kind. Never before had the representatives of so many different nationalities met together for such a purpose. The war had left political, economic and social problems of a magnitude and complexity unknown to earlier statesmen. The traditional governments of some of the largest states on the Continent had collapsed; vast areas were devastated; and Europe's normal economic life was shattered. Millions of soldiers were killed or maimed, and many more millions of civilians were sick with diseases resulting from years of undernourishment. Moreover, the Conference had to make not one but several peace treaties. And, finally, the Conference of 1919 was not a series of negotiations carried on between parties recently at war but a discussion among the envoys of the victors about peace terms to be imposed on the vanquished.

The main responsibility rested on the so-called "Big Four": Woodrow Wilson, the American President; Lloyd George, the British Prime Minister; Georges Clemenceau, the French Premier; and Vittorio Orlando, the Italian Prime Minister. Later, however, Orlando's influence declined, and most of the decisions were left to the remaining "Big Three". Theirs was a stupendous task, for they were called upon simultaneously to rectify political frontiers, meet the claims for reparations, disarm the defeated nations, and lay the foundations of a durable peace. In short, they had to find a middle way between the immediate requirements of national security and the ultimate aims of international idealism. The protagonist of the first of these claims on the attention of the Conference was Clemenceau; the champion of the second was Wilson.

Clemenceau, who was then nearly eighty years old, had twice experienced the invasion of his country by the Germans, and his chief objective was to prevent it happening a third time. Wilson's aim, on the other hand, was, as he himself said, "to make the world safe for democracy". In January 1918 Wilson had submitted to Congress in Washington his famous "Fourteen Points" as the basis of future peace. They included, among other items, the freedom of the seas, the breaking-down of economic barriers between nations, the reduction of armaments, and national self-determination as a principle of political organisation. But his most important point concerned the creation of a League of Nations for the maintenance of international peace and security.

At that crucial hour in the history of the world, the prestige of the United States was extremely high. There were two million Americans under arms, and the United States was the only creditor country. Besides, Wilson was the first American President ever to visit Europe while in office, and many regarded him as the leader of a crusade for the salvation of mankind. But at the conference table his idealism had to give way to the realism of the conflicting claims of the various parties. So Wilson's Fourteen Points were gradually whittled away, and when at length he returned home his own people refused to ratify the treaties and repudiated the League of Nations which he had worked so hard to establish.

THE TREATIES

Five treaties were finally hammered out by the Conference and presented for signature to each of the defeated Central Powers: namely the Treaties of Versailles (Germany), St. Germain (Austria), Trianon (Hungary), Neuilly (Bulgaria)

MARSHAL FOCH (1851–1929)
preme Commander of Allied forces on the Western Front from March 1918.

GENERAL LUDENDORFF (1865–1937)
Supreme Commander of German forces in the West
in 1918.

THE COUNCIL OF FOUR AT THE PARIS PEACE CONFERENCE, 1919
The so-called "Big Four" are (left to right): Lloyd George, Orlando, Clemenceau and Woodrow
Wilson.

WAR DEVASTATION IN FRANCE, 1914–18
A photograph of the ruins of the Cathedral of Notre Dame at Albert, on the Somme, at the end of the First World War.

THE PALACE OF THE LEAGUE OF NATIONS AT GENEVA
This fine building was completed and opened as the permanent headquarters of the League in 1937.

and Sèvres (Turkey). The treaties dealt mainly with four broad subjects: the redistribution of territory, guarantees for the execution of the peace terms, reparations for the damage caused, and the establishment of the League of Nations.

By the treaties the number of sovereign states in Europe was increased from twenty-seven to thirty-three. The six new states were Finland, Esthonia, Latvia, Lithuania, Poland and Czechoslovakia. The Empire of Austria-Hungary disappeared from the map. Austria was reduced to a small land-locked state with a population, entirely German-speaking, of about seven millions, while Hungary was equally isolated with a population, almost entirely Magyar, of about eight millions. Serbia was enlarged, at the expense of Austria and Hungary, by the addition of Bosnia, Herzegovina, Croatia and Slovenia. Montenegro, previously independent, joined this block which, all together, came to be known as Yugoslavia. The treaties added to Rumania both Transylvania (from Austria-Hungary) and Bessarabia (from Russia), to Greece a part of Thrace (from Bulgaria), and to Italy the districts of Trieste and Trentino (from Austria).

The province of East Prussia was cut off from the rest of Germany through the restoration of Poland and the need to grant that new state an outlet to the Baltic. This was achieved by the establishment of what was called the Polish Corridor. This involved depriving Germany of Danzig, which was then the only port in that part of the Baltic and which was placed under an international régime. The Germans, too, had to promise never to attempt to incorporate the diminished Austria in Germany or to change the frontiers of the new Czechoslovakia, which had hitherto formed part of the Austrian Empire.

In the west Germany was forced to restore to France the provinces of Alsace and Lorraine and to cede to Belgium the districts of Malmédy and Eupen on the south-east Belgian border. As a guarantee of security for France against future German aggression, the Rhineland continued in Allied military occupation. For this purpose it was divided into three areas,

EUROPE BEFORE THE FIRST WORLD WAR (1914)

based on the bridgeheads at Cologne, Coblenz and Mainz, to be evacuated respectively after periods of five, ten and fifteen years. But, after these evacuations, the whole of the Rhineland, on both sides of the river, was to remain permanently demilitarised. Germany was also obliged to abolish conscription, to limit her armed forces to 100,000 men, and to abandon the building of warships, submarines, heavy artillery and military and naval aircraft. She also had to demolish the fortifications of Heligoland, undertake to build no more forts on the Baltic, open the Kiel Canal to the ships of all nations, and surrender all her submarine cables.

The conditions imposed by the other treaties were no less onerous and the territorial adjustments even more complicated.

EUROPE AFTER THE FIRST WORLD WAR (1919)

This was especially true in the case of the Turks, some of whom refused to accept the Treaty of Sèvres. In fact, there now occurred in Turkey one of the most extraordinary movements in modern history. While the Sultan at Constantinople was ready to accept the treaty, a National Assembly at Ankara, in Asia Minor, refused to ratify it. The revolt was organised by a great soldier-statesman named Mustapha Kemal (later called Kemal Ataturk, meaning Father-Turk). Having defeated the Armenians, the Italians in Anatolia, the French in Cilicia and the Greeks in Smyrna, Kemal became master of Asia Minor and in 1922 occupied Constantinople. The Allies were thus forced to meet the Turks in conference as equals, and in 1923 the negotiated Treaty of Lausanne replaced the dictated

67

Treaty of Sèvres. Turkey gave up all claims to the Hejaz, to Palestine, Transjordania, Iraq and Syria, which have since become independent, but retained Asia Minor, Constantinople and eastern Thrace to its west.

Germany also had to surrender all her overseas possessions in Africa and Eastern Asia. She had actually lost her most considerable colony, German South-West Africa, in a campaign carried out in 1915 by the forces of the Union of South Africa under the leadership of Louis Botha, to whom the colony was surrendered, while at the time of the armistice a much more difficult campaign by Union forces was still going on against the Germans in East Africa. By the terms of the Treaty of Versailles, these two and Germany's other colonies in Africa were distributed among the South African Union, Britain, France and Belgium, under mandates (explained later, in the section on the League of Nations). Germany's leased port of Kiaochow in China had already been seized by Japan early in the war, and at the end of it the German islands in the northern Pacific were granted to Japan, while German New Guinea went to Australia and German Samoa to New Zealand, all under League mandates.

THE REPARATIONS PROBLEM

Germany was forced to admit her "war guilt", in a clause of the Treaty of Versailles which she afterwards violently repudiated, and to accept responsibility for causing all the loss and damage suffered by the Allied nations. But when it came to calculating how much was to be paid and in what manner the payments were to be made, the Paris Conference undoubtedly faced its most formidable task.

It seemed obvious justice that Germany should foot the bill, since, after all, it was not her lands but those of the victors which had been ravaged. Yet, however high the charge was pitched, it could barely begin to cover the total costs of reconstruction. It was possible to ensure certain payments in kind rather than in cash. For example, it was agreed that the

French should occupy the Saar Valley, under a commission appointed by the League of Nations, as compensation for the destruction of her coal-mines. This was done, subject to a plebiscite, or popular vote, to be held at the end of fifteen years, which, in fact, was duly held in 1935, when, as a result of the vote, Germany regained this area. But the most fantastic figures were seriously suggested for cash payments. In the immediate aftermath of the war, one committee actually assessed the amount at the astronomical total of £14,000 million, a figure which was later reduced to £2,000 million.

Even so, agreement was never properly reached on this question. The truth is that this problem impaled the Allies on the horns of a dilemma. That is to say, if Germany was to pay she must be assisted to recover her full economic stature, but if she so recovered then she might again become a danger to the peace of the world. The consequence was that no reparations figure was actually put into the treaty. It was left in the hands of a Reparations Commission, set up to keep this vital question under constant review. As time went on, it became less and less practicable to enforce the payments. In fact, the Commission gradually scaled them down until by 1932 they had been reduced almost to vanishing-point.

Not until the Allies had completed the draft treaty was it submitted to the German delegates in Paris for their observations. The German envoys recognised that the German people must make sacrifices as a result of their defeat, but they argued that the treaty they were offered was very far from implementing Wilson's Fourteen Points. They protested strongly against the redistribution of territory, especially in the east. They contended that the principle of national self-determination should, if genuine, apply to the vanquished as well as to the victors, and they objected to being excluded from the League of Nations. Finally, they asserted that the reparations bill, with which they were separately presented, was of such monstrous proportions that, if enforced, it would condemn the German nation to perpetual slavery. The Allied statesmen

69

replied that what they were proposing was a peace of justice to the peoples who had been impoverished in defending their native lands. However, the Germans gained something from their protests. One or two small territorial rectifications were agreed, no reparations figure was put into the final treaty, and a door was left open for the possible eventual entry of Germany, among other states, into the League of Nations.

THE CONSTITUTION OF THE LEAGUE OF NATIONS

Incorporated in the text of each treaty concerned with the general settlement following the First World War was the Covenant of the League of Nations. In this way every signatory to the treaties agreed to the establishment of this permanent machinery of international pacification and conciliation. Thus the Central Powers, by their signatures to the treaties, also approved the League even though at that time they were not permitted to join it. The support given to the proposed League indicated the revulsion of feeling from the horrors of war and the general desire to set up a permanent forum in which matters of international concern could be publicly debated, just as, under democratic constitutions, national affairs were ventilated in Parliament. The plan was the culmination of a long series of theoretical projects of internationalism adumbrated by various thinkers and writers through the history of medieval and modern Europe. The theory was for the first time translated into terms of practical politics at the end of the First World War by being made an integral part of the treaties which thus ensured that all the victor signatories should be original members of the League of Nations.

There were twenty-seven original members of the League, which came into being in January 1920. In 1921 forty-eight states were members, and from that time to the outbreak of the Second World War in 1939 the number of member states fluctuated with the admission of new members and the withdrawal of existing ones. In spite of America's refusal to join it, the League, at one time or another, was concerned with the international welfare of fifty states, comprising 75 per cent. of the world's total population and covering about 65 per cent. of the land area of the globe.

The Covenant of the League comprised twenty-six articles. Article 1 stated the rules of membership. Articles 2 to 7 and 14 dealt with the organs of the League, namely the Assembly, the Council and the Secretariat, as well as the International Court of Justice (constituted in accordance with a direction stated in Article 14 of the Covenant). The Assembly consisted of not more than three delegates from each member state, though only one could vote on behalf of his state on any issue. It met at least once a year, usually for about three weeks, and could debate any matter within the sphere of the League affecting the peace of the world. The Council was made up of five permanent members and nine non-permanent members (though both numbers varied as time went on and the membership of the League changed), representing respectively the Great Powers and the smaller nations, the non-permanent members being elected for three years. The Council met as occasion required, in practice generally about four times a year. Its powers were similar to those of the Assembly but, because it was more easily convened and met more often, it dealt with urgent matters between meetings of the Assembly.

The Secretariat was a body of salaried officers permanently employed at the offices of the League in Geneva. Its main functions were to carry out investigations into matters of common interest to all civilised states, to build up permanent records of matters of inquiry, and to prepare reports for submission to the Council and the Assembly.

The International Court of Justice consisted of a bench of eleven judges, representing the different types of law as prevailing in different parts of Europe and the world. The Court was competent to determine disputes submitted to it. Its headquarters were not at Geneva but at The Hague, the seat of the Permanent Court set up by the old Hague Conference.

The League also set up a Mandates Commission. A Mandate

was the authority granted to a particular state (Mandatory) to supervise, on behalf of the League, the government of an area (Mandated Territory) detached by the war from its former allegiance but not yet ripe for political independence. Each Mandatory had to submit to the Commission an annual report on its work under the Mandate.

One other institution associated with the League was the International Labour Organisation (I.L.O.), also housed at Geneva. The plan grew out of the Labour Charter of Rights which, like the Covenant of the League, was made a corporate part of the Treaty of Versailles. For the first time in history a conference of envoys of national governments thus recognised the claims of labour throughout the world and the importance of the part it must play in any durable peace. The International Labour Conference met annually to frame its proposals, and the Organisation did most valuable work. Indeed, its work has continued to this day, for during the Second World War it held meetings in Canada, and survived to become a Specialised Agency of the United Nations Organisation after the war.

The great promise of the League of Nations, as compared with any other plan for the maintenance of peace since the fall of the Roman Empire, lay in the fact that its organs were permanently established. The constitution of the League provided the machinery; it was for the nations to try to make it work.

Chapter 6

THE POST-WAR WORLD

NATIONAL SELF-DETERMINATION

THE sentiment of nationalism, as a state-forming principle, was greatly strengthened by the war. It was in its defence that the various peoples had been called to arms. It was the driving force of their long resistance in spite of the hardships which the war entailed. And it was the ground on which a just settlement was sought when the war was over. National self-determination was President Wilson's watchword, and it was broadly accepted by his colleagues at the Peace Conference. But by the time the Conference met, several of the formerly deprived national minorities had already taken matters into their own hands, either by setting up governments of their own on the ruins of shattered empires or by joining their brethren in neighbouring states. All that the Conference could hope to do, therefore, was to establish satisfactory frontiers for the new states, technically known as Succession States.

It was, of course, beyond human ingenuity to satisfy all the nationalist claims. If every national group had been allowed to create a state of its own, Europe would have become a mere patchwork of states too small and weak to maintain their independence. They would have been regarded as nuisances by the greater states and hence a standing danger to the peace of the continent. Indeed, as events were to prove, even the Succession States, which were recognised by the Conference of 1919, could not long withstand the pressure of their powerful neighbours, whose aggressive attitude towards them ultimately embroiled the world in war once more.

On the other hand, it was not practicable to incorporate every small nationalist group in the state of its choice, and consequently some states found themselves still saddled with alien minorities, as, for example, Germans in Poland and Austrian (or Sudeten) Germans in Czechoslovakia. Some cases, indeed, were so complicated that the Conference agreed to hold plebiscites, so that the minorities could decide by popular vote to which of two neighbouring states they should belong. Such plebiscites were held, for example, to determine the destination of Schleswig as between Denmark and Germany, and of southern Silesia as between Germany and Poland. As a result, both areas were divided and shared, although the division of southern Silesia had to be finally decided by arbitration. In order to ensure that the minorities should not suffer from disabilities at the hands of the majority, the Succession States were obliged to sign treaties with the Allied Powers undertaking to respect minority rights, and permitting an aggrieved minority to appeal to an international authority. Yet such decisions could do no more than settle the immediate question of political allegiance. They did not necessarily ensure to the minority the permanent enjoyment of equal rights with the majority in a given state. The consequent discontent among certain minorities led during the post-war years to the discrediting of parliamentary institutions, and so helped to create a situation favourable to the rise of dictatorships.

A more drastic method of attempting to solve the minority problem was to uproot people from their original homes and to transfer them *en masse* to the state to which they wished to belong. In only one case did this general displacement occur, and that was as between Greece and Turkey after the Turks under Kemal had reconquered some of their lost lands. In 1923, by an agreement between the two countries, Christian Greeks in Asia Minor were transplanted to Greece, and Turkish Moslems in Greece were transferred to Turkish territory, a vast undertaking which naturally involved a great deal of human suffering and distress.

NATIONAL DEMOCRACY AFTER THE WAR

The states of continental Europe enlarged or diminished as a result of the war either maintained their pre-war constitutions, applying them to the enlarged states, or promulgated new ones to meet the changed situation. The six new European states—Finland, Esthonia, Latvia, Lithuania, Poland and Czechoslovakia—without exception became republics, each having an elected President acting through a Cabinet of Ministers responsible to an elected assembly. The constitution in each case, that is to say, was modelled on that of Britain (although a monarchy) and of France (which continued to be governed under the constitution of the Third Republic). In some respects, however, the new constitutions were, in theory at least, more democratic than those of the west, as, for example, in the granting of the franchise to women on equal terms with men. Most of them, too, introduced the method of voting known as Proportional Representation (P.R.), a system under which candidates submit themselves for election in lists and are elected not by a majority but by reaching a quota; that is to say, a number of votes equal to the total of votes cast divided by the number of seats to be filled.

In Poland there were two Houses which, sitting together, elected the President for seven years. A similar presidential election took place in Czechoslovakia, the most truly democratic of these new states and, from the point of view of its birth, the most interesting. The chief architect of the Czechoslovak Republic was Thomas Masaryk, the son of a Slovak coachman and a man of remarkable courage and tenacity of purpose. He became Professor of Sociology in the University of Prague and a member of the Imperial Parliament in Vienna. He organised a revolutionary movement in Prague, but was later forced to flee the country. During the first two years of the war he was in London, and in 1917 he went to Russia, where he recruited a military legion from Czechoslovak prisoners of war which marched across Siberia to Vladivostok

75

and then crossed the Pacific to the United States. In Washington Masaryk gained the support of President Wilson to the creation of a Czechoslovak Republic. This was established in 1918, and, as was just and proper, Masaryk became its first President, an office which he held until 1935.

Equally striking was the emergence of republicanism in each of the pre-war Central and Eastern European Empires. Russia became a republic of a special kind, which will be discussed later. In 1920 Austria became a federal republic, with an elected President and a Ministry responsible to Parliament, for the election of which women were enfranchised. Hungary was proclaimed a republic in 1918. In 1920 it reverted to a monarchical form of government under a regent, but in 1945 became a republic again.

THE WEIMAR REPUBLIC IN GERMANY

Germany provided the most significant example of the constitutional changes wrought by the war. When, in November 1918, the Germans were forced to ask for an armistice, the whole edifice of Bismarck's *Reich* seemed to collapse. The Kaiser abdicated and fled to Holland, the Imperial Chancellor and the Ministry resigned, and a republic was proclaimed. A stop-gap government was formed to see the Armistice through. At one moment it looked as though Germany would go the way of Russia, for the provisional government had to face a serious Communist outbreak, engineered by extremists of the Left and a party known as the *Spartacus* group, led by Karl Liebknecht and Rosa Luxemburg, who were in touch with the Bolsheviks in Russia and, like them, hoped for world revolution. But the movement was not widely supported, and after a short outburst of violence it was crushed. In January 1919 an election took place for a Constituent Assembly which, to avoid clashes in Berlin, met at Weimar, in central Germany. Hence the new régime, which was formulated by this Constituent Assembly, came to be known as the Weimar Republic.

The new republican constitution, which came into force

in August 1919, replaced the hereditary *Kaiser* by a President elected for seven years, by direct universal adult suffrage, every man and woman of twenty-one or over being enfranchised. The same franchise applied to elections to the lower of the two Houses, the *Reichstag*, elections for which were carried out on the basis of Proportional Representation. The change from the Empire to the Republic was made even more radical by the decision that most of the executive powers of the President should be exercised by a Prime Minister (Federal Chancellor) and a Cabinet responsible to the *Reichstag*. Thus the democratic constitution of the Weimar Republic broadly followed the British and French patterns.

The new constitution, however, retained the federal character of Imperial Germany, for the states (now called *Länder*) which had formed the defunct Empire were granted powers of government in all affairs not enumerated as belonging to the general, or federal, authority. But here there were two striking differences from the former régime. First, Prussia lost much of the dominance which it had exercised under the Emperor, who had been also hereditary King of Prussia. Secondly, the Upper House (whose name was changed from *Bundesrat* to *Reichsrat*), while still representative of state interests, lost much of its former influence, owing to the enlarged powers of the *Reichstag* and the establishment of a Supreme Court of Judges to settle disputes between the Federal Authority and the *Länder*.

One very interesting feature of the new German constitution was the introduction of Economic Councils. There were to be set up District Workers' Councils and a Workers' Council of the Reich. These were to combine with representatives of the employers and other classes of the population, both local and national, "for the discharge of their joint economic functions". It was also laid down that any Bills concerned with social and economic legislation should be submitted to the Economic Council of the Reich for its opinion before being introduced in the *Reichstag*, and that the Economic Council might itself propose such legislation. This was a promising plan for combining economic with political interests in Parliament, but, like every other institution of the Weimar Republic, before it had time to establish itself as a working scheme it was engulfed in the Nazi upheaval.

From the beginning the Weimar Republic had to battle against tremendous odds. The Social Democrats, to whom the first President, Friedrich Ebert, belonged, failed to rise to the full responsibilities of government. Nor were other political groups more successful when Ebert died in 1925 and was succeeded by the aged Marshal Hindenburg. Whoever tried to govern Germany under the Weimar Republic had to face the bitter opposition of the Nationalists, who regretted the passing of the glories of the Empire, who considered that the makers of the Republic had betrayed the Fatherland, and who condemned all those who stood for the honourable fulfilment of Germany's obligations under the peace treaty. Moreover, these reactionary forces within the Republic made it an object of suspicion outside, especially with the French who regarded democracy in Germany as a screen covering her real intention to regain her lost prestige.

NATIONALIST REVOLUTIONS IN THE MIDDLE EAST

The spirit of nationalism which the war had heightened in Europe had its counterpart in Asia. The most striking example of it was in the case of Turkey where, as we have seen, a national movement, led by Kemal Ataturk, denounced the Treaty of Sèvres of 1919, to which the Sultan had agreed, and, after a national campaign against Greece and other states, negotiated with the Allies the Treaty of Lausanne in 1923. The new Turkey was a strictly national state, which included only Asia Minor, Anatolia and the region round Constantinople. Its capital was removed from Constantinople, which was now renamed Istanbul (a Turkish name), to Ankara in central Asia Minor. An assembly at Ankara drew up a constitution which declared Turkey a republic with a President and a National Assembly. The constitution provided for the election of an

BREAK-UP OF THE OTTOMAN EMPIRE AS A RESULT OF THE
FIRST WORLD WAR

Assembly, of one Chamber only, by universal suffrage and for the President to be elected every four years.

In theory the President was responsible to Parliament through a Cabinet. In practice, however, there was only one party (the People's Republican Party), of which Ataturk was the leader and which in 1923 elected their leader as President. Ataturk had a remarkable sweep of powers. He held, in fact, a fourfold presidency: of the Republic, of the Cabinet, of the Assembly, and of the only party in it. Ataturk established an enlightened despotism. He made the new Turkey a consolidated and prosperous state, strong internally and respected abroad. On his death in 1938 he was succeeded by his lieutenant, Ismet Inönü, who for some time continued in the fourfold office, but, as you will read later, a remarkable change was to come with the creation of a recognised opposition in the Assembly, and ultimately the opposition party (the Democrats) won a general election and came into power.

The nationalist spirit was also responsible at this time for the movement towards independence of the Arab states: Iraq (Mesopotamia), Transjordan (later called Jordan), Syria, Lebanon, and the Hejaz. They had all formerly been part of the Ottoman Empire, but their separate existence was now recognised. Britain held the mandates, under the League of Nations, for Iraq, Palestine and Jordan. Britain enthroned one son of Hussein, King of the Hejaz, as King of Iraq, and another of Jordan. But not until 1935 did the last of the British troops leave Iraq, while Jordan remained even longer under British tutelage, although granted an elective assembly. In Palestine the situation was complicated by two facts. First, the British had promised to establish Palestine as a new Jewish national home. Secondly, there were more Arabs than Jews there. Each race was violently nationalist, but Jews from all over the world immigrated into Palestine, and this made matters worse between the two peoples. Britain never succeeded in reconciling the two groups, and a final solution, as you will see, was not found until after the Second World War.

Similar difficulties were experienced by the French with their mandate for Syria. The French did their best to meet the nationalist demands by separating Lebanon from the rest, but here again the separate independent Republics of Syria and Lebanon were not established until the Second World War. The Hejaz was the heart of Arabia, embracing the original Mohammedan Holy Cities of Mecca and Medina. It was recognised as independent, but did not establish its sovereignty until 1932, by which time it had joined with the principality of

FREDERICK EBERT (1871–1925)
st President of the German (Weimar) Republic
(1919–25).

THOMAS MASARYK (1850–1937)
First President of the Republic of Czechoslovakia
(1918–35).

THE NATIONAL THEATRE, WEIMAR
Where the National Assembly debated and approved the constitution of the German Republic
in 1919.

KEMAL ATATURK (1880–1938)
Creator and first President of the Turkish Republic (1923–38).

SUN YAT-SEN (1866–1925)
Father of the Chinese revolution and first President of the Chinese Republic (1912).

A CENTRAL SQUARE IN ANKARA, THE NEW TURKISH CAPITAL
A magnificent city, built by the Turks since 1923, beside an ancient town, as a new capital to replace Istanbul (Constantinople). Its population now exceeds half a million.

Nejd, the combined state being known as the Kingdom of Saudi Arabia.

Persia, too, had its revolution during the years following the First World War. The nominal head of the state was the Shah, but in the 1920's Reza Khan (or Pahlavi), a leader of humble origin, set up a National Assembly and persuaded it to depose the Shah and elect him instead. He modelled his conduct and policy on those of Kemal Ataturk, of whom he was a great admirer, and introduced several reforms. Particularly he encouraged the growth of a national consciousness by emphasising the teaching of the distinctive language and history of Persia, and, following this line, he officially restored to Persia its ancient name of Iran.

Egypt, although linguistically Arabic, could not be regarded as an Arab state, and it followed a distinctive line after the First World War. Egypt was nominally a part of the Ottoman Empire, but, as you may remember, it was under a virtual British Protectorate, established in 1882 when Gladstone promised that the British would eventually evacuate the country. In December 1914 the British Protectorate was formally declared, but after the war, with the collapse of the Ottoman Empire, Britain considered that the time had come to begin to redeem Gladstone's pledge. In 1922, in response to Egyptian nationalist demands, Britain agreed to the establishment of a constitutional monarchy, with a descendant of the original Khedive family as King. By this constitution the King was given a status rather like that of the British monarch, the King acting through a Ministry responsible to a Parliament, made up of a Senate, partly nominated and partly elected, and an elected Chamber of Deputies. By the Anglo-Egyptian Act of 1936 Egypt became a sovereign state, and the British military occupation was terminated, subject to certain safeguards concerning British interests in the Suez Canal Zone and the Sudan. However, further discussion was delayed by the outbreak of the Second World War, in which Egyptian territory was to prove a focal point and an essential base of British strategy.

All these unsolved problems presented by the growth of militant nationalism in the Near and Middle East came up for further discussion and settlement after the Second World War, as you may read in Part Three of this book.

CONSTITUTIONAL EXPERIMENTS IN THE FAR EAST

In the Far East it seemed, at a time well before the outbreak of the First World War, that Japan might successfully assimilate and apply European political ideas, for in 1889 the Mikado established a constitution on the Western model with a Prime Minister and Cabinet responsible to a Parliament, or Diet, consisting of a House of Peers, partly hereditary, partly nominated and partly elected, and a House of Representatives, elected for four years by adult male suffrage. But the hope of steady constitutional progress which this constitution seemed to justify faded after the First World War through the expansionist policy of the dominant party in Parliament. This was a war party, which led the country first into the venture of the conquest of China and then into the folly of an alliance with Germany and Italy and the undeclared attack on the Western Powers which brought America into the Second World War. After her defeat in 1945, Japan, as you will see later, was given a second chance to establish liberal institutions under the ægis of the United States as the chief Occupying Power.

Nor was the attempt to establish constitutional government in China ultimately any more successful than in Japan, although it failed for different reasons and was finally extinguished by a régime inspired by a European tradition of much more recent origin than that of parliamentary democracy. The revolution of 1911–12, which overthrew the Manchu dynasty and set up a republic in its place, was the culmination of years of devoted work on the part of Dr. Sun Yat-sen. He was a liberal and humane leader whose three objects, as set forth in his lectures, published after his death, were nationalism, democracy and the welfare of the people.

The Constitution of the Republic, promulgated in 1912,

established an elective Presidency, an executive Ministry with a Premier at its head, and a Parliament composed of a Senate and a House of Representatives. But Sun Yat-sen was more of a political philosopher than a practical politician, and he was soon superseded in Peking. He was, however, supported by a nationalist party known as the *Kuomintang*, with whose help he later established a government at Canton in southern China. Meanwhile, in the north the central government broke down, and effective power passed into the hands of land-grabbing local "war lords", with whom Sun could not come to terms.

During the First World War, which China entered on the Allied side in 1917, Japan took advantage of the preoccupation of the Western Powers elsewhere to strengthen her position in northern China, while, after the Bolshevik Revolution in 1917, Communism began to spread in certain parts of southern China through Soviet propaganda, which urged the expulsion of foreigners and so harmonised with the aims of national unity. When the blending of nationalism and Communism was ultimately accomplished, the Communist Revolution triumphed. But for the moment the only hope seemed to be in the strength of the *Kuomintang*, which, after Sun's death in 1925, passed under the control of a forceful leader named Chiang Kai-shek.

Chiang made a tremendous drive against the northern war lords, and in 1928 entered Peking as a conqueror. Peking was renamed Peiping, and the government of the Chinese Republic was transferred to Nanking, where Chiang was proclaimed President. Actually he became a dictator, since he held simultaneously the Presidency of the Republic, the command of the army, and the chairmanship of the *Kuomintang*, which was soon declared to be the only permitted party in the country. How Chiang Kai-shek and the *Kuomintang* fared against the aggression of Japan and the growing strength of the Chinese Communists, especially after the destruction of the Japanese power in 1945, you may read in a later chapter.

83

Chapter 7

POST-WAR BRITAIN AT HOME AND OVERSEAS

INDUSTRIAL UNREST

BRITAIN emerged from the war, in which she had played so decisive a part, with her land unscathed, her navy supreme, her Empire intact, and her international prestige higher than it had ever been before. Relief at the victorious end to the war led many people to imagine that the country could now quietly slip back to the peace and comfort of pre-war days. But the world could never be the same again after so intense and universal an upheaval as the War of 1914–18. The war, in fact, marked the end of an epoch and the beginning of a new age of political, economic and social revolution which Britain and the British Commonwealth could not escape any more than the rest of the world.

During the war the British Government had assumed the control of services vital to the national effort, including food, transport, mines, wages, prices and foreign exchange. While these controls continued there was a brief period of post-war prosperity, but as soon as they were removed the boom declined and prices fell. Widespread distress and unemployment caused strikes, especially of the mine workers. In 1919 a commission of inquiry into the mining industry, presided over by John (afterwards Lord) Sankey, had recommended the nationalisation of the mines. When the government finally refused to act on this proposal, the miners struck in 1921. The strike failed, and between 1922 and 1924 nearly all trades had to accept a fall in wages. After a slight revival of prosperity, trade became again depressed, and this prepared the way for a renewal of the struggle in 1926. In that year the miners struck once more against further wage reductions, and appealed for support not only to the unions of railwaymen and transport workers (with which the miners formed what was called the Triple Alliance) but to all unions.

In March 1926 the Trade Union Congress (T.U.C.) called a conference of trade union executives in London and authorised a general strike in sympathy with the miners. Such a sympathetic strike was something new in British industrial warfare. It involved the withdrawal from vital national services of the labour of $2\frac{1}{2}$ million men, most of whom were not directly involved in a trade dispute. They hoped thus to force the government to negotiate, but the government, supported by public opinion, refused to recognise the strike as legal. After nine days of complete disruption of normal life, while industry and trade were at a standstill, the T.U.C. called off the strike. The miners continued their resistance for several more months, but had finally to return to work at the same wages, though for longer hours.

The General Strike of 1926 had serious consequences for the trade union movement. In 1927 the Trade Disputes Act declared a general strike illegal, and prohibited the imposition of a political levy by a trade union on its members, permitting the contribution to be taken only from those members who "contracted in"; that is to say, made it voluntarily. In the period following the strike, trade union membership fell from 8 to 5 millions, while after 1930, as the world depression spread, unemployment increased, particularly in such basic industries as engineering, shipbuilding, textiles and coal. The proportion of unemployed for the whole country remained round about 12 per cent., but in the coal-fields of Durham and South Wales it sometimes rose to 60 per cent. With thousands of men and youths living "on the dole", the government increased insurance payments, instituted development schemes in depressed, or special, areas, and improved the operation of the Poor Law. The Local Government Act of 1929 abolished the Guardians and transferred their powers to County and County Borough Councils. These measures emphasised the new conception of the democratic state as an instrument for the establishment of a true social democracy.

THE FIRST LABOUR GOVERNMENTS

In 1918, under Lloyd George's Coalition Government and while the war was still on, Parliament passed two Acts of great social and political importance. The first was the Education Act, designed by H. A. L. Fisher, a great scholar and educationist, who was then President of the Board of Education. The Fisher Act raised the school-leaving age to 14, abolished all school fees for any kind of public elementary education, made the medical inspection of school-children universal, and proposed the setting-up of part-time day continuation schools. The second measure was the Representation of the People Act which gave the vote to all men of 21 or over and to many women of 30 or over, whether married or single, besides making them eligible for election to the House of Commons. The Act added to the electorate 8 million voters, of whom 6 million were women.

In December 1918 a general election was held on the new register of voters, and as a result Lloyd George's Coalition Government was returned to power. But in 1922 the Coalition broke up, and the three parties—Liberal, Conservative and Labour—fought a general election separately. The Liberals were hopelessly divided as between the followers of Asquith and of Lloyd George, whose breach was never healed, and the Conservatives were returned with 344 seats, under the leadership of Bonar Law, who became Prime Minister. Lloyd George's National Liberals gained only 57 seats, while Labour secured 138. In the following year Bonar Law retired and was succeeded as Prime Minister by Stanley Baldwin, who decided to revive Joseph Chamberlain's policy of tariff reform and to seek the support of the electorate. In the ensuing election of

1923 the Conservatives, with 258 seats, failed to gain an absolute majority over the two sections of the Liberal Party (together 158) and Labour (191) combined. As the Labour Party was thus the second largest in Parliament, the Liberals agreed that, for the first time in British history, it should form the Government of the Day.

The head of the Labour Ministry which set forth on its new adventure in 1924 was Ramsay MacDonald, who had been the first Secretary of the Labour Party and had entered Parliament in 1906. Although of humble origin, he became a highly cultivated man, and was greatly helped in his career by his marriage to a niece of the great scientist, Lord Kelvin. In his first Cabinet the new Prime Minister had a number of able colleagues, including Philip Snowden who was appointed Chancellor of the Exchequer. But after only nine months the Liberals, on whom MacDonald depended for his majority in the Commons, withdrew their support when he proposed that the British Government should officially recognise Soviet Russia. This forced another general election, as a result of which the Conservatives under Stanley Baldwin recovered their absolute majority, gaining 413 seats against Labour's 151 and only 40 Liberals, who were thus reduced to a mere "rump" of Gladstone's great party.

Baldwin's second administration carried some measures in the direction of Protection, as well as the Trade Disputes Act of 1927 (following the General Strike), and the Representation of the People Act of 1928, which finally gave all women the vote on the same terms as men, thus increasing the electorate to 27 millions, of whom $14\frac{1}{2}$ millions were women. The first of these measures caused widespread dissatisfaction, the second alienated the workers, and the third introduced a new incalculable electoral element. At the General Election of 1929 the Conservative seats were reduced to 261, while Labour gained 287, which, again with Liberal help, brought MacDonald back to 10 Downing Street. But hardly had this second Labour Government got into its stride than the depression began in the United States and soon spread to the rest of the world. In 1931 the depression caused a financial crisis in Britain, which led to cuts in salaries and in unemployment insurance benefit.

To meet the crisis MacDonald appealed to the two other parties to form with him a National Government. The vast majority of MacDonald's own party repudiated him, and, in the election which followed, the Coalition was returned with the amazing majority of nearly ten to one (554 to 61). Mac-Donald remained Prime Minister, but in his Cabinet of twenty members there were only four Labour Ministers. The rest comprised four Liberals and eleven Conservatives, of whom the leading men were Baldwin and Neville (son of Joseph) Chamberlain. This Parliament passed an Act imposing a duty of 10 per cent. on certain imports. But, following this measure at home, it was agreed at the Imperial Conference held at Ottawa in 1932 that certain Empire products should be admitted to Britain free of duty, while in the case of others, such as wheat, butter, fruit and timber, the Dominions should be given a preference by being required to pay a smaller duty than that imposed on foreign imports. The Dominions, however, undertook not to flood the British market with their products to such an extent as to damage the agricultural industry of the homeland. They also agreed to impose duties on foreign imports so as to give British exports a fair chance.

Thus Joseph Chamberlain's dream largely came true after a lapse of thirty years, and Britain was committed to a policy of Protection. But it caused the resignation of Philip Snowden and the Liberal statesman Herbert Samuel from the Cabinet. After this the government became, in effect, a Conservative Ministry. In 1935 MacDonald retired from the Premiership in favour of Baldwin, and in 1937, in failing health, almost blind and shunned by his former Labour colleagues, he died. Meanwhile, in 1936 Baldwin had had to deal with the difficult situation created by King Edward VIII's proposed marriage, which led to his abdication and the succession of his brother, George VI. In 1937 Baldwin resigned his office of Prime Minister and went to the House of Lords as Earl Baldwin. He was succeeded by Neville Chamberlain, who remained Prime Minister until after the outbreak of the Second World War.

REBELLION IN IRELAND

At the outbreak of war in 1914, as you may recall, Home Rule for Ireland had been postponed until the war should be over. Ulster, naturally, was staunch in its support of the British cause in the war. So were many southern Irish, who followed the lead of John Redmond. But there were also many extremists in the south, belonging mostly to the Irish Republican Brotherhood and an anti-British political organisation called *Sinn Fein* (a native Irish term meaning "ourselves alone"), which had been founded in 1905 as a cultural movement by a journalist named Arthur Griffith. These malcontents, who realised that the war in Europe offered an excellent opportunity to establish the independence of Ireland, formed a citizen army, and on Easter Monday, 1916, under the leadership of Arthur Griffith and his two lieutenants, Michael Collins and Eamon de Valera, they rose in rebellion. In Dublin 15,000 men seized key-points, including the Post Office, from which they proclaimed the Irish Republic. The government suppressed the rebellion, executed 7 of the insurgents, reprieved 75 others, and held 2,000 more as prisoners. The executions caused much bitterness among the southern Irish, and, in spite of the failure of the rebellion, De Valera began to organise *Sinn Fein* as "a mass republican movement".

In the General Election of 1918, which was held in Ireland also, John Redmond's Home Rule Party was virtually wiped out, being reduced to 6 members, while *Sinn Fein* candidates won 73 seats, and the Unionists, mostly, of course, in Ulster, returned 26 members. The Sinn Feiners refused to take their seats at Westminster and organised their own local Parliament (*Dail Eireann*) in Dublin. They proclaimed the Irish Republic, and elected De Valera as President and Collins as Vice-President. They set up their own organs of local government and

89

their own law courts. They turned the Volunteers into the Irish Republican Army (I.R.A.), and sought international recognition of their status. They made attacks on police, burned down the houses of the landlords, and drove their cattle away. By way of reprisals for these acts of sabotage, the British Government recruited a special police force, known as the "Black and Tans", which, between July 1920 and July 1921, took armed action against the Republicans. At the same time, in Belfast, a body of Unionists was organised to make attacks on Catholic workmen in Ulster. Thus the whole of Ireland was a seething cauldron of disruption and lawlessness.

Meanwhile, in 1919 a new Government of Ireland Bill, to replace the now unworkable Act of 1914, was introduced in Parliament at Westminster. It provided for two Irish Parliaments, one for the six counties of Ulster, and the other for the remaining twenty-six counties, each with limited powers. The Bill, which became law in November 1920, was reluctantly accepted by Northern Ireland but rejected by the South. At the ensuing Irish elections the Unionists gained a large majority (40 to 12) in the North and set up their separate government in Belfast. In the rest of Ireland the Republican candidates captured practically all the seats and reconsitituted themselves as "The All-Ireland Republican Legislature". The government then decided to invite the Irish Republicans to send delegates to London to discuss the whole matter. In the summer of 1921 a truce was arranged and a delegation, headed by Griffith and Collins, met government representatives, and after much discussion a treaty was signed in December 1921. By this treaty Southern Ireland was granted the status of a Self-governing Dominion, under the name of the Irish Free State.

The treaty was ratified by the Parliament at Westminster, and in January 1922, in spite of the impassioned opposition of De Valera, it was ratified also by *Dail Eireann*, in Dublin. Griffith was chosen as head of a "pro-treaty ministry" and Collins as Prime Minister. The Republicans under De Valera continued to boycott the new Parliament, and the conflict flared up into a fierce civil war. Griffith died a little later and Collins was killed, but William Cosgrave, who succeeded Griffith as head of the Provisional Government, finally got the new constitution of the Irish Free State through the *Dail* in October 1922, though the armed struggle did not cease until April 1923.

Thus Southern Ireland ceased to be a part of the United Kingdom. The treaty allowed for the ultimate union of Ulster and Southern Ireland, but Ulster refused, as she has consistently refused ever since, to leave the United Kingdom of Great Britain and Northern Ireland. The Irish Free State, meanwhile, was governed under the Constitution of 1922 which, as in Canada and the other Self-governing Dominions, provided for a Governor-General to represent the King and an executive council under a President, or Prime Minister responsible to a legislature of two Houses—a nominated Senate (*Seanad*) and a House of Commons (*Dail Eireann*). The Constitution could, under its rules, be amended by the Irish Free State, so long as such amendments were not repugnant to the treaty of 1921. And this is what the Irish Free State later did. In 1927 De Valera at last agreed to enter the *Dail*, and formed a new party (*Fianna Fail*), whose object was "to remodel Irish institutions on republican lines, while preserving the 'external relation' with the British Commonwealth and refusing to accept the final severance of Northern Ireland from the rest of Ireland".

Hence the constitution of Eire, as Southern Ireland is now called, was modified after the re-establishment of the ascendancy of De Valera in Irish politics. A new constitution was promulgated in 1937, introducing an elected President as head of the state. Later still, and especially as a result of the Second World War, further changes were made. So it came about that when in 1948 Southern Ireland demanded the status of an independent republic, the British Government consented to the change.

THE SELF-GOVERNING DOMINIONS

The Self-governing Dominions had given powerful support to Britain in the First World War. Their help was generously given, not only because the Dominions were conscious of their kinship with Britons at home and of their loyalty to the British Crown, but also because of the need for a common imperial defence against a common danger. The Dominions, in fact, realised that Britain was the centre and mainstay of a maritime Empire to which they all belonged and without which they could not survive. Yet, in spite of this common need, the people of each Dominion had a growing sense of their importance as a separate nation. This feeling of individuality among the Dominions was emphasised by the changes in the structure of the Empire which had been taking place under the influence of the New Imperialism dating from the later years of the nineteenth century.

The New Imperialism imposed upon Britain additional world-wide responsibilities in tropical areas and among native peoples quite different from those of the Dominions. There were the new colonies acquired at the end of the nineteenth century in Africa, Malaya and the Far East. Added to these new colonies there were the Mandated Territories in Africa and the Middle East for which Britain took responsibility under the League of Nations after the First World War. In each of these under-developed areas, moreover, Britain introduced modern methods of hygiene and medicine which tended to increase the native population, while the growing production of petrol facilitated transport in the more remote and primitive regions. Finally, the use of the Suez Canal as an imperial waterway gave new economic and strategic importance to India and Malaya.

These developments emphasised the difference between a Colony and a Dominion. While the affairs of the colonies were directed from Whitehall, each Dominion was autonomous in domestic matters. It had the power to regulate its own tariffs, to make its own immigration laws, to administer its own military needs, and to amend its own constitution. The First World War gave the Dominions a new status in world affairs, and when it was over they separately signed the Peace Treaties and sent delegates to the Assembly of the League of Nations at Geneva. At the Imperial Conference held in London in 1926 it was unanimously agreed that "Britain and the Self-governing Dominions are autonomous communities within the British Empire, equal in status, in no way subordinate one to another in any aspect of their domestic or external affairs, though united by a common allegiance to the Crown, and freely associated as members of the British Commonwealth of Nations".

Five years later this decision was given the full force of law by the Statute of Westminster of 1931. This Statute laid down that no law made in future by a Dominion should be "void or inoperative on the ground that it is repugnant to the law of England or to the provisions of any existing or future Act of Parliament of the United Kingdom". It also declared that no future Act of Parliament of the United Kingdom should extend to a Dominion "unless it is expressly declared in that Act that that Dominion has requested, and consented to, the enactment thereof". In another section of the Statute a distinction was drawn between a Dominion and a Colony in these words: "The expression 'colony' shall not, in any Act of Parliament of the United Kingdom . . . include a Dominion or any Province or state forming part of that Dominion."

So the Statute of Westminster gave legal expression to the new conception of the British Empire as a Commonwealth of Nations, so far as the Self-governing Dominions were concerned. The Crown remained the sole legal unifying force. Thus, just as the law refers to "Her Majesty's Government in the United Kingdom", so it refers to "Her Majesty's Government in the Dominion of Canada", "Her Majesty's Government in the Commonwealth of Australia", and so on for each of the other Self-governing Dominions which form part of the British Commonwealth.

INDIA

India presented to Britain a quite different problem from that of the Dominions, on the one hand, or the Colonies, on the other. Here was not a mere country but a continent covering an area of over $1\frac{1}{2}$ million square miles with a rapidly growing population, now more than 400 millions, but even at the time of the First World War well exceeding 300 millions, or about four-fifths of the population of the Empire and about one-sixth of the human race. Its people were, as they still are, composed of several races with many different creeds and grades of society (or castes), and varying languages, traditions, cultures and customs. Of the adherents of the various religions, about 65 per cent. were, and are, Hindus, and about 25 per cent. Mohammedans, or Moslems, and between these existed mutual hostility and constant feud.

The problem of governing such a vast and varied country was complicated by its political division into two types of area: British India and the Native States. British India was divided into provinces, while the Native States, covering about two-fifths of the area of India and containing about a quarter of the total population, were ruled by Indian princes, most of whom had made treaties with the British who controlled their external relations. In 1858, following the suppression of the Indian Mutiny of 1857, the East India Company had been abolished and Queen Victoria had become Sovereign of India, though not actually proclaimed Empress until 1877. The Act created the office of Secretary of State for India, a member of the British Cabinet, who was assisted by a Board in London, on which sat one Indian representative (later increased to two). The Governor-General, or Viceroy, represented the Queen, and a Governor was appointed to each province. The administration was carried out by a civil service composed of Britons, whose numbers at no time exceeded 6,000, and about 200,000 Indians, while the defence was maintained by an army in the proportion of five soldiers—one British and four Indians—to 6,000 of the civil population.

To assist them in the government, the Viceroy had a Council at the capital, transferred from Calcutta to Delhi in 1912, and each Governor had a Provincial Council. By a series of Acts passed in 1861, 1892 and 1909, Indian representatives were brought in increasing numbers on to these Councils. In 1917, towards the end of the war, in which Indian contingents played a notable part, an official report proposed a plan whose object was "the gradual development of self-governing institutions with a view to the progressive realisation of responsible self-government in India". The subsequent Act of 1919 set up a Council of State and a Legislative Assembly for the country as a whole, as well as a similar two-chamber legislature for each of the provinces. A large proportion of seats on these Councils were allotted to Indians. In the provincial assemblies a considerable measure of responsible self-government was proposed by the device known as Dyarchy, or dual government. The subjects to be dealt with by the Assembly were divided into two: those "reserved" to the Governor and those "transferred" to the Indians. The transferred subjects included agriculture, health, education and public works. Where these were concerned the Indians were to form their own ministries, each to be responsible to its own Assembly.

This offer of Home Rule, or *Swaraj* as the Indians called it, was at first fairly well received by the more moderate elements among cultured Hindus, who were organised in the political association called the National Congress (founded in 1885), and Moslems, who belonged to the Moslem League (established in 1907). Unfortunately, just when the new constitution was about to come into force in 1919, violent strikes and riots occurred in the Punjab, where in one case, at Amritsar, a British general ordered the troops to fire on the crowd. In spite of the bitterness caused among Indians by this unhappy incident, elections were held in 1920, and, with the co-operation of the moderates, the new plan was initiated.

There now emerged as a vital force in Indian politics the crusade of Mahatma Gandhi (1869–1948), a Hindu who had studied law at the University of London. Gandhi was one of the most remarkable figures of modern times. In middle life he renounced all worldly goods and became an ascetic, living on a vegetarian diet and generally wearing nothing but a loin-cloth. Early in 1919 he began a revolutionary movement against the British régime, based not on force but on non-violent non-co-operation. He gathered a great number of followers, who pledged themselves to refuse to pay taxes, or to send their children to school, or to buy certain imported goods. With this vast following Gandhi launched a campaign of "civil disobedience" to the Act of 1919, which handicapped it from the very beginning.

Nevertheless, the British persevered, and in 1927, in fulfilment of the promise contained in the Act, appointed a Commission (under John Simon) to inquire into its working up to that time. The Simon Report, which finally appeared in 1930, was followed by meetings in London of representatives of all parties concerned at a Round Table Conference, whose deliberations led to the passing of a new Act in 1935. This proposed practically full responsible government in the Provinces and a federal system to cover the whole of British India, and to include any Native States whose rulers agreed to join an All-India Federation, in which responsible government was also to operate. The constitution projected in the Act of 1935 was fated never to be fully realised. With the support of the National Congress, provincial elections took place in 1937, and in those Provinces where the Congress Party gained a majority Indian ministries were set up. The Federation proposed by the Act. however, never came into being at all. Indeed, before the new constitution could get fully to work India was heavily involved in the Second World War, and when it was over, as you will see, the plan of 1935 had become obsolete.

STANLEY (AFTERWARDS EARL)
BALDWIN (1867–1947)

Conservative Prime Minister (1923 and 1924–9)
and in the National Government (1935–7).

JAMES RAMSAY MACDONALD
(1866–1937)

First Labour Prime Minister (1924 and 1929–31)
and in the National Government (1931–5).

THE GENERAL STRIKE, 1926

Volunteers in Hyde Park, helping in the distribution of emergency milk supplies to the people of
London.

THE DEPRESSION IN THE UNITED STATES IN 1931
A "bread line" in New York, showing how unemployed workers queued daily for loaves, a common sight in all American cities during the worst period of slump (1931–3).

THE IMPERIAL ECONOMIC CONFERENCE AT OTTAWA, 1932
The Governor-General of the Dominion of Canada opening the Conference, attended by delegates from Britain and various parts of the Commonwealth, which reached new trade agreements on the basis of Imperial Preference.

Chapter 8

EUROPE AND AMERICA

THE EARLY YEARS OF THE LEAGUE

In the years immediately following the war, while each nation was struggling with its own internal difficulties, the League of Nations was doing its best to cope with the international situation. But from the beginning the League suffered from three fundamental weaknesses. First, it was never as universal as it was intended to be. Not only did the United States never join it, but at no one time did the League embrace even all the great nations of the world. Germany was not admitted until 1926, but by the time Soviet Russia entered it in 1934, Germany and Japan had already withdrawn from membership. Secondly, the League Covenant was made an integral part of the treaties. This fact led many people to conclude that its main object was to preserve the settlement of 1919 at all costs. While this suited those who had gained from the settlement, it did not satisfy the losers, who naturally desired to see its effects reversed. Thirdly, the League was based on the assumption that all nations desired peace, an assumption which was soon proved to be false.

Nevertheless, during the first decade of its existence the League did invaluable work for peace and proved itself a powerful instrument of international aid and conciliation. In 1923, for example, it settled a dispute between Italy and Greece which might otherwise easily have led to hostilities. In the same year it helped to restore the finances of Austria and of Hungary, both economically weakened by their detachment from each other and by the disintegration of the old "Ramshackle Empire". Also in that year the League's officers supervised the complicated task of settling in Greece the Greek refugees from Asia Minor under the terms of the Treaty of Lausanne. In 1925, again, the League composed a frontier quarrel between Greece and Bulgaria.

Over the same period, too, the League discharged several obligations under the treaties. It supervised and kept under review the allotment of mandated territories, such as the former German colonies, and the international control of the Free City of Danzig. Meanwhile, the League Secretariat collected and collated from all over the world information connected with the international aspects of labour and health, and drafted rules for the suppression of various social evils, such as the traffic in pernicious drugs. In short, the League became a storehouse of facts and a clearing-house of ideas about truly international affairs, and on this side of its work promised to be of the greatest benefit to Europe and the world at large.

THE RUHR AND THE PACT OF LOCARNO

While this pacific work on the part of the League was proceeding, complications beyond its control occurred in Western Europe. Towards the end of 1922 Germany asked the Allies for a moratorium, or delay, of two years in her reparations payments. The British were prepared to consider the proposal, but the French refused to listen and decided to use force. In 1923, therefore, French troops invaded the Ruhr, which was the heart of Germany's economic life, with the object of appropriating the output of the coal-mines there as compensation for loss of reparations. The French, no doubt, had the legal right to take such a step, but it failed to achieve its immediate object, for the German workers in the Ruhr adopted a policy of passive resistance, so that before the end of the year the French were forced to abandon the project. Nevertheless, the French action induced the Germans to reconsider their policy of resistance to the Treaty of Versailles and move towards co-operation in its fulfilment.

The Ruhr episode of 1923 also had the effect of persuading

the Western Powers that new arrangements must be made concerning the payment of reparations. Consequently, in 1924 the parties concerned opened negotiations for revision, assisted by a body of financial experts under the chairmanship of the American banker, Charles Dawes. The resulting Dawes Plan, as it was called, arranged that, while the originally agreed total of Germany's payments should not be reduced, the period over which they were to be made should be lengthened. At the same time, the whole machinery of reparations was placed under the supervision of a neutral agent-general, and Germany undertook to do her best to stop the inflation of the currency and to try, by taxation and other means, to restore the mark to its pre-war value.

All this cleared the international air. A new government in France brought Aristide Briand to the Foreign Office, while in Germany Gustav Stresemann, the leader of the People's Party, became Chancellor and Foreign Minister. Briand was not only a strong supporter of the League of Nations but a believer in the practicability of creating a United States of Europe, for which he actually worked out a constitution before his death in 1932. Stresemann, although an Imperialist at heart, seemed to be prepared to set aside his beliefs in the interests of peace. The result was that these two statesmen, together with Austen Chamberlain, Britain's Foreign Minister, worked in harmony for a time, and in 1925 Britain, France and Germany, as well as Italy and Belgium, signed a number of agreements known collectively as the Pact of Locarno.

By the Pact of Locarno Germany freely pledged herself to maintain the Rhineland as a demilitarised zone (a condition which had been *forced* on her at Versailles), guaranteed the frontiers of France and Belgium, and undertook not to disturb the boundaries of Poland and Czechoslovakia except by agreement or arbitration. Britain at the same time guaranteed the Franco-German and Germano-Belgian frontiers. By the Pact, too, France and Germany solemnly promised never to go to war with each other again. In the following year, 1926, Germany was admitted to the League of Nations and was found a seat on the Council. The "spirit of Locarno", though ridiculed by extremists in various countries, prevailed during the next few years.

Indeed, so universal was the atmosphere of optimism engendered by Locarno that in 1928 the American Secretary of State, Frank Kellogg, was persuaded to join Briand in drawing up the Briand-Kellogg Pact, otherwise known as the Pact of Paris. The Pact was signed by the representatives of almost all nations, including the United States, though not a member of the League. The Pact of Paris was merely a verbal condemnation of recourse to war as a means of solving international differences. No state gave any pledges beyond its good faith in the intention to outlaw war. The pacific spirit hovered over Europe long enough to see the withdrawal of the last of the Allied troops from Germany in 1930, five years earlier than the time fixed by the Treaty of Versailles, and the virtual conclusion of the reparations controversy in 1932. But by that time, as you will see, there were taking place in Germany the preliminary moves of a revolution, to the causes of which events in America unconsciously contributed.

THE REPUDIATION OF PRESIDENT WILSON

When President Wilson returned to America from the Paris Conference in 1919, with the treaties he had signed and the Covenant of the League he had created, the Senate repudiated both. In order to understand how such a repudiation was possible, it is necessary briefly to examine the working of the American Constitution, which differs in several respects from the British Constitution. First, in Britain the executive power is exercised by the Prime Minister and his Cabinet colleagues who are responsible to Parliament, and every Minister must be a member of either the House of Commons or the House of Lords. In the United States, on the contrary, the executive power, exercised by the President and his Cabinet Officers, is quite separate from the legislative power, which is exercised by Congress, and, although the President delivers periodical Messages to Congress and the Vice-President is Chairman of the Senate, no other executive officer is allowed to sit or speak in either House of Congress.

Secondly, the nature and function of the two Houses of Congress differ from those of the two Houses of Parliament. The House of Commons is elected and the House of Lords hereditary; whereas both the House of Representatives and the Senate are elected, though under different rules as to time. Again, while in Britain the lower House, the Commons, is much the more powerful of the two, in the United States the reverse is the case, the Senate having much more influence on affairs than the House of Representatives. This is specially true in matters of foreign policy and in the ratification of treaties, which requires a two-thirds majority in the Senate. The reason for this is that, in such common concerns, each of the states has surrendered its powers to the Federal Authority, and all states, however small or large, are equally represented (namely by two members each) in the Senate, while the House of Representatives is elected on a population basis.

Thirdly, whereas in Britain there is only one type of national general election (namely for the House of Commons), in the United States there are three: for the President, for the Senate and for the House of Representatives, though they may take place at the same time. In Britain, again, a general election for the House of Commons may occur as frequently or as seldom as the political situation demands, so long as the total life of any one Parliament does not exceed the statutory maximum of five years. In the United States, on the other hand, election periods are fixed by the Constitution and cannot be varied. The President is elected every four years, each of the two Senators for each of the states is elected for six years, and the whole of the House of Representatives is elected every two years. Generally, when the President is elected his party in the Senate and House of Representatives get a majority with him, but at the mid-term elections—that is, after he has been in office for two years—he may lose that majority in one or both of the Houses.

This is what happened to President Wilson in the middle of his second term in 1918. Wilson belonged to the Democratic Party, but he made a serious mistake in taking as his advisers to Paris only Democrats (except one), for he thus alienated the Republicans, who at the mid-term elections of 1918 had gained a majority in both the Senate and the House. The Americans, in any case, were by now suffering from a revulsion of feeling against being entangled in Europe's troubles, and this general sentiment of sullen isolationism, added to the outraged feelings of the Republicans at Wilson's high-handed conduct in not taking them into consultation on these great issues affecting the peace of the world, sealed the President's fate. When the Senate refused to ratify the Treaties and the League, Wilson set off on a speaking tour of the country in the hope of gaining the support of the nation to his plans, but his health gave way and he was stricken with paralysis.

From his sick-bed he had to listen, helpless, to the news of the overwhelming victory of the Republican candidate, Warren C. Harding, at the Presidential election of 1920. In July 1921 Congress resolved that "the state of war declared to exist between the Imperial German Government and the United States of America, by the joint resolution of Congress, approved April 6, 1917, is hereby declared at an end". With these brief words did the Americans officially end their participation in the First World War. Woodrow Wilson died in 1924, and with him went his unrealised dream of America's leading the world to a new era of peace and security. But it was by no means the end of America's concern with European affairs.

THE UNITED STATES AFTER THE WAR

The war had left Europe desolate, prostrate and bankrupt; it left America physically unscathed and economically enriched. Before the war the United States was among the debtor countries; after the war it was the foremost creditor country in the world. In fact, the effect of the war was to shift the centre of economic gravity from the Eastern to the Western Hemisphere. Nevertheless, America had its post-war disturbances, especially in the industrial field, where in 1919 there was an epidemic of strikes in almost every industry and service.

Two reforms—one social, the other political—were hastened by the war, and both were such as could be carried only by amendments to the Constitution. The first of the two amendments—the eighteenth—prohibited the manufacture, sale and transportation of intoxicating liquor throughout the United States. The amendment became effective in 1920, but it did not work. It led to all sorts of subterfuges and breaches of the law, and thirteen years later another amendment was carried repealing Prohibition, so that it was again left to any individual state to decide whether it would be "wet" or "dry". The second of these post-war amendments—the nineteenth—said "that the right of citizens of the United States to vote shall not be denied or abridged by the United States or by any State on account of sex". Thus, in time for the Presidential Election of 1920, all women in the United States had the same right to vote as men, and thus woman suffrage was more completely carried in the United States by the amendment of 1920 than it was in Britain by the Act of 1918.

The defeat of the Democrats in 1920 began a succession of three Republican Presidents—Warren Harding, who died in office in 1923, Calvin Coolidge (1923-9) and Herbert Hoover (1929-33). In the midst of the post-war prosperity there was wild speculation in stocks and shares; vast fortunes were made and lost, and generally there was an atmosphere of materialism. What was called the "Coolidge prosperity" saw a boom period in which the national debt was reduced and the standard of living rose. Herbert Hoover, who succeeded Coolidge in 1929, had been at the White House only a few months when the boom was suddenly halted. The mad speculation led to a crash on the American stock market. This was in October 1929, and it was the premonitory sign of a depression which was to be prolonged and world-wide.

Throughout the 1920's, although the United States had no official part in the League of Nations or the affairs of Europe, many Americans remained, for various reasons, active in the international field. The idealists, who regretted Wilson's defeat, wished to see their country play an active part in the International Court at The Hague. At one time the Senate Foreign Relations Committee actually reported favourably on the proposal that America should accept a seat on the Bench of the World Court. But nothing positive was done at the time, and in 1935 the proposal was finally dropped.

The moneyed interests in America, however, were much concerned to collect the war debts arising from the vast amounts that the United States had advanced to the Allies during the war. In 1922 Britain agreed to a settlement of her debts to America, but most of the other European debtors contended that the question of debts should go hand in hand with that of reparations due to them from Germany under the Treaty of Versailles. America refused to admit that the two went together, and the absurd situation was reached in which America was advancing loans to Germany, without which she would not have been able to make even the inadequate payments of reparations that she did manage to achieve. With the advent of the depression, America was unable to continue making loans to Germany, who consequently defaulted again. At last, in 1931, America for the first time agreed to consider debts and reparations together and President Hoover declared a moratorium for one year. After that, although at no time did the United States recognise their cancellation, debt payments by Europe to America were never resumed.

Another way in which America retained her interest in international affairs after the war was through her naval position. In peace-time, America had no desire to maintain large land forces, and as soon as the war was over she rapidly demobilised her vast armies. But on the sea it was a different matter. There her interests were world-wide, for she had to safeguard her future both in the Atlantic and in the Pacific. She therefore realised the importance of maintaining her naval strength in relation to other Powers, and especially the two largest, namely Britain and Japan. If America had continued the programme launched during the war, she would, by 1924, have become the strongest naval power in the world. In order, therefore, to maintain the balance without being involved in this vast programme, she sought an agreed limitation of naval armaments among the Powers. To this end, in November 1921 President Harding invited Britain and Japan, together with France, Italy, China, The Netherlands, Belgium and Portugal, to a Conference at Washington. All accepted the invitation.

At the Washington Naval Conference America proposed a "naval holiday" for ten years. What this really meant was an agreed ratio for the various nations in the building of capital ships. But the only result was a race in the building of auxiliary ships, which were not mentioned in the proposals. Among other important results of the Washington Conference was a treaty by which America, Britain, France and Japan agreed to respect each other's rights in the Pacific, and, in view of this decision, there was no longer any need for the Anglo-Japanese Alliance. Other treaties, signed by all nine Conference Powers, guaranteed the territorial integrity of China, and allowed her full control over her own tariff system.

These agreements seemed to hold out a bright prospect for the future peace of the world. But during the next few years the prospect faded, and in 1936, when Japan refused to bind herself any longer to her quota, the whole project collapsed. By that time, as you will read later, the world-wide depression had done its work, the aggressors were in the saddle in Europe and Asia, and the world was clearly heading for another universal clash of arms.

Chapter 9

THE WAR AND SOCIAL CHANGE

THE LOST GENERATION

THE First World War not only brought about many political changes: it also had a revolutionary effect on social conditions. The principal factor contributing to social change was the loss in man-power suffered by most of the thirty nations which took part in the war. Besides the eight million young men who were killed, several millions were wounded and many were maimed for life. Thus a large proportion of the young men of that period never reached mature manhood, or, if they did, were prevented by their war disablement from making the full contribution which they might otherwise have made to social progress. It is no wonder that the youth of Europe which was destroyed between 1914 and 1918 is sometimes referred to as the "Lost Generation".

The effect of these losses was to disturb the normal balance of age groups in the population and to increase the proportion of women to men. This, in most countries, tended to give women a much more important place in society than ever before, a tendency hastened by the part they had played in the war itself. Women in their millions worked both directly and indirectly in war services and in civilian occupations where they replaced men on war service. Thus many worked in the armed forces, in hospitals, canteens and camps, while many more were occupied on the land and the railways, in road transport and the postal service, in factories, offices, banks and commerce generally. All this made the demand of the women for a more direct and active share in politics irresistible, and,

106

as we have seen, several of the older states which had not already done so, such as Britain and the United States, granted women the vote, while woman suffrage was introduced into the constitutions of almost all the new states which the war created. The First World War thus precipitated a movement giving women a heightened status which has grown and spread since in most parts of the world, including Asia and Africa.

DISENCHANTMENT

The return from a war to a peace economy involved all states in many complications which had far-reaching social consequences. The unprecedented cost of the war left most nations impoverished. Added to huge debts which had to be met at the end of the war, there was in all the countries involved the question of rehabilitating wounded soldiers and the payment of war pensions to them. In some also, and in particular France and Belgium, there was the colossal problem of restoring devastated areas. Besides, each nation had to reabsorb its demobilised Service men. When you consider that in the war from beginning to end there were no fewer than sixty-five million men under arms, you may appreciate the enormity of the social problem involved in returning them to civilian life.

Nor was the situation made any easier by the increased feeling of nationalism, for not only were there more states than before the war but each adopted a policy of tariffs to protect its own post-war industrial growth, and this retarded the restoration of the flow of international trade, without which domestic production was bound in its turn to be restricted. Consequently there were fluctuations in trade, resulting in alternations of inflation and deflation which affected the composition of the new society. The landed aristocracy on the Continent was mostly ruined and in Russia disappeared. In Eastern Europe generally the peasants profited from the change, many of them becoming peasant proprietors. But the middle classes, in many countries, suffered badly from the depreciation of the currency to which governments resorted in an attempt to meet the vagaries of world economy. In Germany, in the middle 1920's, the mark fell so low that the war bonds, in which the middle class had invested, became valueless, while in France during much the same period government stock fell to about one-fifth of its original value. In Russia the Communist Government simply repudiated its predecessor's debts. The new Austria was cut off from its pre-war markets; Italy's poverty made her the scene of violent strikes and Communist agitation; and even Britain was supporting more than a million unemployed on the dole.

Thus the first flush of optimism which came with a sense of relief from the strain of war gave way to a phase of disillusion, which was described by one well-known English writer as "disenchantment". The view of a great many people seemed to be that, when mankind had suffered so much, it should receive some recompense. When the recompense was not forthcoming they became despondent about the future, and felt that life had no longer any serious purpose. The result was a considerable change in manners and customs. This phase of disenchantment, moreover, synchronised with the growing popularity of the public cinema and the arrival of wireless broadcasting. Although these two mass media had their educational importance, the general effect of their diffusion was to produce a new generation of passive lookers and listeners. The disillusionment following the war also led to a decline in religious observance and church-going.

In America the post-war spirit was seen in the spread of racketeering and gangsterism, which were encouraged by the popular determination to evade the Prohibition laws. But even among law-abiding citizens there developed a passion for possessions, judged from a purely quantitative standpoint. The accepted materialism of the period was well illustrated in a speech of President Hoover, in the course of which he said: "The slogan of social progress is changing from the full dinner pail to the full garage." As two American historians have written: "Cities were bigger, buildings taller, roads longer, fortunes greater, automobiles faster, colleges larger, night-clubs gayer, crimes more numerous . . . than ever before in history." That seems to sum up perfectly the general spirit of materialism, the social unrest, and the decline of manners in the Western world after the war.

Much of the social malaise of the post-war period was reflected in the Arts. Artists in almost every medium appeared to be deeply affected by the unrest and insecurity engendered by four years of war. Many of them repudiated the older forms of artistic expression which they felt to be irrelevant to the new society. In poetry the revolt took the form of free verse, without metre or rhyme as understood by poets of an earlier age. In prose it led some novelists, for example, to search for a new kind of word- and sentence-construction which in some extreme cases made the writing quite incomprehensible even to a reasonably cultured reader. In painting there appeared new forms called "cubism" and "surrealism"; while in sculpture the watchwords were "primitiveness" and "abstraction". In music the post-war years were marked by the growth of Jazz.

It must not be supposed, however, that all writers, painters, sculptors and musicians were infected at that time with a spirit of anarchy, or that many of them who sought new modes of expression did not produce works of great beauty. One of the good effects of the war on music, for example, was to send composers in search of traditional songs and dances which had become obscured by the passage of time, a search which encouraged a revival of interest in folk music. In the realm of dancing, too, there was a marked growth in the popularity of the ballet. Finally, a perfect harmonising of the arts of sculpture and architecture was achieved in some of the war memorials erected in many different parts of the world to symbolise the self-sacrifice of those who had died and the sense of loss sustained by those who survived.

INDUSTRY AND COMMUNICATIONS

The momentum of advance in science and technology during the later half of the nineteenth century and the opening years of the twentieth century was greatly increased by the demands of war, and after it society reaped the benefit of the inventive skill which the war had encouraged. The production of coal and iron, the life-blood of machine development, although it fell off somewhat in Britain, rose steeply in the United States and Russia, as well as in Japan, China, India and certain parts of Africa. At the same time there was some increase in cotton output and slightly more in wool. With a change in fashions after the war there was a big demand for silk, particularly in connection with lighter garments and stockings. Indeed, such was the demand that the output of natural silk was not enough. This led to the invention of processes for the manufacture of artificial silk, or rayon. At first this was thought to be a menace to the prosperity of producers of natural silk, but later the two industries became almost indistinguishable, and most manufacturers of natural silk also produced artificial silk.

After the war, too, household and office needs were met in an ever-increasing and improving flood of articles, such as furniture, tools, canning and refrigerating plant, leather, pottery, china and typewriters. Electricity, which the scientists of the nineteenth century had discovered, came into much more widespread use in industry and transport and in the home for both lighting and heating. In many parts of the world water-power was used for generating electricity, and hydro-electric plant was installed. In the leading industrial countries, however, only about 25 per cent. of the potential hydro-electric power has so far replaced coal for the driving of turbines.

Transport and communications advanced after the war in step with industrial developments. Those great inventions of the nineteenth century—the steamship, the railway, the telegraph and the telephone—which had made tremendous strides up to the outbreak of war in 1914, all played an important part in it and in the peace which followed. Steamships increased in number, tonnage and speed. Railways expanded, especially in newly industrialised countries in outlying parts of the world. The telegraph eased communication for business and social purposes. The telephone, too, came into much more general use in business and domestic life. Telegraphy and telephony, indeed, were rapidly transformed after the war by the development of wireless, a process hastened by the training during the war of many wireless technicians.

There had been considerable progress in wireless telegraphy since Marconi's experiments at the turn of the century, and by the outbreak of war in 1914 it was already widely in use for communication between ships. This proved a real boon to sailors during the war itself. In the 1920's there was an even more rapid development of wireless telegraphy, especially after the institution in 1925 of Marconi's "beam" service, which afforded cheap telegraphic communication over vast distances. By 1927 communication of this kind had been established between Britain, Canada, South Africa and Australia, and between European countries and America. Wireless threatened to render the cable entirely obsolete, but more recently the laying of telephone cables has given the submarine system a new lease of life.

Radio-telephony, which achieved the transmission not merely of messages by code but of speech and music, made parallel strides with wireless telegraphy. In 1927 the American Telegraph and Telephone Company and the British Post Office jointly set up a wireless telephone service between London and New York, and soon there was similar communication between the countries of continental Europe on the one hand and the North American continent on the other. Within the next few years similar services were established between Great Britain and India, South Africa, Australia and New Zealand. Meanwhile, broadcasting, in its more familiar sense, expanded at great speed. It first came into use in the United States in 1921, and in Britain in 1922 with the formation of the British Broadcasting Company, which was succeeded in 1927 by the British Broadcasting Corporation (B.B.C.). Such were the beginnings of the world-wide system of wireless broadcasting that we know to-day.

PROGRESS IN AERONAUTICS

Transport was further revolutionised during and after the war by the rapid development of motor-driven vehicles, a form of traction which was only in its infancy before 1914. The progress of the motor-car was most marked in the United States, where the number of cars increased from $1\frac{1}{4}$ millions in 1914 to nearly 4 millions in 1920, the latter figure being multiplied eightfold in the succeeding fifteen years. Mass-production methods, similar to those used in America, though on a smaller scale, caused rapid progress in motor-car production also in Britain and the countries of Western Europe. The spread of automobilism led to a vast expansion of oil and rubber production, and a great development of arterial roads.

Even more remarkable was the growth of aviation. Flying, in both lighter- and heavier-than-air machines, received a great stimulus by the demands of war in which, as we have seen, airships and aeroplanes played some part in action, though, as compared with that in the Second World War, only a minor role. The airship, or dirigible motor-driven balloon, had been first produced in Paris in 1898 by a Brazilian named Santos-Dumont who had settled in France, where in 1901 he made his first successful flight from St. Cloud, in the western suburbs of Paris, to the Eiffel Tower. He was soon followed by the German, Count Zeppelin, who constructed his first airship in 1900 and made his first series of flights in 1906. Meanwhile, in 1903 the Wright brothers had achieved their first successful flights in a heavier-than-air machine.

From that time aviation, in both airships and aeroplanes, made striking progress. The Wrights and others in America improved on their pioneer efforts. In France Santos-Dumont, turning from airships to aeroplanes, made a flight of twenty-five miles in 1906, while in 1909 Louis Blériot made the first flight across the English Channel from Calais to Dover. Most of the major belligerents in the war developed a considerable air force. Britain, for example, possessed some 300 planes at

A LONDON BUS CONDUCTRESS IN 1917

One of the many civilian occupations in which women replaced men during the First World War.

THE MENIN GATE AT YPRES, BELGIUM

Above the central arch of this impressive war memorial, completed in 1927, appears the following inscription: "To the armies of the British Empire who stood here from 1914 to 1918 and to those of their dead who have no known graves."

THE FIRST TRANSATLANTIC WIRELESS MESSAGE, 1901

Marconi (centre) and two colleagues (Messrs. Kemp and Paget) waiting at Signal Hill, New-foundland, to receive the message which at length triumphantly arrived.

THE FIRST TRANSATLANTIC FLIGHT, 1919

How John Alcock and Arthur Brown landed in a bog at Clifden, Ireland, after their epoch-making flight from Newfoundland.

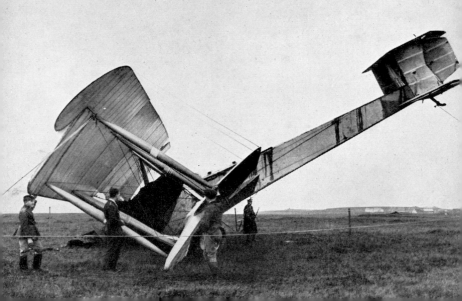

the beginning of the war. At the end of it the R.A.F. had nearly 23,000. After the war civil aviation also made rapid progress, although it was in Denmark, which was neutral in the war, that the world's first air-line company was formed in 1918.

In June 1919 the first transatlantic crossing was made by two English pilots, John Alcock and Arthur Brown, who flew from Newfoundland to Ireland, covering about 1,890 miles in about sixteen hours. In 1927 the American, Charles Lindbergh, made his famous solo non-stop flight from New York to Paris. In the same year another American, Admiral Richard Byrd, flew to the North Pole, and in 1929 flew over the South Pole. In 1928 the first transatlantic crossing took place from east to west. Women, too, took part in this development. The English woman pilot, Amy Johnson, flew alone from England to Australia in 1930; while in 1932 the American, Amelia Earhart, achieved the first solo transatlantic flight ever made by a woman. She also flew across the Pacific in 1935. In 1933 an American pilot, named Wiley Post, flew alone round the world from New York in less than eight days; two British aviators, Charles Scott and Campbell Black, flew from England to Australia in less than three days; and a British plane flew over Mount Everest at an altitude of 31,000 feet.

As to the parallel development of the airship, in 1924 Britain adopted a programme of airship construction. Under this plan two airships, the R.100 and the R.101, were completed in 1929. But the R.101, on her maiden voyage to India in 1930, was destroyed, and a distinguished company, including the Secretary of State for Air and the Director of Civil Aviation, perished. This disaster caused a slowing-down of British airship construction, and later it was abandoned altogether. Meanwhile, the airship was making remarkable progress in Germany. In 1929 the *Graf Zeppelin* not only crossed the Atlantic but circumnavigated the globe in twenty days. The future, however, was not with the airship but with the aeroplane, which, by 1939, had reached such a stage of development that it changed the whole character of warfare.

A. SUMMARY OF PART ONE

Chapter 1. When the twentieth century opened, Europe was still the economic centre of the world. Progress in transport and communications was annihilating distance and causing the world, in effect, to shrink. Thanks to medical science, the population of the world was growing at twice the annual rate of the nineteenth century, in which it had doubled itself, and that of Europe continued to grow despite the great increase in emigration overseas. The ideal of national democracy was realising itself through responsible parliamentary government in most Western European countries, while in Central and Eastern Europe autocracy, in varying degrees, survived. In America, Canada had become a Self-governing Dominion, the United States had completed the opening-up of the West and gained the Philippines from Spain, and in the centre and south the independence of the Latin American republics was fully established. Meanwhile, the New Imperialism of the Western Powers had brought about the dismemberment of China and the partition of Africa.

Chapter 2. The South African War (1899-1902) ended with the Treaty of Vereeniging, and was followed by the grant of self-government to the Transvaal (1906) and the Orange Free State (1907), and the establishment of the Union of South Africa (1910). In Britain the Liberals, returned with a large majority in 1906, carried out a programme of social reform, including old age pensions, labour exchanges and trade boards, National (health and unemployment) Insurance, and amendment of the Poor Law. Lloyd George's Budget of 1909, proposing taxes on land values, was rejected by the Lords, but, after two elections in 1910, the legislative power of the House of Lords was restricted by the Parliament Act (1911). The Trade Disputes Act of 1906 undid the effect of the Taff Vale Case (1901) and the Trade Union Act of 1913 that of the Osborne Judgment (1909), while the introduction of payment of Members in 1911 helped the growth of the Parliamentary Labour Party.

The militant movement for woman suffrage grew in violence, and the threat of civil war in Ireland, against the third Home Rule Act, was averted by the outbreak of war in 1914.

Chapter 3. Following the Anglo-Japanese Alliance of 1902, Britain ended her isolation from European entanglements through the understanding (*Entente Cordiale*) of 1904 with France and the Triple Entente of 1907 with France and Russia (the latter weakened by her defeat in the Russo-Japanese War of 1904–5). Germany, allied to Austria and Italy, pursued an active policy in North Africa, leading to the three Moroccan Crises (1905–11), and in the Balkans and Near East, while her naval policy led to Anglo-German rivalry in warship building. Many international societies worked for peace, but the second Hague Conference (1907) could not stop the race in armaments. In the Balkans the Young Turk Revolution of 1908 led to the formation of the Balkan League against Turkey and to the two Balkan Wars of 1912 and 1913, which left Serbia the strongest Balkan state and the object of Austrian animosity. The murder of the Austrian Archduke Ferdinand in Bosnia on June 28, 1914, was the spark which set Europe ablaze.

Chapter 4. The German plan to end the war quickly in 1914 by a decisive victory in the west before the Russians could fully mobilise was foiled by the French at the Marne, which saved Paris, and by the British at Ypres, which saved the Channel ports. The Western Front then became fixed in a continuous line of trenches, and the consequent frontal attacks by both sides (e.g. at Verdun, Somme and Passchendaele) were costly failures. The British Navy relentlessly blockaded Germany, whose counter-policy of unrestricted U-boat warfare brought America in against her in 1917; while Bolshevik Russia went out of the war and made with Germany the separate Treaty of Brest-Litovsk (March 1918). In the summer of 1918 the Allies, under Foch, having survived repeated German attacks, took the offensive on the Western Front as the Americans rapidly swelled their ranks. Meanwhile, the Turks were expelled from Palestine (1917) and from Mesopotamia (1918), and the Italians were at last successful against the Austrians. Thus the resistance of the Central Powers broke down and the war ended in a series of Armistices, signed September-November, 1918.

Chapter 5. The Peace Conference at Paris (1919) made five treaties: Versailles (Germany), St. Germain (Austria), Trianon

(Hungary), Neuilly (Bulgaria) and Sèvres (Turkey). By these treaties the victors disarmed the vanquished, redistributed their territories, imposed reparations on them, and instituted the League of Nations. Germany lost some of her European territory, including Alsace-Lorraine to France, and all her overseas possessions. The Empire of Austria-Hungary disappeared, leaving Austria and Hungary as small separate states; Serbia was enlarged to Yugoslavia; Czechoslovakia was one of six new sovereign states. The Ottoman Empire was broken up, although by the later Treaty of Lausanne (1923) the Turks regained some of their lost territory. The question of reparations was left to a special Commission which gradually scaled down the payments until by 1932 they had practically ceased. The Covenant of the League of Nations was incorporated in the Treaties and the League was established at Geneva in 1920 with an original membership of twenty-seven states, which rose to forty-eight by 1921, but never included the U.S.A.

Chapter 6. All the new states created after the war and based on the principle of national self-determination, promulgated republican democratic constitutions which granted the franchise to women and adopted P.R. The diminished Austria also became a republic, while Hungary ultimately emerged as a republican state. In Germany the Weimar Republic established responsible parliamentary government, an elected President replacing the hereditary Emperor. It also set up Economic Councils. The new nationalist spirit led also after the war to the Turkish Republic under Kemal Ataturk, to the movement towards independence of the Arab states, and to a revolution in Persia. Egypt became a constitutional monarchy in 1922 and an independent state in 1936 (with British reservations concerning the Sudan and the Suez Canal Zone). In Japan the military party became dominant in Parliament after the war, and adopted an expansionist policy against China, where Chiang Kai-shek became the leader of the Nationalist Party (the *Kuomintang*) after the death of Sun Yat-sen, the creator of the Chinese Republic, in 1925. As President, with dictatorial powers from 1928, Chiang had to face both the aggression of the Japanese and the growing power of the Chinese Communists.

Chapter 7. In post-war Britain industrial unrest reached its climax in the abortive General Strike of 1926, which was made illegal by the Trade Disputes Act of 1927. Schooling was improved by the Education Act of 1918, women were enfranchised by the Representation of the People Acts of 1918 and 1928, and the powers of the Poor Law Guardians were transferred to County and County Borough Councils by the Local Government Act of 1929. The first Labour Government (1924) was short-lived, and the second (1929) ended in 1931, when Ramsay MacDonald, in face of the financial crisis, formed a National Government and was deserted by most of his party. In 1932 Imperial Preference was initiated at the Ottawa Conference. Civil strife in post-war Ireland ended with the establishment of the Irish Free State (1922). The Imperial Conference of 1926 recognised the full independence of the Self-governing Dominions, and this was given legal force by the Statute of Westminster (1931). The Government of India Act of 1919 introduced partial responsible government (Dyarchy), against which Gandhi launched his "civil disobedience" campaign. The Simon Report and the Round Table Conference (1930) led to the Act of 1935 granting full responsible government in the Provinces and proposing an All-India Federation.

Chapter 8. In its early years the League of Nations did useful international work. The French failure to gather reparations by invading the Ruhr was followed by the Dawes Plan (1924), under which the period and method of payment were revised, and by a new international spirit; hence the Pact of Locarno (1925), Germany's admission to the League (1926), the Briand-Kellogg Pact (1928), and the withdrawal of the last of the Allied forces from Germany (1930). The American Senate having refused to ratify the treaties or join the League, Congress simply declared the war with Germany at an end (1921). At the Washington Naval Conference (1922) nine Powers agreed to proportionate restrictions on the building of capital ships. The eighteenth and ninetenth amendments to the American Constitution introduced Prohibition and enfranchised women (1920). Under the Republican President Coolidge (1923–9) there was growing prosperity, but under Hoover (1929–33) a depression set in and gradually spread all over the world.

Chapter 9. The First World War deeply affected the economy of states and the organisation of society. The loss of a generation of young men disturbed the balance of the sexes, and women gained a new social and political status. The disillusionment following the war prompted the growth of a materialistic view of life which was

117

reflected in art and religion. The inventive skill encouraged by the war led after it to a spread of public and private amenities (e.g. electricity, telephone, cinema and wireless), and to a striking advance in aeronautics, in which both men and women accomplished remarkable feats. For example, the Atlantic was flown, the South Pole reached by air, and the globe circumnavigated. Gradually, the aeroplane completely superseded the airship, and the consequent revolution in civil and military aviation not only introduced new modes of everyday travel but changed the character of warfare.

B. FURTHER STUDY

I. IMPORTANT WORDS

(Needing to be clearly defined in the reader's mind)

Abdication, aeronautics, aftermath, aggression, allegiance, anarchy, arbitration, aristocracy, assassination, assembly, attrition, autocracy, automobile, barrage, belligerent, blockade, broadcasting, cable, census, coalition, conciliation, confederation, conscription, constitution, convoy, copyright, covenant, creditor, currency, deflation, demobilisation, democracy, denomination, depreciation, depression, devastation, dictatorship, diplomacy, disarmament, disillusion, dole, economy, emigration, enfranchisement, executive, exploitation, federation, flank, franchise, gangsterism, hegemony, idealism, immigration, imperialism, improvisation, incorporation, inflation, judiciary, kingdom, legion, legislation, legislature, littoral, majority, mandate, manœuvre, materialism, minority, mobilisation, moratorium, nationalisation, neutrality, offensive, pacification, phenomenon, plebiscite, principle, prestige, prohibition, propaganda, protagonist, racketeer, realism, reconstruction, recruitment, régime, reparations, representative, republic, salient, secretariat, statute, suffrage, superstructure, supertax, tank, tariff, technology, telegraphy, telephony, transport, turbine, ultimatum, veto.

2. IMPORTANT TECHNICAL TERMS

Afrikaans, Anglo-Japanese Alliance, Berlin-Baghdad Railway, Black and Tans, Boers, Bolsheviks, Briand-Kellogg Pact, budget, *Bundestag*, Cabinet, "civil disobedience", Congress, Conservativism, Constituent Assembly, Co-operative Society, Czar, "Dark Continent," Democratic Party (U.S.A.), Die-hard, Dreadnought, Dual Alliance,

Dual Monarchy, *Duma*, Dyarchy, Economic Council, *Entente Cordiale*, Expeditionary Force, foreign exchange, "freedom of the seas", Friendly Society, Guardians, heir-apparent, House of Representatives, hydro-electric power, Imperial Preference, Irish Republican Army, Kaiser, *Kuomintang*, Labour Exchange, *Land* (German state), Latin America, Liberalism, Machine Age, Marconi's Beam Service, Mikado, Money Bill, National Self-determination, Navy League, Olympic Games, Osborne Judgment, Pact of Locarno, passive resistance, political levy, Poor Law, "Ramshackle Empire", Red Cross Society, *Reich*, *Reichsrat*, *Reichstag*, Republican Party (U.S.A.), Responsible Government, Rhineland, Round Table Conference, Royal Commission, Ruhr, Schlieffen Plan, Self-governing Dominion, Senate, Shah, *Sinn Fein*, Slavs, Social Democrats, social security, Spartacus Group, Succession States, Supreme Court, *Swaraj*, Taff Vale Case, Tariff Reform, Trade Union Congress, Trialism, Triple Alliance, Triple Entente, *Uitlanders*, Ulster Volunteers, unearned increment, Universal Postal Union, Universal Telegraph Union, U-boat, Young Turks, *Zeppelin*.

3. IMPORTANT PERSONS

Abdul Hamid II, Alcock (aviator), Asquith, Baldwin, Balfour, Blériot, Black (Campbell), Bonar Law, Botha, Briand, Brown (aviator), Burns (John), Byrd, Campbell-Bannerman, Carnegie, Carson, Chamberlain (Joseph, Austen and Neville), Chiang Kai-shek, Clemenceau, Collins (Michael), Coolidge, Cosgrave, Cromer (Lord), Dawes, De Valera, Earhart (Amelia), Ebert, Edward VII, Edward VIII, Ferdinand (Archduke), Fisher (H. A. L.), Foch, French (General), Gandhi, George V, George VI, Grey (Edward), Griffith (Arthur), Haig, Haldane, Harding (Warren), Hindenburg, Hoover, Humbert (King of Italy), Joffre, Johnson (Amy), Kellogg, Kemal Ataturk, Kitchener, Kruger, Liebknecht, Lindbergh, Lloyd George, Ludendorff, Luxemburg (Rosa), MacDonald (Ramsay), Marconi, Masaryk (Thomas), Nobel, Orlando, Pankhurst (Mrs.), Pétain, Pethick-Lawrence (Mrs.), Redmond, Roberts (Lord), Roosevelt (Theodore), Salisbury (Lord), Samuel (Herbert), Sankey (Lord), Santos-Dumont, Scott (C.W.A.), Simon (John), Snowden, Stresemann, Sun Yat-sen, Tirpitz, Victoria (Queen), Victor Emmanuel III, Zeppelin (Count), Wiley Post (aviator), William II (*Kaiser*), Wilson (Woodrow), Wright (Wilbur and Orville).

4. IMPORTANT DEVELOPMENTS (in chronological order)

Technological progress, world shrinkage, and population trends; end of the Frontier in U.S.A.; the New Imperialism in relation to (a) the expansion of Europe, (b) the Spanish-American War, (c) the dismemberment of China and the awakening of Japan, (d) the partition of Africa and the South African War; the effect of the Act of 1902 on education in Britain; Liberal reforms and the Parliament Act of 1911; the approach of the First World War, with special consideration of alliances and balance of power, international peace agencies, and the Balkan Wars; phases of the war; the treaties and the League; the making of the post-war political constitutions; constitutional experiments in Japan and origin and growth of the Chinese Republic; background and emergence of the Irish Free State; post-war Britain, with special reference to the first Labour Governments and what followed them; growth of Dominion Self-government and the significance of the Imperial Conference of 1926 and the Statute of Westminster of 1931; Responsible Government in India and the Act of 1935; work of the League of Nations and the effect of the Pact of Locarno; America and the spread of the Depression; social effects of the War.

5. NOTES ON SPECIAL POINTS

(a) *Monarchy and Republic*

In contemporary Europe the terms Monarchy and Republic no longer indicate any real difference between the states so called. There are only six monarchies left, but most of them are quite as democratic in their government as the republics. In the Kingdom of Britain and of Denmark, for example, the hereditary monarch exercises political power through ministers who are responsible to Parliament, just as the elected President acts in, for instance, the Republic of post-war Italy. Hence Britain has been described as a "Crowned Republic".

(b) *The House of Lords as the Final Court of Appeal*

It is a very ancient function of the House of Lords to act as the final Court of Appeal, but the present composition and procedure of the Court were laid down in an Act of 1876. Any civil case tried in the High Court may be taken by a dissatisfied party to the Court of Appeal, but, if one party is still dissatisfied, permission may be granted for the case to be finally considered by the House of Lords. Only the Law Lords (i.e. the Lord Chancellor, ex-Lord Chancellors and "Lords of Appeal in Ordinary") are present to hear appeals, generally five at any hearing, and the decision of the majority is binding. The House of Lords also acts, though more rarely, as the final Court of Criminal Appeal, in which case, again, it sits as a special Court, as constituted by an Act of 1907.

(c) *Proportional Representation (P.R.)*

P.R. cannot be worked in single-member constituencies, as we have them in Britain, since it requires in each constituency a number of candidates so that the voter can express his preferences. There are many different forms of P.R. Here is an example of the working of one method, known as the single transferable vote. Let us suppose that there are ten candidates for four seats in a given constituency. The voter may express his preferences by placing against four of the names the numbers 1, 2, 3, 4, so that, if the vote for his first choice is not wanted because the candidate has reached the quota without it, that vote can be transferred to the voter's next choice, and so on through the series.

(d) *Some American Constitutional Factors*

(i) *Senatorial Life.*—In the U.S.A. a third of the Senate retires every two years, so that each Senator is elected for six years and the two Senators for each state are elected at different times, namely at two of the biennial Congressional elections within the six-year period. In other words, any state misses one election for Senator in every series of three general elections. Any Senator is eligible for re-election.

(ii) *Presidential Election.*—The original intention of the founders of the Constitution was that the President and Vice-President should be elected by an Electoral College in each state composed of a number of representatives equal to the number of members for that state in Congress. Nowadays, American citizens, in electing the Electoral College, actually vote for a known candidate nominated by the party for which he stands. Thus the election of the College has become a mere form and the President and Vice-President are, in fact, directly elected by the people.

(iii) *Amending the Constitution.*—An amendment to the American Constitution may be proposed either by two-thirds of the total membership of each House of Congress or by a convention specially called for the purpose when the legislatures of two-thirds of the states of the Union petition Congress to call it. If, as a result of either of these procedures, an amendment is agreed on, then it does not become effective until three-quarters of the states (now, with Alaska and Hawaii added [1959], numbering 50) ratify it.

(e) *Cable and Wireless*

The development of wireless communication in the twentieth century threatened to render obsolete the transatlantic telegraph cable (originally laid in 1866). But the radio-telephone system between Europe and America could not bear the strain of the growing use of it (e.g. over 100,000 calls in 1954). The consequent crowding of wave-lengths and atmospheric interference with wireless speech led to a joint Anglo-United States-Canadian project for a two-way transatlantic telephone cable. The first of the twin cables was laid in 1955 and the second in 1956.

6. READING AND REFERENCE

Among the many books on this period any of the following may be helpfully read or consulted.

(a) *General.*—Bowen: *The World in the Twentieth Century*; Brummel: *The Changing World*; Cruikshank: *Roaring Century*; Happold: *This Modern Age*; Ogilvie: *Our Times*; Thomson: *World History (1914–1950)*; Lipson: *Europe in the 19th and 20th Centuries*; Barker: *Britain and the British People*; Somervell: *British Politics since 1900*; Carrington: *The British Overseas*; McInnis and Reid: *The English-speaking Peoples*; Strong: *Dynamic Europe, Modern Political Constitutions*, and *The Story of the American People*; Nevins and Commager: *America, The Story of a Free People*; Pratt: *The Expansion of Europe in the Far East*; Hudson: *The Far East in World Politics*.

(b) *Biography.*—Jones: *Lloyd George*; Baker: *Woodrow Wilson*; Adams: *Clemenceau*.

(c) *Britain before the First World War.*—Ensor: *England (1870–1914)*; Churchill: *Liberalism and the Social Problem*; Maurois:

The Edwardian Era; Sackville-West: *The Edwardians*; Gore: *Edwardian Scrapbook*.

(d) *The First World War and After.*—(i) *Historical Accounts*: Churchill: *World Crisis. 1911–1918*; Mansergh: *The Coming of the First World War*; Cruttwell: *History of the Great War*; Liddell-Hart: *History of the World War*; Zimmern: *The League of Nations and the Rule of Law*; Mowat: *Britain Between the Wars*.

(ii) *Fiction, Poetry and Drama:* Aldington: *Death of a Hero*; Barbusse: *Under Fire (Le Feu)*; Hemingway: *A Farewell to Arms*; Monkhouse; *The Conquering Hero*; Mottram: *The Spanish Farm* (a trilogy); Raymond: *Tell England*; Remarque: *All Quiet on the Western Front*; Tomlinson: *All Our Yesterdays*. War Poems by Laurence Binyon, Rupert Brooke, Julian Grenfell, Wilfrid Owen and Siegfried Sassoon (to be found in most anthologies of modern verse); R. C. Sherriff's play about trench life, *Journey's End*.

C. TOPICS FOR ESSAYS AND DISCUSSIONS

1. In what sense was the world shrinking as the twentieth century opened?

2. How did the Empires in Eastern Europe differ in their political organisation from the states of Western Europe before the First World War?

3. Explain the significance of the South African War in British history.

4. Describe the main Liberal reforms of the period 1906–14, and explain their importance in the growth of social security.

5. Imagine yourself a member of one of the voluntary organisations working for peace before the First World War, and account for the failure of your association, in conjunction with the others, to prevent the outbreak of war in 1914.

6. In what respects did the First World War differ from earlier wars, and what were the main causes of the defeat of the Central Powers?

7. Describe the main territorial changes in Europe made by the Paris Peace Conference in 1919. Illustrate your answer with two maps showing the political divisions before and after the war.

8. Outline the organisation of the League of Nations and show in what respects it was new as a project of internationalism.

9. Give a brief account of (*a*) the nationalist movements in the Near and Middle East after the First World War; (*b*) the early years of the Chinese Republic; (*c*) the effect of the war on Japan's position in the Far East.

10. Suppose yourself a representative of one of the Dominions at the Imperial Conference of 1926 and, in the light of the discussions there, say how far you consider the Statute of Westminster to have satisfied the claims of the Dominions to independence.

11. Describe the situation in the United States after the war, in the form of a letter to a friend at home as if you were on a visit to America at the time.

12. What were some of the effects of the First World War on European society? Include in your answer a brief passage (in prose or verse) describing your thoughts in pondering on the "Lost Generation" or in looking at a war memorial.

13. Debate the following propositions, as though the members of the form were contemporary with the events to which the topics refer:

(*a*) That Tariff Reform will inevitably lower the workers' standard of living (1903–5).

(*b*) That the Parliament Act, curtailing the powers of the House of Lords, is a necessary step in the growth of democracy (1911).

(*c*) That Home Rule will reconcile the Catholic Irish to their continued political association with Britain (1912–14).

(*d*) That Germany can prevent war by not supporting Austria in her demands on Serbia (1914).

(*e*) That the United States of America should:
 (i) remain neutral in the war against Germany (1917);
 (ii) join the League of Nations (1920).

(*f*) That the General Strike is an attack on the British Constitution (1926).

(*g*) That Mr. Ramsay MacDonald should resign rather than form a National Government with his political opponents (1931).

(*h*) That P.R., although in theory a good democratic device, in practice makes stable government difficult (1919–32).

(*i*) That the war (of 1914–18) was fought in vain. (Any time between 1918 and 1928.)

PART TWO

THE DICTATORS AND THE SECOND WORLD WAR

Chapter 10

THE MAKING OF SOVIET RUSSIA

THE BACKGROUND OF THE RUSSIAN REVOLUTION

PARLIAMENTARY democracy, which became almost universal in Europe in the period immediately following the First World War, proved in many states to be short-lived. In those states the parliamentary system was violently replaced by a dictatorship, whereunder the ruling power imposed its will on the rest of the community, which was thus denied any real share in the control of its own political destiny. Such a dictatorship is a modern development of an earlier type of personal rule variously referred to as tyranny, absolutism, autocracy and despotism. In the states of Central and Eastern Europe the tradition of autocracy was much more real and deep-seated than was the parliamentary principle, which accounts in those states for the apparently easy triumph of dictatorship. In essence, the modern dictator's power is based on the strength of a single party which forcibly excludes all others and sets itself up as the only authority in the state. Such a régime is therefore called authoritarian. In the exercise of his authority through a single party the dictator dominates all aspects of the people's lives, and hence his rule is called totalitarian.

The Russians were the first to repudiate the methods of Western constitutional government which they had only recently and very superficially adopted, and to build up a new authoritarian and totalitarian system in its place. But when they did so in 1917, in the crisis of the First World War, the basis of the despotism which the revolutionaries imposed was quite different from that of the older autocracy of the Czars. It was, in theory at least, based on what Karl Marx had called the Dictatorship of the Proletariat. There have been few, if any, more dynamic movements in all history than the Bolshevik Revolution of 1917. To understand its success and to account for the survival of the system it created, while most of the other inter-war dictatorships have since been overthrown, it is necessary to consider its peculiar background, so different from that of the others, whether in Italy, Germany, Spain or elsewhere.

Russia, in its history, its interests and its existing extent is as much Asiatic as European, and at the present time, although three-quarters of its total population are concentrated in Europe, four-fifths of its area lie in Asia. Russia's history thus made her the victim of the conflicting pulls of East and West. On the one hand, her contiguous Asiatic interests gave her a different outlook from that of the rest of Europe and tended to cut her off from its life and progress. On the other hand, the more enlightened leaders of the European majority of her people cherished the hope that she might develop politically according to a Western pattern.

At the opening of the twentieth century, Russia remained by far the most backward of the larger states of Europe. Although serfdom had been abolished in 1861, most of the peasants remained poor and underfed. Only 15 per cent. of the population lived in towns, most of which were little more than enlarged villages, while 80 per cent. of Russians remained illiterate. Nevertheless, towards the close of the nineteenth century there had begun an industrial development which revealed, though in a milder form, many of the characteristics of similar changes in the West. It created the beginnings of a middle class (*bourgeoisie*), aided by foreign, and especially French, capital. It produced a class of industrial workers (proletariat), mostly from the emancipated serfs who provided a reservoir of cheap labour. Yet Russia remained an overwhelmingly agrarian society, and while this partial industrial revolution went far enough to create conditions of unrest, it was not sufficiently widespread of itself to bring social and political reform in its wake. It was, in fact, a series of external events, namely the disasters of the Russo-Japanese War (1904–5), which brought about a crisis.

The war was hopelessly mismanaged and the government became gravely discredited. The middle-class leaders demanded a share in the government through constitutional reform, while the workers' representatives met to air their grievances in improvised councils or *soviets* (a Russian word meaning councils). While the Czar's government was considering the constitutional proposals, the workers staged a series of strikes, culminating in a great demonstration in St. Petersburg on Sunday, January 22, 1905, when the police opened fire on a procession, and thus, by so much spilling of blood, made this day memorable as Red Sunday. In October the Czar issued a manifesto summoning a *Duma*, or Parliament, to be elected on a fairly wide franchise. The first Duma met in May 1906, and the Russian parliamentary experiment began. But it was evident from the beginning that the Czar's advisers were not prepared to observe the conditions of the October Manifesto. The Ministry, composed of Liberal members, responsible to the Duma, were denied control of the armed forces, foreign policy and even finance; while an attempt was made to exclude the Social Democrats, who generally represented the workers' interests, on the ground that they were disloyal to the throne.

In these circumstances the constitutional experiment made a poor start. The first Duma was dissolved after six weeks, and the second, which assembled in March 1907, lasted only three months. The third, however, ran its full five-year term until 1912, and succeeded in passing a number of laws for the reform of justice and local government and the improvement of agriculture and education. It even introduced state insurance for workers. The fourth Duma, elected in 1912, though not quite so successful as the third, remained in existence until the débâcle of 1917. The Russian Duma was far from enjoying the power of the parliaments of Western, or even of Central,

Europe. Nevertheless, it went a considerable way towards modifying the autocratic régime of the Czar, and but for the war might have gone on in later years to achieve a more solid democratic status. As it was, it lacked the strength to cope with the rising tide of social and political unrest aggravated by war losses and deprivations. Thus the constitutional experiment failed, and this failure at length opened the flood-gates of revolution.

LENIN AND THE BOLSHEVIK REVOLUTION

The Russian Revolution of 1917 passed through two phases: first the political revolution in March which destroyed the Czarist autocracy, and secondly the social revolution in November (October, according to the old Russian calendar) which created the Workers' Republic. In the first weeks of 1917 discontent was rampant. In Petrograd (as St. Petersburg had by then been renamed), Moscow and other cities there were bread riots, strikes and demonstrations against the war and the Czar. Troops called out to quell the rioters refused to fire on them. By March 15 the situation had become so ugly that the Czar was persuaded to abdicate, and the opposition leaders in the Duma set up a Provisional Government, later reconstructed and led by a revolutionary lawyer named Alexander Kerensky. But now a curious system of dual control emerged, for the workers were again organising themselves in soviets, as they had done in 1905. This time, however, they were much more effective. Soviets, composed of industrial workers, peasants, soldiers and sailors, appeared in every town and village, and when the Petrograd Soviet summoned a Congress of Soviets, it rapidly became more powerful than the Duma.

At this crucial moment there returned to Russia Vladimir Ulyanov, better known as Lenin, which was the name under which he wrote as a journalist. Lenin has been described as "the greatest revolutionary genius of modern times", and it is certainly true that the Revolution which he directed changed the course of world history. Born in 1870, the son of a schoolmaster,

VLADIMIR LENIN (1870–1924)
Founder of the Soviet State, as he was in 1917.

JOSEPH STALIN (1879–1953)
Successor to Lenin, as he was in 1928.

THE ALL-RUSSIAN SOVIET CONGRESS
Delegates from every part of the U.S.S.R. are seen in this picture of a meeting held in the White
Hall of the Kremlin, Moscow.

INDUSTRIAL DEVELOPMENT IN THE U.S.S.R.

Combing machines in a synthetic rubber factory in western Russia, capable of an annual product of more than seven million tyres for cars .commercial vehicles and aeroplanes.

COLLECTIVE FARMING IN THE U.S.S.R.

Harvest workers on a collective farm in the Ukraine taking their midday meal in the fields.

he became a lawyer in St. Petersburg, but spent most of his time there moving among factory workers, educating them politically and building up the Social Democratic Labour Party. For these activities he was sent to Siberia, whence he escaped, living for a time in London. He returned to Russia during the disturbances of 1905, but had to escape again when the rising was suppressed. Meanwhile, there had been a split in the Russian Social Democratic Party, which had been founded by Marxists in 1898 and to which Lenin belonged. At a conference of this party held in London in 1903, the majority (*Bolshinstvo* in Russian) voted in favour of a more active and militant membership of the party against the minority (Russian, *Menshinstvo*), who stood for a looser organisation. Thus originated the two sections, Bolsheviks and Mensheviks. In 1912 the Mensheviks were expelled from the party by the Bolsheviks, who later formed the official Russian Communist Party which, under the leadership of Lenin, carried through the revolution of 1917.

At the outbreak of the Revolution in March 1917, Lenin was in Switzerland. In April the Germans, seeing this as a heaven-sent opportunity of making the Russian confusion worse confounded, gave Lenin a "safe-conduct" to Russia. During the next four months Lenin's influence grew, as Kerensky's hope of keeping Russia in the war against Germany faded, and he at length came to the decision to destroy the Provisional Government and the Duma in favour of the Bolsheviks and the soviets. Now, Lenin was a disciple of Karl Marx, and he determined to establish a Communist state on the basis of the dictatorship of the proletariat, as Marx had taught. Yet none of the conditions which Marx had prognosticated for the carrying out of such a revolution existed in Russia at that time. Nevertheless, the conditions favoured Lenin and falsified Marx. The very absence of a strong middle class weakened the Duma and thus opened the way for the triumph of the soviets. Moreover, in advocating the taking over of the land by the peasants, Lenin deviated from the Marxist creed, but thereby secured the strongest possible bulwark for the Bolshevik Revolution.

Gradually, under Lenin's sure guidance, the Bolsheviks built a majority in the soviets at Petrograd (now called Leningrad), Moscow and other cities. The Petrograd Soviet was by then presided over by another remarkable leader, and a stalwart champion of Lenin, named Leon Trotsky, who had recently returned from America. Under Trotsky's inspiration the Petrograd Soviet set up a Military Revolutionary Committee and began to recruit and drill a Red Army. On November 7, 1917, in the middle of the night, Red Guards occupied key-points in Petrograd and made themselves masters of the city. The soviets of other towns quickly followed Petrograd's example. Meanwhile, a Constituent Assembly had been called to consider a new political constitution. In January 1918, when this Assembly met, it rejected a Bolshevik resolution to the effect that "Russia is a Republic of Soviets", whereupon Lenin forcibly dissolved the Assembly and proclaimed the Soviet Government to be the "Government of all Russia".

Thus, by a *coup d'état*, Lenin achieved his purpose. The new government took the land from the landlords without compensation and arranged for the election of committees to redistribute it among the peasants. It placed the factories in the hands of committees elected by the workers, and nationalised the banks, the railways and the larger industrial undertakings. Lenin then issued an appeal to all nations to reach "a just and democratic peace". When the appeal failed he was forced to accept from the Germans, in March 1918, the shameful peace of Brest-Litovsk, by which Russia was deprived of vast territories, including Georgia and the Ukraine, Finland, Poland and the Baltic lands, besides having imposed on her a huge war indemnity.

The Soviet Republic was thus out of the world war, but it was soon involved in a civil war. In this war the Bolsheviks had to face the opposition not only of the dispossessed classes, assisted by the Western Powers, but also of the Mensheviks and other anti-Bolshevik revolutionary groups. For the next two years Russia was the unhappy cockpit of the opposed "Red Terror" and "White Terror". But the counter-revolution failed, and by 1920, thanks to Lenin's leadership, Trotsky's organising ability, and the toughness of commanders like Joseph Stalin, the Soviet power stood supreme.

THE TRIUMPH OF STALIN

While Lenin lived he remained the unquestioned leader of the revolution and of the Communist Party. When he was at the helm in those early years, the Russian Revolution made a strong appeal to Socialists all over the world, and many believed that a new age of enlightenment would follow the Russian success. But when Lenin died in 1924 there ensued a struggle for leadership between Stalin and Trotsky which ended in the triumph of Stalin. "Stalinism", as the new policy came to be called, seemed to drain the Revolution of its pristine idealism. As this change was gradually appreciated, it caused widespread disillusion among those who had originally expected so much from the destruction of the Czarist autocracy, and turned the tide of world opinion against the Soviet régime.

Stalin, the son of a shoemaker in Georgia, in the Caucasus, was born in 1879. He was originally intended for the priesthood, but in 1896 was expelled from his theological college because of his political opinions, and from that time waged incessant war against the Czarist régime. Leon Trotsky, whose real name was Levi Bronstein, was born in 1877, the son of a Jewish farmer in the Ukraine. He escaped from Siberia, to which he had been exiled, and, exiled once more, he made his way to America, whence he returned on the outbreak of the Revolution in 1917.

At the moment of Lenin's death Stalin was Secretary of the Central Committee of the Communist Party and Trotsky the Commissar of War. Theirs was a battle of personalities: it was also a battle of ideas or ideologies. It had always been assumed by Marxists that the revolution in Russia would be followed by similar revolutions in the capitalist countries of the rest of the world. Lenin believed this, and therefore strongly supported the *Comintern* (otherwise known as the Third International), which was established in Moscow in 1919 as "the general staff of world revolution". But, in fact, the Revolution did not spread, as expected, and where it was attempted immediately after the war, as it was in Germany and Hungary, it failed.

In spite of all the evidence against it, Trotsky, after Lenin's death, persisted in his belief in "permanent revolution" spreading throughout the world. Stalin, on the other hand, was a realist who knew that world revolution, at least at that period, was a dream. He realised that revolutionary Russia could survive only through industrial development, and that this would require for a long time to come the machinery and technical aid which other countries could alone provide. If, by cultivating commercial relations with other states, Russia could thus get the requisite technical equipment, then, Stalin believed, it was practicable to maintain what he called "Socialism in one country". Trotsky and his followers held the opposite view. Therefore Stalin decided to destroy all Trotskyists. As Secretary of the Communist Party, Stalin controlled the party machine, and he ruthlessly "purged" the party of all opponents to his plan, whether they were Bolsheviks on the Left or on the Right. Thus, within five years of Lenin's death Stalin had driven Trotsky into exile, and had "liquidated" all unrepentant Trotskyists. Trotsky, in fact, remained in exile until in 1940 he was assassinated in Mexico.

THE FIVE-YEAR PLANS

In pursuit of his policy of "Socialism in one country", Stalin carried out a series of Five-year Plans for the development of heavy industry, transport and electrification, the first of which was launched in 1928. This was in some respects an extension of Lenin's earlier schemes. During the civil war in Russia (1918–20), all industries had been taken over by the state, private trade prohibited, and the necessities of everyday life completely communalised, while the peasants were forced to yield a quota of their produce to feed the armies and the towns. When the civil war ended, Lenin modified this "War Communism" and introduced what he called the New Economic Policy (N.E.P.). The state retained ownership of the forests, mines, banks, railways and heavy industry, and the absolute control of foreign trade, but retail trade was again permitted, peasants were allowed to sell produce in the open market, private enterprise was partially restored, and payment of wages replaced token payments. Lenin then introduced a fifteen-year scheme of electrification by utilising water-power to be obtained through the building of huge dams on the Dnieper, Volga and other great rivers.

It was this policy of Lenin's that Stalin took up and extended in 1928. New factories, railways and roads were built, new mines opened, and new furnaces and engineering plants set up. On the execution of the Five-year Plan all the national energies were concentrated, and life was lived with Spartan rigour on the barest necessities in order to release exports with which to pay for the necessary imports of vital machinery which Russia could not then herself produce. In 1932 the Second Five-year Plan was launched, and was completed in 1937, some months ahead of schedule. These first two Five-year Plans revolutionised the industrial life of Russia. By 1937 Russia was producing three or four times as much coal, iron, steel, cement, oil and paper as in later Czarist days. She was also manufacturing goods not hitherto produced there, such as motor-cars, tractors, aeroplanes, bicycles and gramophones, besides copper and aluminium products and synthetic rubber. In fact, by the middle 'thirties Russia was producing over 200,000 motor-cars a year, and more tractors and locomotives than any other country in the world. By 1937, twenty-five million people were engaged in industry where only eight million had been so employed fifteen years before.

It was not until the opening of 1939 that the details of the third Five-year Plan were announced. It was, of course, not completed at the time of the German invasion in 1941, when it was modified and adapted to war purposes. Its object was said to be to make Russia "independent economically and technically, and its defences invulnerable". It concentrated on a maximum output of the "means of production"—machinery, metallurgy, fuel and electric power—and, only secondarily, on the production of consumer goods to ease the lives and encourage the morale of the people. Its most interesting feature was the shift of the centres of new production eastward to the region of the Volga and the Urals, and even beyond to Siberia and the Far East, a change which assumed a vital significance when the west of the country was overrun by the Germans.

This planned industrialisation could not have been carried out without a corresponding development of agriculture, in which, for some time after the Revolution, methods and implements remained quite primitive. The expropriation of the great landed estates and peasant proprietorship were not enough to meet the new industrial situation with the increasing numbers of urban mouths to be fed. Moreover, the policy of expropriation and redistribution, left to itself, tended to create a class of wealthy peasant farmers, known as *kulaks*, which threatened to become a new kind of *bourgeoisie*. Stalin saw that Russia could become a truly Socialist state only if land, as well as the means of industrial production, distribution and exchange, were state-owned. In 1928, therefore, he introduced the policy of "collectivisation", which meant combining peasant holdings in large farms under a system of collective ownership and production. The project had three objects: to feed all the members of the collective group, to gather a quota for the government, and to produce a surplus which might be sold in the open market. The policy met with the violent resistance of the peasantry, whose refusal to co-operate caused an acute economic crisis. But Stalin crushed the opposition with utter ruthlessness and proceeded with the scheme. Indeed, so efficiently was the policy of collectivisation carried out that by the end of the Second Five-year Plan, 90 per cent.

THE MAKING OF SOVIET RUSSIA

of the peasants were working within the framework of collective farming in one form or another.

Thus the industrial and agrarian revolutions were complementary to each other. In other words, agriculture was planned to intensify food production in order to meet the needs of the industrial population and to pay for certain industrial machinery which had to be imported. Industry, in its turn, produced the machinery to intensify agricultural production so that by the end of the period of the third Five-year Plan there remained only a negligible amount of farmland not cultivated by mechanised methods.

POLITICAL ORGANISATION OF THE U.S.S.R.

The original constitution of the Soviet Republic, promulgated in 1918, was prefaced by a "Declaration of the Rights of the Labouring and Exploited Peoples". In this Declaration, which Lenin himself drafted, Russia was proclaimed to be a "republic of soviets of workers', soldiers' and peasants' deputies", chosen by the workers in the factories, by the soldiers in the various army units, or by the peasants in the villages. Lenin made this primary assembly the base of a sort of pyramid in a new kind of democracy, rising to the apex, which was known at first as the All-Union Congress of Soviets, and is now called the Supreme Council or Soviet. This constitution differed from Western modern constitutions in various ways. First, it deliberately disfranchised all those who employed hired labour for profit or lived on an income not derived from their own labour, as well as all those engaged in private business. Thus the only citizens were the workers, and the slogan was "he who does not work shall not eat". Secondly, the election to the central Soviet was indirect; that is to say, delegates to the next higher soviet were elected by the soviet immediately below. Thirdly, the constituency was not territorial, as we know it, but occupational, or functional.

This was all very well on paper, but Lenin himself, in his pamphlet, *State and Revolution*, said: "What the revolution establishes is not socialism or democracy but a transitional state, the dictatorship of the proletariat, in which all the powers are used to dispossess and hold down the old exploiting class. In it the party, the fully conscious minority who are the natural leaders of the whole working-class and the guides and teachers of all the exploited classes, directs and organises the new social order." What, then, is this dictatorship of the proletariat, which Lenin called a transitional state? Stalin, in his book, *Leninism*, gave the answer when he quite frankly stated that "the dictatorship of the proletariat is substantially the dictatorship of the Communist Party as the force which guides the proletariat", and added that "no important political or organisational problem is ever decided by our soviets and other mass organisations without directives from the party". The party executive powers were, in fact, from the beginning in the hands of a small body known as the Presidium, composed of Communist leaders, while the heads of the various departments of government were also leading Communists called People's Commissars.

Lenin's Constitution of 1918 originally applied to the Russian Soviet Federated Socialist Republic (R.S.F.S.R.), which comprised most of Russia proper in Europe. In 1923 the Union of Soviet Socialist Republics (U.S.S.R.) was established. The Union was created in the first place by the voluntary federation with the original Soviet State of three other states, including the Ukraine, each of which had already constituted itself closely on the model of the R.S.F.S.R. The powers of the Federal Authority, which were specifically stated, as in the United States of America, included defence, diplomacy, transport, communications and the control of heavy industries, while the unstated powers remained in the hands of each federating unit. Since then the U.S.S.R. has grown by the incorporation of further Soviet Republics, until it now covers the whole of European and Asiatic Russia.

In 1936 Stalin promulgated a new Constitution for the U.S.S.R. While it was based on the original Communist ideology and retained the fundamental nature of the Soviet State, it introduced certain changes which seemed to owe something to Western models. For example, the Supreme Soviet was reconstituted, with two Houses; namely the Council (or Soviet) of the Union and the Council (or Soviet) of Nationalities. The first was to consist of 596 members elected by all citizens, both men and women of 18 and over (for men and women in Soviet Russia are equal in their rights in every respect). The second was to consist of deputies to be elected by each federating unit in numbers, according to its status, as laid down in the Constitution. Both Councils were to be elected for four years and to have equal legislative power.

Such was the theoretical democracy of the U.S.S.R., as distinct from its authoritarian practice, which requires that candidates for election shall be in lists drawn up by special electoral commissions. In the first general election to the Supreme Soviet, held in December 1937, all those submitted and elected, though not all were actual members of the Communist Party, supported Stalin and his policies. At that election no fewer than 90 million people voted out of a total register of 93 million, and of the votes cast 98 per cent. were in favour of Stalin.

Stalin certainly achieved his purpose of establishing "Socialism in one country", and thereby consummated the Bolshevik Revolution in Russia. He gave the Russian people all sorts of social services which they had never before enjoyed. But he remained throughout the supreme dictator, a position which, as you will see, was strengthened when he was called upon to organise the defence of his country and to fight for the vindication of Russian Communism against the German onslaught in the Second World War.

Chapter 11

FASCISM IN ITALY

THE MARCH ON ROME

THE First World War left Italy with many problems, political, social and economic. The nation was suffering from exhaustion and war-weariness. The Peace Treaties did not satisfy what the Italians regarded as their just claims. Industry and trade were disorganised, causing much unemployment, particularly in the towns of the industrial north. In Parliament in 1920, as a result of the general election of November 1919, the Prime Minister, Giolitti, led a majority of Liberals who, however, could not agree on a united policy. The next largest party were the Socialists, holding 150 seats out of a total of 574. But they were weakened by the growth of a strong Syndicalist, or militant trade union, movement in the north, where the workers demanded control of the factories. Giolitti, in an attempt to mollify the workers, granted a measure of factory control. This surrender to the Syndicalists placed a strong weapon in the hands of those who were opposed to the old parliamentary system, for it enabled them to pretend that Italy was the victim of an extreme Left conspiracy and hence a prey to anarchy.

Benito Mussolini, the founder of Fascism, was born in the Romagna in 1883, the son of a working man who was an ardent Socialist. Mussolini worked hard to gain his education and, after being by turns a teacher, a mason and a blacksmith, became a journalist. As a young man he was a rabid Syndicalist and ventilated his political views in a journal which he edited called *Avanti* (meaning Forward!). The outbreak of war in

138

1914 caused him to change his views, and he became a fiery nationalist. During the first year of the war, while Italy was neutral, he demanded Italy's intervention on the Allied side, pleading his cause in a new journal which he founded called *Popolo d'Italia*. Italy entered the war in 1915 and Mussolini fought in it. After being invalided out of the army, he returned to journalism and watched with a growing disgust what he regarded as the betrayal of Italy's rights at the Peace Conference and the inability of the government to cope with the post-war situation. He then determined on personal action.

In Milan, in March 1919, he founded what he called the Fascist fighting groups (*fasci di combattimento*). His use of the word *fasci* indicated his purpose, which was to fire the national spirit with a sense of the imperial greatness of its Roman past. For the word *fascio* (singular of *fasci*) is derived from the Latin word *fasces*, signifying the bundle of twigs fastened round an axe which the old Roman lictors, or magistrates, carried when they accompanied the consuls, symbolising the right to inflict corporal and capital punishment. Actually, some nineteenth-century revolutionaries in Sicily had already revived the term *fasces*, but Mussolini gave it a new significance. The Roman *fasces* were an emblem of constitutional law and order. Mussolini's *fasci*, on the other hand, formed an unofficial and illegal militia created with the set purpose of opposing by force the constituted government of the day and of intimidating those, whether of the Right or the Left, who supported it. In this sense he applied the tactics urged by the Syndicalists, whose theories he himself had originally supported, but with a nationalist rather than a Syndicalist object. In fact, he turned his force with equal vigour against the Syndicalists, whom he now called Communists.

The Fascist militia had its own uniform (Blackshirts) and carried arms. It was commanded by its founder, who gave himself the grand title of *Duce* (from the Latin *dux*, meaning leader). Its members were drawn from various sections of the community, and at first it consisted largely of ex-Service men and students. Mussolini's gift for organisation turned this scattered body of local groups into a national body of action, and the movement spread rapidly through the towns and villages. At the first annual Fascist Congress in 1919 twenty-two groups were represented, constituting a total membership of 22,000. At the third congress in 1921 there were representatives of over 2,000 groups with a total membership of nearly half a million. This rapid rise emboldened Mussolini to challenge the government, a step in which he was encouraged by the fact that he was joined by another revolutionary party called National Syndicalists and made up of original Syndicalists who, like Mussolini, had changed their views. They were led by Edmondo Rossoni, who later became Mussolini's Minister of Labour.

Other discontented sections, political and cultural, joined Mussolini, and, at a congress held at Naples in 1922, he declared that if the government were not handed over to the Fascists they would march on Rome. In October, 1922, they did, in fact, march on Rome. While Fascist militiamen encamped outside the city, Giolitti resigned, and the King, Victor Emmanuel III, to avoid bloodshed, called on Mussolini to form a Cabinet. For that moment, but no longer, Mussolini acted constitutionally. He formed his Cabinet, although there were then only 35 Fascists and 10 National Syndicalists in the Chamber of Deputies. But Parliament was thoroughly scared, and it granted Mussolini, in spite of his thin minority, dictatorial powers for a year. Having been granted these emergency powers, Mussolini proceeded to use them in order to destroy the Italian parliamentary democratic state.

THE FASCISTS IN POWER

The Duce quickly proved his efficiency, at least in the administrative and technical spheres of action. He reformed the Civil Service, reorganised public transport, and launched schemes for the construction of buildings, bridges and roads, and for the reclamation of hitherto unproductive land. In return for these purely material blessings he demanded the unquestioning obedience of every citizen, and anyone who dared by word or deed to disparage him was liable to imprisonment. In fact, the new régime, working through the Fascist Party, forced its attention on every activity of the national life and ruthlessly destroyed every kind of civil and political liberty.

Only those associations of men and women, whether political, social or cultural, which supported Fascism were allowed to continue; the rest were abolished. In 1924 the electoral law was altered so as artificially to produce a Fascist majority in the Chamber of Deputies, while the King obligingly made appointments to the Senate so as to "swamp it with Fascists". All these manœuvres, however, were only a sort of constitutional cloak for Mussolini's unconstitutional intentions. In the end it did not matter how Parliament was constituted, because the real governing body was the Fascist Grand Council, through which Mussolini always worked. By a law of 1926 this Council was definitely established as "the supreme organ co-ordinating all the activities of the régime which arose out of the revolution of 1922". The law stated, moreover, that the Council of Ministers (i.e. the Cabinet) were, *ex officio*, members of the Grand Council, so that the executive authority was identified with the Fascist Party.

Meanwhile, local government was superseded by officials appointed by the central government, an act which completely destroyed all local democracy. The legal system was also revised in an authoritarian direction, while the great safeguard of the nation's legal rights, the jury system, simply fell into desuetude. Public education, too, was deprived of all liberty, and the Duce imposed on all schools the compulsory use of a textbook on the origin, aims and institutions of Fascism. Going with this destruction of cultural freedom was the institution of a censorship of the Press, so that newspapers could exist only at the whim of the government and then only print news or express views which the official censors approved. All this was reinforced by a perpetual propaganda extolling the virtues of the Duce and his régime.

Mussolini thus destroyed the political Liberalism on which parliamentary democracy in Italy had been built up during the preceding half-century. In doing so he pretended to respect the monarchy, but, in fact, a law of 1925 said that the King must maintain him in power indefinitely. He also pretended to respect Parliament, to the extent at any rate of keeping it in being, although in fact, by his irresponsible executive machinery and his electoral jugglery, he reduced it to impotence. Meanwhile, he openly expressed his utter contempt for the rights of man and for any social or political system which might secure them. His one concern was to glorify the state: "Everything in the state, nothing outside the state, nothing against the state," he declared. Such was the Totalitarian State, which Mussolini himself defined as "the state that absorbs in itself, to transform and make them effective, all the energy, all the interests, and all the hopes of a people".

THE CORPORATE STATE

The application of these anti-liberal ideas was soon seen in Mussolini's plan for the creation of what he called the Corporate State. It was thus that the Fascist revolution entered its second phase, in which an entirely new economic structure was to be built. This was to be done through a scheme of National Syndicalism. Syndicalism implied self-government in industry, but Mussolini aimed at the complete national control of industry, using the device of state-sponsored trade unions to reconcile these two opposite ideals.

As early as 1924 a special commission had been appointed to explore the possibilities of this scheme. On the basis of its report a new Syndical or Trades Union Law was passed in 1926. There were to be three kinds of unions: of the employers, of manual workers, and of intellectual workers. No citizen was forced to join his appropriate union, but had to pay the annual contribution—one day's pay—whether he joined or not. As no unofficial union was recognised, any worker not joining the official union would obviously be entirely unprotected in his professional rights. The second part of the Act of 1926 established special courts, known as the Magistracy of Labour, to which recourse, in the case of all disputes, was obligatory. The third part of the Act prohibited all strikes and lock-outs, under pain of the most rigorous penalties for its breach.

Later in 1926 a special decree filled in the details of the Trades Union Law. Its most significant feature was the statement that any person over the age of 18 might join a syndicate "if of good moral and political conduct"—a clear indication of the determination of the régime to ensure that all young workers were good Fascists. The Law and the Decree were followed in 1927 by the publication of the Charter of Labour. The purpose of Labour, said this Charter, "may be summed up as the well-being of the producers and the development of the national strength". It added an important statement, which gives the key to its whole purpose and shows how utterly different in conception and practice Italian National Syndicalism was from British Trade Unionism. It said: "Professional or syndical organisation is free, but the recognised syndicate alone, under the control of the state, has the right of legally representing the employers, of stipulating for collective labour contracts for all belonging to its category, and of imposing contributions on them."

Thus by 1927 the foundations of the new economic structure were laid. It remained to build the political superstructure, which took some years to complete. For the time being, the Chamber of Deputies was allowed to remain, but in an even more enfeebled state than that to which the electoral law of 1924 had reduced it. By a law of 1928 a new electoral procedure was laid down. Under it the general councils of the thirteen National Syndicates met in Rome and nominated a list of 800 candidates. This list was next reduced by the Fascist Grand Council to 400. Then the whole list of 400 was submitted to the country for each voter to give a simple yes or no to the question on the ballot paper: "Do you approve the list of deputies designated by the National Grand Council of Fascism?" But such was the terror with which Fascist methods had by then filled the average citizen that in the election of 1929 the official list received an overwhelming majority of votes. It shows how truly Mussolini spoke when he said that Fascism had "buried political Liberalism".

The next development was the creation of Corporations designed to furnish the connecting-link between the syndicates of employers and the syndicates of employees. There were twenty-two such Corporations, which were solemnly installed by Mussolini in 1934. It took five years for the Corporations to get into full working order. Then in 1939 the final step was taken in the establishment of the Corporate State in Italy. In that year the Chamber of Deputies was abolished and replaced by what Mussolini called the Chamber of Fascios and Corporations, which was opened by the King. It had 682 members, called National Counsellors, of whom about two-thirds were delegates of the Corporations, mostly leading officials of the Syndicates, and the remainder officials of the Fascist Party. There was no sort of popular election: merely the Duce's approval of the delegates. The Senate, by then largely filled with Fascists, remained, and the new Chamber bore the same relation to it as the old. But there was no longer even a pretence of legislative power left to the two Houses. The functions of the new Chamber of Fascios and Corporations were purely advisory and the Duce was in no way responsible to it.

There was little chance to judge of the success or failure of the completed scheme of Mussolini's Corporate State, for he was soon caught in the toils of Hitler's war as the result of his foreign policy, which will be described in a later chapter. Mussolini, of course, could never have carried through the Fascist revolution without the active support of large sections of the Italian people, and at least the toleration of most of the rest. The support came largely from the middle classes, who were weary of the apparent lethargy of parliamentary institutions and the lack of national prestige in foreign affairs. They looked to a dynamic personality like Mussolini to get things done. Some direct help, too, came from certain Leftish groups, which hoped for social betterment.

Undoubtedly, Mussolini's plan of the Corporate State had behind it a sound idea, which was to get the economic aspects of the national life represented in the institutions of the state. As worked out, however, the plan simply flouted every principle of democracy and was, in any case, ruined by the Dictator's arrogance. And in the end the Italian people paid a bitter price for their support or toleration of Mussolini, on whom they wreaked a bloodthirsty revenge in the course of the Second World War. Nor did a trace of the Corporate State remain in the constitution of the Italian Republic which replaced the monarchy after the war.

Chapter 12

THE NAZI UPHEAVAL IN GERMANY

ADOLF HITLER AND THE FOUNDATION OF NATIONAL SOCIALISM

THERE is no stranger spectacle in the history of the modern world than the rise to supreme power of Adolf Hitler, who established in Germany a dictatorship far more tyrannical and terrible than that created by Mussolini in Italy. Hitler's plans to dominate the German nation matured about a decade later than Mussolini's to dominate the Italian nation. There were several superficial likenesses between the two régimes, and Hitler acknowledged his indebtedness to Mussolini in many of his methods. There was the same intolerance of any but a single party, with its uniformed militia, its aggressive salute, and its unquestioning devotion to the leader. There was the same uncompromising disrespect for traditions, rights and institutions, the same ruthless drive and the same terrorisation of all opponents. Yet there were many differences in background and personality, which made Nazism a much graver menace not only to German liberty but to the peace of the world.

No national leader ever had origins more obscure than Hitler's or a childhood and youth less likely to produce a popular hero. He was not a military genius like Napoleon, a master of statecraft like Bismarck, or a diplomatist like Cavour; not an experienced politician like Clemenceau or Lloyd George; not a thinker like Lenin, an organiser like Trotsky, or a planner, like Stalin, although he possessed a diabolical flair which was a sort of amalgam of all their qualities. He did not even, like Mussolini, belong to the nation which he afterwards led to its doom, for he was not a German but an Austrian. He was born in 1889 in the little Austro-German frontier town of Braunau-on-the-Inn, in Upper Austria, the son of a petty Austrian government official who had formerly been a peasant-cobbler and had changed his name from Schickelgruber to Hitler. When Hitler was 13 his father died, and for the rest of his youth he was strongly under the influence of his mother, an ill-educated woman of uncertain temper. On leaving school he had the ambition to become an artist or an architect, and went to Vienna in the hope of being trained. But he failed to get into an art school and was forced to work as an artisan painter. He was, however, frequently unemployed, and his unhappy experiences warped and embittered him.

In 1912, at the age of 23, Hitler left Vienna to settle in Munich, the capital of Bavaria, which was to become the cradle of the Nazi movement. He threw off his Austrian nationality and fought in the German Army in the First World War, in which he did not rise above the rank of lance-corporal. Towards the end of the war he was badly wounded, and was in hospital at the time of the Armistice. "The more I tried to glean some definite information of the terrible events that had happened," he afterwards wrote, "the more my head became afire with rage and shame." At that moment Hitler convinced himself that the German Army had not been defeated but had been the victim of a "stab in the back" by the politicians and civilians. Released from hospital, he determined to take up political work.

Hitler returned to Munich and lived for a time on occasional work and a mere pittance. As he wandered aimlessly through the streets, he made contact with a group of agitators who called themselves the German Workers' Party. He undertook to lead this group, and before long, with a much-increased following, he formulated a twenty-five-point programme. In February 1920 the party hired a beer cellar in Munich, and at an enthusiastic meeting Hitler's programme was adopted. At this meeting the Party gave itself the fuller name of National

Socialist German Workers' Party (in German *Nationalsozialistische Deutsche Arbeiterpartei*, which became popularly shortened to Nazi). The Nazis, as we may now call them, next acquired a newspaper which became the organ of the Party, and Hitler presented them with their famous emblem, the *Swastika*. Soon the numbers swelled by the addition of ex-Service men who formed "strong-arm squads" for street-fighting, and were called Brownshirts, from their uniform, or Storm-troopers (*Sturmabteilung*, shortened to S.A.). Later emerged the more important blackshirted S.S. (short for *Schutzstaffeln*, meaning defence-formations). Originating as Hitler's personal bodyguard, the S.S was later built up by Heinrich Himmler into a formidable private army of party fanatics pledged to unquestioning support of the leader, or *Führer*, as Hitler called himself.

THE RISE TO POWER

By 1923 the Nazi Party was well established, with a growing membership, a salaried staff, an office in Munich, and one or two branches beyond the city. When the French occupied the Ruhr in that year Hitler, in agreement with certain Bavarian political leaders, organised a raid (*Putsch*) on the government in Munich. At the critical moment the Bavarian leaders recoiled, and the Nazis, left to carry on the fight alone, were mown down in the streets by the state forces. Sixteen Nazis were killed and most of the rest, including Hitler himself, were imprisoned. The Party was dissolved and the movement prohibited; its members were killed or imprisoned or otherwise scattered. How, then, could it ever rise again? We shall see.

While in prison, Hitler began to write his famous autobiography, *Mein Kampf* ("My Struggle"). It contained much false history, but as a prophecy it proved to be remarkably accurate, for the programme of future action that Hitler sketched in it was destined to be carried out in almost every detail, except, of course, his own final defeat and suicide. With plenty of time for reflection, the imprisoned Hitler came to the conclusion that his rebellious action in Munich had been premature and shortsighted. In future, he vowed, he would proceed by strictly constitutional means; that is to say, through the creation of parliamentary strength, thus concealing his ultimate purpose by a veil of legality while quietly building up his armed reserves.

Although he received a five-year sentence, Hitler was released from prison at the end of 1924. He immediately set about reviving the Nazi Party and working towards the constitutional victory which he had now decided must precede the establishment of his dictatorship. His platform was based on certain half-baked ideas which he had picked up through his personal contacts and a certain amount of desultory reading. These ideas were chiefly three. The first was that only those of pure German race or blood (*Blut*) can rightly claim membership of German political society. The second was that the state is made up of the whole people or folk (*Volk*), without distinction of class. The third was that national cohesion or solidarity can be secured only through the principle of leadership (*Führerprinzip*).

Most of these ideas are to be found, in one form or another, in earlier German writings. An Englishman, turned German, named Houston Stewart Chamberlain, had in 1899 published a book called *Foundations of the Nineteenth Century*, in which he argued that the Germans were a race apart, a people of lords and masters (*Herrenvolk*). This was the ground of Hitler's anti-Semitism which led to the slaughter of millions of Jews in Germany. The idea that the state was absolute and all-powerful was, of course, to be found in the attitude towards government of such leaders as Frederick the Great and Bismarck. It was also set forth in the books of such philosophers as Johann Fichte (1762–1814) and Georg Hegel (1770–1831), of the historian, Heinrich von Treitschke (1834–96), and of the social philosopher, Friedrich Nietzsche (1844–1900). Nietzsche saw a vision of the world overwhelmed by vast social upheavals and devastating wars, from the consequences of which mankind was only to be saved by the emergence of a superman. Hitler conceived himself as such a superman. Such a vision may even have inspired him deliberately to carry out what one of his earlier adherents later called a "revolution of destruction".

Between 1925 and 1929 Hitler devoted himself to the regeneration of the National Socialist Party on constitutional lines, which was necessarily a slow and difficult process. He kept both the nationalist and the socialist sides of it going, as he built up a parliamentary party, and maintained his own position by playing off one side against the other. The political and economic situation in Germany favoured him. There were, outside the Nazi Party, but inside the *Reichstag*, both Nationalist and Socialist Parties. The Nationalists supported Hitler in his opposition to the *Diktat* of Versailles and in his determination to undo it. The middle classes were hit by the spreading depression. They hated the Socialists and feared the Communists, and so turned to the Nazis as the only hope of salvation. All this time, while he had the aid of the Nationalists, Hitler was able to criticise the government because he himself was not in a responsible position. In the *Reichstag* election of 1928 the Nazis gained twelve seats; in 1930 the number increased to 107, so that by then they were the second largest party to the Social Democrats. It was a great constitutional triumph for Hitler. The day of reckoning, he said, was at hand, and he prophesied that when that day arrived "heads would roll" in the coming conflict with those who had "betrayed the Fatherland". And how right he was!

In 1932 there was an election for the Presidency of the Republic, which Marshal Hindenburg had held since 1925. Hitler decided to test his position with the people by standing as a candidate. The result was surprising, for, in a second ballot, necessitated by the fact that in the original election no candidate had gained an absolute majority over the rest combined, Hitler actually secured 13 million votes against Hindenburg's 19 million. As a result of the *Reichstag* elections in the same year the Nazis, although their total vote fell by 2 millions from that gained at the election of 1930, nevertheless became the strongest party in the *Reichstag*. The President was therefore persuaded to call on Hitler to form a Cabinet. Hitler thus became head of a coalition government. So, in January 1933, the former house decorator and lance-corporal became Chancellor of the Reich. He had reached the end of his constitutional journey, and the stage was now set for his "revolution of destruction".

THE ESTABLISHMENT OF THE DICTATORSHIP

Hitler could not have achieved the Chancellorship without the votes of the people who had elected 200 Nazi candidates to the *Reichstag*. Nor could it have happened if the political forces of the Left and Centre had not been hopelessly weak and divided. Moreover, he gained the support of the great landowners and industrialists, who broke down the aged Marshal Hindenburg's personal objection to appointing the ex-lance corporal, Hitler, to be his Prime Minister. On the one hand, a large body of ordinary German citizens thought of Hitler as the "People's Chancellor". On the other hand, the landowners and industrialists thought that Nazi violence would be sobered by the responsibilities of office, and fondly imagined that in Hitler they had, as they said, a "Chancellor in chains". They were both soon proved wrong. Hitler was not concerned with popular rights but with political power, and he was strong and skilful enough to break any chains which the people in high places might attempt to forge. No sooner was he in office than he proceeded, by a series of deliberate and ruthless steps, to destroy the foundations of the constitutional state and to build on its ruins his own absolute dictatorship.

Although he began his Chancellorship with a coalition Cabinet drawn from several parties, he soon turned his régime into a one-party government. In 1933, during the preparations for a new election, the *Reichstag* building was burned down. The Nazis made it appear that the Communists were the perpetrators of this outrage. The prospect of a Communist revolution, which the Nazis had thus deliberately engineered, so frightened the President that he approved an emergency decree permitting the government to impose restraints on personal liberty and on freedom of speech, press, association and assembly, and to search private houses and confiscate property. As a result, the government banned the Communist Party as an illegal organisation and, in the panic which followed, the Nazis won nearly half the seats in the *Reichstag*. Trading on the public fears, Hitler intimidated the *Reichstag* into passing an Act conferring on him, for a period of four years, the power to promulgate and enforce new laws without recourse to Parliament. From that moment the Weimar Republic was dead.

Hitler now proceeded to suppress all other parties as he had outlawed the Communists. The Catholic Centre and the Nationalists were "liquidated", and in July 1933 a decree went forth declaring that the only legally constituted organisation in Germany was the National Socialist Party. The whole country, as in Fascist Italy, became, in effect, one vast constituency with a single imposed list of candidates requiring the voter's mere yes or no to the entire list. But, in any case, the *Reichstag* ceased to be a deliberative and legislative assembly; it became, in fact, a mere occasional audience for the Führer's rhetorical outbursts. Next, he rendered the *Reichsrat*—that is, the Federal House—superfluous by simply abolishing the federation. In January 1934 he issued a "Law for the Reorganisation of the Reich", containing fewer than a hundred words, which destroyed the federal principle that had characterised the German state for more than a thousand years. By this law he transferred all the powers of the states to the central government and replaced them by decrees which the Führer issued and which were executed by Nazi officials.

Hitler now felt sufficiently secure to rid himself of those members of his party who honestly believed in the Socialist side of the original National Socialist programme, for which he no longer had any use and which he now identified with such disruptive forces as Communism. He therefore decided on a purge. So occurred, on June 29 and 30, 1934, the terrible "blood bath", as it was called, in which about a hundred eminent Nazis were murdered in cold blood. Among the victims of the "purge" were also certain leading Germans who, though not members of the Nazi Party, had tried unsuccessfully to work in association with Hitler. These murders were officially declared by the Reichstag to be legitimate "acts in defence of the state". Even worse was the organised massacre of the Jews, which Hitler, by his diatribes against them as anti-German agents, inspired. Those Jews who escaped slaughter were deprived of all their rights as citizens, while thousands of them were sent to concentration camps where they joined all those who dared to question the omnipotence of the Führer and the superiority of his followers.

In August 1934 the aged Hindenburg died, but, instead of proceeding to the election of a new President, Hitler calmly announced that the two offices of President and Chancellor were combined in his own person as Führer. To this action he sought, after the event, the approval of the nation by means of a plebiscite, or mass popular vote. In the previous year he had successfully used this device to gain approval of his decision to withdraw Germany from the League of Nations. This had greatly increased his prestige, for thereby the Germans seemed to regain their self-respect. Nearly 90 per cent. of the electorate now approved the concentration in Hitler's own hands of the two highest offices in the state.

THE AUTHORITARIAN STATE

Hitler did not confine himself to the reorganisation of the political field. He also revolutionised the economic and social life of Germany. He endeavoured to make Germany economically a self-sufficient state (*Autarky*), so that it should be free from dependence on imports. In an effort also to abolish unemployment, he destroyed the employers' associations and the trade unions, and replaced them by a common government organisation known as the Labour Front. While Hitler had risen to power on the depression, he now exploited his success on the strength of the world recovery. But it was made to appear that improved economic conditions, which were due to world causes, resulted from Hitler's policy. He was for ever talking in terms of battle, as when he referred, for example, to the "subsistence battle" and the "employment battle". In fact, he now placed everything on a war footing. Hermann Göring, in charge of the economic plan, talked of "guns before butter", and, because the people were enjoying the benefits of full employment through the building up of armaments, they accepted personal deprivations for the sake of the national resurrection.

Hitler had been granted four years of personal rule, but before that period expired he had carried his dictatorship to such a point that he was under no necessity to ask anybody's permission to continue his absolutist régime. He instituted an entirely new basis of national allegiance and state power. The rights of individuals and associations were abolished. The organs of the Republic established by the Constitution of 1919 were entirely scrapped. A federal democracy was thus forcibly transformed into a centralised autocracy.

Meanwhile, the very lives of the people were at the mercy of the Nazi octopus, whose poisoning arms stretched out to the most obscure recesses of German society. The Secret State Police, familiarly known as the Gestapo, originally created by Göring, had complete authority to invade any home and to violate the sanctities of family life. Every child was claimed for the state, every youth obliged to join the national youth organisation known as the *Hitler-Jugend*, and every school forced to shape its curriculum according to the pitiless doctrines of Nazism.

Here, then, was the authoritarian state as Hitler conceived it and as he and the Nazis built it. It was a state more absolutist than Mussolini's and one without precedent in the conditions of the modern world. It claimed a universal range of powers exercised and enforced through an all-pervading political party which totally excluded all others. It demanded only duties from the people who received in return no corresponding rights. The Nazi philosophy pretended that the individual can fully realise himself and find his true happiness only in blind service to the state, without reference to any standards of judgment which the individual himself helps to create. The state, according to this theory, does not recognise society as having anything but a political existence, and therefore does not regard itself as a means to the achievement of social good, but as an end in itself—the end of political power. In short, in Hitler's Germany the state was nothing but a governmental instrument which bludgeoned out of the individual all political intelligence and all sense of the interplay of rights and duties.

If Nazism could have confined itself to Germany, the rest of Europe and the world might have been content to tolerate it. But Nazism could not, by its very nature, keep within the German frontiers. Hitler's whole purpose was to undo the effects of the treaties which had ended the First World War, and his internal policy was shaped to this external end. His race theory implied an eventual breaking down of recognised political frontiers, for if all nations of Teutonic origin were to form what Hitler called "one people and one *Reich*", not only must Austria be incorporated with Germany but other neighbouring states must be annexed to it. Again, the Nazi argument that the Germans were a superior race of *Herrenvolk* demanded that their superiority must be exercised not only over helpless non-Germans, such as the Jews, in their midst, but also over what they regarded as the inferior races, such as the Russians, around them. Besides, Hitler cried out for more "living space" (*Lebensraum*) for the Germans, which meant the subjugation of neighbouring peoples.

In short, Hitler aspired to be something more than a mere German Führer: he was infatuated enough to believe that he could conquer Europe and establish a "New Order" which, as he said, was to last for a thousand years. How he ultimately failed in that object we shall see.

Chapter 13

THE SPREAD OF AUTHORITARIANISM

THE DEMOCRATIC WEST

THE success of Communism in Russia, of Fascism in Italy, and of Nazism in Germany had inevitable repercussions in neighbouring states, where parliamentary institutions were a comparatively recent innovation. In fact, no country altogether escaped some Communist infiltration and certain manifestations of the Fascist trend. Even in Britain, where the Communist Party never grew to serious proportions, a Fascist movement was started in 1932. From then until the outbreak of war in 1939 the British Fascists, in their black shirts, marched and paraded, held noisy meetings, and caused disturbances and even destruction in Jewish quarters. But their propaganda made no impression whatever on the established democratic institutions. In France, where a strong Communist Party grew up in the Chambers, the Fascist movement was much more serious. There had always been a powerful body of French opinion, generally royalist in origin, which was opposed to the parliamentary institutions of the Third Republic. In 1906 there had been founded a militant nationalist and royalist organisation known as *Action Française*. After the First World War it intensified its anti-parliamentary campaign, and joined forces with an association called the *Croix de Feu*, composed mostly of young men bent on undermining the influence of the parties of the Left: Radicals, Socialists and Communists.

In 1936, to strengthen their resistance to the increasing threat from the Right, the French Radicals, Socialists and Communists formed a new parliamentary *bloc*, known as the

156

Popular Front (*Front Populaire*), whose declared intention was "to place French liberties beyond the reach of Fascism". The combined parties gained a majority at the election of 1936 and formed a Cabinet under the Premiership of the Socialist leader, Léon Blum. This coalition Cabinet lasted for thirteen months, but, after a break, Blum formed another government from the same party combination. Although Blum's two Popular Front administrations had a stormy parliamentary existence, they managed to hold the fort against the anti-democratic attacks until the nation was called upon to close its ranks in face of the renewed menace of German aggression. But the ideological conflict and party strife of those years so sapped the strength of France that she was unable to resist the Nazi assault when it was at length let loose upon her.

In the three Scandinavian kingdoms of Norway, Denmark and Sweden democratic institutions were fully maintained during this period, generally under Liberal or Socialist governments. The same was true of the Netherlands, Belgium and Switzerland, although in each of these three there were small Communist groups who gained a few parliamentary seats, but not enough to disturb the balance of political forces. In Belgium, however, two groups with Fascist tendencies grew up outside the three traditional parliamentary parties: Liberals, Socialists and Catholics. One was the Rexist Party, founded by Léon Degrelle. In the general election of 1936 the Rexists gained twenty-one seats, but from 1937 they began to lose popular favour. The other was a Flemish movement. It adopted a Nazi ideology and developed an anti-Belgian and pro-German policy. Although neither of these parties made much headway in peace-time, they proved to be a weakening agency for Belgium in the Second World War, when some of their members collaborated with the German invaders.

AUSTRIA, HUNGARY AND CZECHOSLOVAKIA

Austria was perhaps the most harshly treated of all the states by the Peace Conference of 1919. It was so restricted and confined that it could not resist interference from its neighbours, and its post-war history is one long tale of political and economic crises. The two main political parties in the new republic were the Social Democrats and the Christian Socialists, the latter being what we should call Conservatives. At first these two parties combined to form a government but later separated, and for two periods between 1922 and 1929 the Chancellorship was held by a priest named Ignatius Seipel, the leader of the Christian Socialists. The extreme Left Wing of the Social Democrats were mostly Marxists, though not all of them were professed Communists. The extreme Right Wing of the Christian Socialists, all ardent Nationalists, were divided into two sections, one looking for a restoration of the monarchy, the other forming a National Socialist group in favour of collaboration with the Nazis of Germany.

The Austrian Nazis grew in size and strength after the retirement of Seipel in 1929. As the depression spread and poverty and distress became acute, the Nazis gained the sympathy of the middle class, and soon became openly Hitlerite, ready to swallow his whole programme, including the incorporation of Austria with Germany. All this, of course, became much more dangerous as Hitler moved inexorably towards dictatorial powers in Germany; so much so that Engelbert Dollfuss, who had succeeded Seipel as leader of the Christian Socialists and Chancellor, came to the conclusion that parliamentary institutions were no longer workable in Austria. He thereupon decided to set up a dictatorship of his own to forestall a worse one under the Nazis. In 1934, therefore, he suspended the constitution and proposed a new one based broadly on Mussolini's scheme of the Corporate State. In support of this he organised a new party, called the Fatherland Front. He dissolved the unofficial Nazi army and, after bombarding the working-class districts of Vienna, also suppressed the Social Democrats. This was followed by the promulgation of the new constitution.

The answer of the Nazis was to try to snatch the government

by force, and during these riotous proceedings they assassinated Dollfuss. At that moment Hitler would no doubt have liked to intervene, but he was dissuaded from doing so by the insistence of Mussolini, who feared that Germany's annexation of Austria would weaken his own position, a view which in the long run proved correct. Hitler was not at that time prepared to risk alienating Mussolini, and so for four years the strange Christian Corporate State continued in Austria under the new Chancellor, Kurt von Schuschnigg, until, in fact, Hitler was finally ready to strike decisively.

Hungary's post-war difficulties were scarcely less acute than Austria's. Budapest, like Vienna, lost its former glamour, and, deprived of its original sources of supply, became an island of economic distress. The monarchy, as explained earlier, was nominally restored after the first attempt to form a republic and the failure of the Communist *coup* in 1919. Between 1920 and 1930, therefore, the government was in the hands of a regent, Admiral Horthy, who maintained much of Hungary's traditional political system with the help of a succession of sympathetic Prime Ministers. But Horthy could not prevent the growth of a Nazi Party, called the National Unity Party, which, with Hitler's support, gradually gained a dominant position in the state. This dominance had dire consequences for Hungary in and after the Second World War.

The new republic of Czechoslovakia was deeply affected by the rise of Nazism in Germany and its influence on Austrian and Hungarian affairs. Czechoslovakia was an entirely artificial state. The Czechs, mainly concentrated in Bohemia and Moravia in the west, had formerly been under Austrian rule. The Slovaks, mainly in the eastern provinces, had been under the control of Hungary. Little love was lost between these two poeples, who together made up a bare majority of the total population. The rest included powerful minorities of Sudeten Germans in the west and Hungarians in the east, both politically detached from their fellow nationals outside solely by strategic requirements. The Sudeten Germans, in particular, formed an increasingly powerful Nazi cell within the Czechoslovak Republic. Until Masaryk's retirement in 1935, his prestige held the state together, but not long after, when Hitler began his policy of external aggression, it was seen how loose was the cement which bound its diverse parts.

THE SITUATION IN THE BALKANS

In the decade following the First World War all the Balkan states had a hard struggle to maintain their democratic institutions, and in the 1930's not one of them escaped the trial of some form of dictatorship. The Kingdom of Yugoslavia was, like the Republic of Czechoslovakia, an amalgam of national groups which the new state failed to fuse into a real political whole. The Serbs wished to maintain a unitary state; the Croats wanted a federal state in which they could enjoy autonomous powers. There were frequent fights between Serb and Croat deputies in the Chamber, and in 1928 this bitter struggle reached its climax when a Croatian leader and some of his followers were killed.

The King, Alexander, felt that the only way to end this strife was to establish his own personal rule. In 1929, therefore, he suspended the constitution and proclaimed himself dictator. Although, two years later, he promulgated a new constitution, his dictatorship was only slightly modified. It was, however, brought to a violent end when, in 1934, while on a visit to Marseilles, he was assassinated by the agent of a Croat exile. The throne was left to Peter II, a boy of eleven. The regency set up on his behalf slightly relaxed the harsh rule of Alexander. But Yugoslavia suffered badly from the depression. She could not sell her produce except to Germany, and this made her increasingly dependent on Hitler. Meanwhile, the emergence of a Communist Party, leaning towards Russia, complicated the internal conflict which was still unsettled when Yugoslavia became involved in the Second World War.

Other Balkan states similarly failed to operate their parliamentary institutions. In Rumania, King Carol II, who had

LEON BLUM (1872–1950)
ch Socialist Prime Minister in the "Popular
Front" Governments of 1936 and 1938.

MARSHAL JOSEPH PILSUDSKI
(1867–1935)
The strong man of Poland, who headed a dictatorial
régime from 1926 to 1935.

ENGELBERT DOLLFUSS, AUSTRIAN CHANCELLOR, WITH HIS
MINISTERS IN VIENNA, 1934.
A photograph taken on May Day 1934, twelve weeks before his assassination during disturbances
caused by his Nazi opponents.

ANTONIO SALAZAR
(born 1889)

Portuguese Prime Minister and Dictator since 1939.

GENERAL FRANCISCO FRANCO
(born 1892)

Spanish leader (*El Caudillo*) and Dictator since 1939.

THE SPANISH CIVIL WAR (1936-39)

Franco's troops arriving at Le Perthus in the extreme north-east of Spain, on the French frontier, in 1939.

been excluded from the throne, regained it in 1930 by a *coup d'état*. There thus arose a curious situation, in which the King, who ruled as a dictator, banned a Nazi Party, called the "Iron Guard", which naturally wanted a dictatorship but not Carol's. In 1939 the King promulgated a new constitution in which he attempted to give his dictatorship a legal form. After the outbreak of the war, however, he became completely discredited and was compelled to abdicate and leave the country. His dictatorship was then replaced by that of General Antonescu, a Nazi sympathiser, who in 1941 led Rumania into war against Russia on Germany's side.

In Bulgaria intense party conflicts developed between a militarist government elected in 1926 and a Communist Party which grew up, under Russian influence, after the war. This party strife caused a reaction in 1934, when a group of Fascist army officers overthrew the government and set up a dictatorship. In the following year, however, King Boris II, who had so far remained in the background, asserted his authority and set up a royal dictatorship.

In Albania a democratic republic was established after the First World War under a priest named Fau Noli, who had lived for some years in the United States. In 1925 the Presidency was assumed by a young Mohammedan army officer named Ahmed Zog, a member of a leading Albanian clan, who had held office previously in the republican government. In 1928 he was proclaimed king, and retained the throne with dictatorial powers until 1939, when, as you will read, he was dethroned by Mussolini's aggression.

Greece during this period provided the most striking example of the ding-dong struggle for power between democracy and dictatorship. Continuing as a monarchy immediately after the war, Greece became, by a plebiscite held in 1925, a democratic republic. Between 1928 and 1933 the veteran Liberal statesman, Venizelos, struggled as Prime Minister to maintain the republican constitution, but in the latter year was replaced by a royalist politician, against whom a revolt was organised in 1935. Venizelos joined the revolt, but it was suppressed with much bloodshed, and Venizelos fled abroad and died in the following year. King George II was then restored to the throne. He did not himself exercise power, but called on General Metaxas, who, as Prime Minister, established a dictatorship which continued until the outbreak of war in 1939.

Strangely enough, of all the post-war states which had arisen out of the Balkan tangle, the most stable and progressive was Turkey. Under the inspiring leadership of Kemal Ataturk, who, as we have seen, was an enlightened, though firm, dictator, the new republic, with its centre of gravity moved to Asia Minor, was well established as a national state and Turkish society was reformed largely on Western European lines.

POLAND AND THE BALTIC STATES

Poland was the largest and most powerful of the states which were created out of the pre-war German, Austrian and Russian Empires. The Poles had a strong national feeling, made more intense by their long struggle for renewed liberty. Poland also had great economic potentialities, if only she could be left alone to exploit them. But her international position was very insecure because of the nature of her frontiers which impinged on the peripheral problems of neighbouring nations. Germany and Russia, who had lost most territory through the creation of Poland, were her natural enemies and always ready to quarrel with her. At the same time, two of the new states, by which she was bounded—Czechoslovakia and Lithuania— were constantly in dispute with her. Consequently, Poland's problems caused difficulties beyond her borders, a fact which gave point to Aristide Briand's remark that Poland was "the rheumatism of Europe", meaning that her malaise set up aches and pains which ran through the whole continent.

The constitution of the Polish Republic, as established after the first war, was based on that of France. The middle class were most anxious to make it work, but the people were largely illiterate peasants, and in other ways the problem of the non-

Polish peoples incorporated in the state made the constitution unworkable. There were in Poland Russians whom the Poles governed by police methods, Ukrainians who looked forward to the establishment of an independent state, and Germans to whom the Polish Corridor was a standing outrage. Moreover, the Jews in Poland were regarded as responsible for many national difficulties. In 1926 Marshal Pilsudski, a popular hero of the First World War and of the war which followed with Soviet Russia, decided to set up a strong government. This meant modifying the constitution and removing the existing government. He forced both the Prime Minister and the President to retire, and, appointing a President of his own choice, he himself became Prime Minister.

With a large army behind him, Pilsudski formed a nationalist ministry which greatly weakened the power of Parliament. Although he denied that he was a dictator, he in fact exercised dictatorial powers, and continued to do so until his death in 1935. Just before he died he promulgated a new constitution by which the powers of the President were increased and those of Parliament further diminished. The years following Pilsudski's death were difficult for Poland, with Soviet Russia pressing on one side and Nazi Germany on the other. The Poles signed non-aggression pacts first with Russia and then with Germany, but neither pact ultimately saved them from the aggression of their two powerful neighbours.

The three Baltic states—Lithuania, Latvia and Esthonia— recognised as independent by the treaties of 1919, had a very chequered career in the inter-war years. Lithuania failed to operate her new democratic institutions. In 1926 General Anton Smetona seized the Presidency of the republic, and in 1928 a new constitution gave legal sanction to his dictatorship, based on government by a single party. In Latvia a dictatorship replaced the constitutional republican régime in 1935. A similar move took place in Esthonia in 1934. Both states had to contend with a growing Communist movement, which they attempted to suppress. All three Baltic states were pressed by

163

German and Russian propaganda in the approaches to the Second World War, which finally engulfed them.

THE PECULIAR CASE OF PORTUGAL

Dictatorships also emerged in Portugal and Spain, but they took a somewhat different form from those in other countries and from each other. Moreover, unlike the Fascist and Nazist régimes in Italy and Germany, they survived the Second World War, in which they took no armed part, and, indeed, continue in existence to this day. In Portugal a revolution in 1910 had driven King Manoel into exile and established a democratic republic in place of the monarchy. The new constitution, however, did not work well, and there was much poverty and unrest following the First World War. In 1926 an army commander, General Antonio Carmona, with the object of ending the disorders, set up a military dictatorship. He suspended the constitution and in 1927 was formally elected President, at first for four years and afterwards for seven.

To assist him in the government Carmona chose a remarkable man, Antonio Salazar, a professor of economics in the University of Coimbra. In 1928 Salazar became Minister of Finance and four years later Prime Minister. In 1933 Salazar formulated a new constitution which had some unusual and interesting features. According to this constitution, there was to be a President elected for seven years and a Prime Minister and Cabinet responsible to a legislature of a single Chamber, called the National Assembly, of ninety members elected by the head of each family, whether man or woman. In practice, however, parliamentary candidates were exclusively those put forward by the government. Besides the Assembly, there was to be a Corporative Chamber, somewhat on the lines of Mussolini's scheme and of the Economic Council of the Weimar Republic in Germany, consisting of representatives of local authorities and of industrial and commercial corporations, including organisations of employers and employees. The Corporative Chamber had no legislative powers, but all Bills had to be submitted to it for its opinion before the National Assembly gave its final vote.

Thus Salazar established his undisputed ascendancy which he still holds in Portugal. He has suppressed all revolutionary agitation, prohibited strikes and lock-outs, and instituted compulsory state arbitration on all labour disputes. He has restored the country's finances and given the workers the protection of labour laws which they never before enjoyed. He is certainly a dictator, but of a much milder and more creative kind than were either Mussolini or Hitler. Salazar has succeeded where Mussolini and Hitler failed, first because his authoritarianism has been comparatively moderate; secondly because he has created a régime suited to Portuguese conditions; and thirdly because, unlike his Italian and German counterparts, he has been satisfied to confine his activities to his own land and not to become warlike and aggressive.

FRANCO AND THE SPANISH CIVIL WAR

The story of dictatorship in Spain has been much less happy than that of her Iberian neighbour. From 1876 to 1923 Spain was a constitutional monarchy, with an elected Parliament (*Cortes*) and a Ministry appointed by the monarch and responsible to the legislature. In September 1923 an army officer named Primo de Rivera (Marqués de Estella) seized power by force of arms at Barcelona, whereupon the King, Alphonso XIII, summoned him to form a government. Having done so, de Rivera suspended the constitution and set up a dictatorship, called the Directory. He carried out a number of reforms, but by 1930 the nation had grown tired of the dictatorship. He then resigned, and the constitution was restored.

In April 1931 municipal elections resulted in a large majority in favour of a republic. The republican leader, Niceto Zamora, demanded the King's abdication. To avoid civil war Alphonso left the country. He hoped that he might one day be recalled, but he never was and he died in exile in 1941. Zamora proclaimed Spain a republic and put himself at the head of a Provisional Government. In June 1931 elections were held for a Constituent Assembly to draw up a new constitution. A very mixed body resulted, representing every shade of opinion, but with a majority of Conservatives, Liberals, Socialists and Radicals, who formed a coalition. This Assembly promulgated a republican constitution setting up a Presidency with a Cabinet responsible to a single Chamber legislature (*Cortes*), to be elected by adult suffrage, including women for the first time. Zamora remained President, and Manuel Azana, a writer, became Prime Minister.

An election held in 1933 resulted in a majority of moderate republican groups, against which the Radicals, Socialists and Communists formed a union calling itself, like its French counterpart, the Popular Front. Another election, in 1936, resulted in a majority for the Popular Front. Thereupon Zamora resigned and was succeeded in the Presidency by Azana. The Popular Front government wished to carry out a programme of social reform, but it could not stop its more extreme supporters from indulging in acts of violence. In the country peasants seized land, and in the towns there were violent strikes in which the strikers burned and looted important buildings, including churches. Various conservative groups, including a Fascist type of organisation called the *Falange*, founded in 1933, determined to put a stop to what they regarded as a drift towards anarchy. The general attack on the republican government was precipitated by General Francisco Franco, commander of the Spanish forces in Morocco, who in July 1936 launched an armed rebellion.

Crossing the Straits of Gibraltar with an army largely composed of Moorish troops, Franco was joined by the bulk of the regular army, as well as a large part of the navy, and in October these adherents recognised him as their official leader, or *Caudillo*, a Spanish word broadly corresponding to *Duce* in Italian and *Führer* in German. Franco having overrun southern and western Spain, set up an opposition government at Burgos in the north. In the next month his forces reached

the suburbs of Madrid. Consequently, the republican government transferred itself to Valencia, and began to recruit levies
from the supporters of the Left and from the Basque and
Catalan groups which always stood for regional rights.

So began a civil war which turned Spain into a kind of
ideological cockpit. Soviet Russia sent help to the Republicans,
although the Communists formed only a section of Republicans
in Spain. Also an International Brigade, composed of men of
Leftist sympathies in various countries, fought in support of the
Republican cause. To Franco, on the other hand, much more
considerable help in men and armaments was sent by Hitler and
Mussolini, who frankly used the occasion to give their forces
some military training under war conditions. With this powerful support, Franco gradually broke down the republican resistance. In January 1939, having divided the Republican forces in
the east, he occupied Barcelona, and in the following March the
Republicans abandoned the defence of Madrid, which Franco
entered in triumph.

The Spanish Civil War had lasted nearly three years. It
caused the loss of a million lives and untold damage to property,
and left the Spanish people impoverished and embittered.
Franco set up a military dictatorship which destroyed all traces
of the republican parliamentary system and ruthlessly suppressed its supporters, driving many of them to seek asylum
abroad. Franco's dictatorship, although it had some of the
characteristics of Fascism and Nazism, was in many respects
unique. All political parties were declared illegal except the
Falange, although Franco was not the founder or leader of it,
as Mussolini was of the Fascists and Hitler of the Nazis.
Franco's Spain was quickly recognised by most European
governments (though not by Russia) and by the United States.
His régime thus became firmly established, and, as he managed
to remain neutral between 1939 and 1945, his dictatorship, like
Salazar's in Portugal, survived the Second World War.

Chapter 14

ROOSEVELT AND THE NEW DEAL IN AMERICA

FRANKLIN DELANO ROOSEVELT

In the year 1649, when the colony of New York still belonged to Holland and had not yet changed its name from New Netherland, there settled in the city of New Amsterdam, as New York was then still called, a Dutch immigrant named Roosevelt. From the grandsons of this colonist there descended two branches of the Roosevelt family, one of which produced the twenty-sixth President of the United States, Theodore Roosevelt, and the other the thirty-second President, Franklin Delano Roosevelt. Both branches of the family remained, throughout the generations, in the State of New York, the elder branch on Long Island, the younger at Hyde Park, on the Hudson River, where F. D. Roosevelt was born in 1882.

After graduating at Columbia University, Roosevelt became a lawyer in New York, and soon afterwards married his cousin, Eleanor Roosevelt, a remarkable woman who helped to shape his career. He then became interested in politics, but, instead of joining the ranks of the Republicans, to whom his family had always belonged, he threw in his lot with the Democrats. He supported Woodrow Wilson in the election of 1912, and took office under the new President as Assistant Secretary to the Navy, a post which he held through the First World War and until the Republican victory of 1920. In the following year, when only thirty-nine, he was struck down with polio-myelitis which crippled him for the rest of his life. But with incredible courage and will-power he fought through this frightful disability and in 1928 was elected as Democratic Governor of the State of New York.

In that position he watched the growth and spread of the depression under the Republican Presidency of Hoover, and slowly surrounded himself with friends and supporters who stood by him in the Presidential Election of 1932, in which, as Democratic candidate, he promised to carry out "a drastic change in economic governmental policies". On this programme Roosevelt swept the country.

THE DEPRESSION AND THE NEW DEAL

When F. D. Roosevelt took the oath of office as President of the United States in March 1933, he was confronted with an unprecedented situation. The slump had begun in America in October 1929, with a "crash on Wall Street", the centre of American finance. That is to say, there was a sudden fall in the price of stocks and shares after a wave of confidence had sent them soaring to impossible heights. The consequent depression, however, affected not only the money market but the whole of American society. By 1933 industrial production and farm income had fallen to less than half the figure of 1929, and the total national income from 80,000 million dollars to less than 40,000 million. General business and exports dropped to the lowest mark of the century. The banking system practically collapsed; in 1932, 1,400 banks failed, and in 1933 most of those in the larger cities suspended their normal business.

Such a situation meant dire misery and even starvation for many American citizens. The unemployed figures rose to some fifteen millions, and queues of people seeking public relief ("bread lines") were daily sights in every town. Thousands of families were evicted from their homes because they could not pay their rent. Some of them moved from the towns to the country in search of work, which few farmers had to offer. It was, therefore, the new President's first task to restore the public morale. In his Inaugural Address he said, "The only thing we have to fear is fear". The immediate business was to get the people back to work. The American people, he said, must move "as a trained and loyal army", and he intended to use his executive power "to wage a war against the emergency" as he would if the land were "invaded by a foreign foe". Despite the opposition of some leading politicians who regarded this utterance as a threat of dictatorship, Congress granted the President the necessary powers for immediate action.

First he declared a bank moratorium, or delay, during which the banking system was to be thoroughly overhauled and re-started under government control. Next, to reduce public expenditure, the salaries of all government officials and employees were cut by 15 per cent. Thirdly, in order to increase the public revenue and in anticipation of the repeal of Prohibition, already agreed upon, an Act was passed permitting the manufacture and sale of light wines and beers. Finally, the President was authorised to establish a Civilian Conservation Corps to carry out public works, such as building and re-afforestation, which reduced the figure of unemployment by half a million in the first year.

These were the preliminary steps in the carrying out of a vast plan of legislative and administrative action which went under the general name of the New Deal. To assist him in this vast project the President selected his Cabinet with great care, and included in it, for the first time in American history, a woman Cabinet officer, namely Miss Frances Perkins, who was appointed Secretary of Labour. He also engaged a body of experts, popularly known as the Brains Trust.

The New Deal legislation was divided into five main sections: finance, agriculture, industry and public utilities, labour organisation, and social security. In finance, prices were raised through inflation, and the banking system was improved and stabilised. In agriculture, farmers were encouraged to reduce their acreage to avoid waste, in return for payments to compensate them for loss. They were also helped with government loans to prevent mortgage foreclosure. In 1934 Congress passed the National Industrial Recovery Act, "a two-year emergency measure for the purpose of providing employment and stimulating industry". Money was provided for federal, state and local schemes of slum clearance, new housing, and the building of new roads and schools. All these schemes were to be financed with federal loans raised by encouraging public lending. The Federal Government also undertook the direct organisation of certain public utilities, such as the setting-up of the Tennessee Valley Authority (T.V.A.), which was empowered to build dams, to install electrical power plant, to launch a programme of flood control, re-afforestation and prevention of soil erosion, and to manufacture explosives and fertilisers from nitrogen products.

As to labour organisation, the immediate objective of this part of the New Deal legislation was to get as many people as possible back to work. The depression and consequent unemployment had resulted in the lowering of wage scales, the increase of industrial accidents through the decline in supervision of safety devices, and the overworking of women and children because their labour was cheaper. The new legislation, therefore, aimed at improving the conditions of labour, regulating hours of work, and making sure that proper wages were paid. The law encouraged the extension of trade unions and the use of collective bargaining with the employers' organisations which consequently grew up. Federal Labour Exchanges and Boards of Arbitration were set up. To round off all this labour legislation came the Social Security Act of August 1935, providing for unemployment insurance, old age pensions, payments to poor mothers, crippled children and the blind, and financial aid to public health work.

OPPOSITION TO THE NEW DEAL

Some Americans regarded the New Deal as the perfect remedy for the social evils of the time; others felt that it was contrary to the American spirit of free enterprise. In the eyes of his supporters Roosevelt was the saviour of society; in those of his opponents he was a socialist and a would-be dictator.

The truth is that in the public provision of social services the United States had, by European standards, been unprogressive. The type of social security contemplated in the New Deal had long been effected in Germany, Britain and the Scandinavian countries, and Roosevelt's programme in this respect was no more Socialism than that carried out by the Liberal Government in Britain between 1906 and 1914. The capitalist economy was essentially maintained in America under Roosevelt as it had been in Britain under Asquith.

Some recent historians of America have referred to the changes made under the New Deal as the Roosevelt Revolution. But if it was a revolution, it was only a mild one. And, indeed, as some American historians themselves have pointed out, much of the new legislation merely gave legal expression to doctrines already held by organised bodies in agriculture, industry and commerce. What Roosevelt wished to achieve, as he himself said, was "balance between agriculture and industry, and balance between the wage-earner, the employer and the consumer".

The problems raised by the New Deal are difficult for a British citizen to understand, because the political organisation of the United States is so different from that of the United Kingdom. Britain is a unitary state, in which the central Parliament is supreme. The United States, it cannot be too often emphasised, is a federation, in which each state retains the powers not surrendered by the Constitution to the Federal Authority. If any Act passed by the federal Congress is challenged on the ground that it infringes state rights as secured under the Constitution, it is for the Supreme Court to decide whether or not the Act is constitutional. In other words, in Britain the law is what Parliament says it is; in the United States the law is what the Supreme Court says it is. Much of the New Deal legislation was challenged as unconstitutional, and this brought the Supreme Court into action.

The Federal Government argued that it was responsible for the welfare of the nation as a whole, and defended the New

Deal legislation on the simple ground that it was necessary to meet the emergency. This did not prevent the Supreme Court invalidating both the Agricultural Adjustment Act and the Industrial Recovery Act because they infringed state rights, and thus forcing Congress to pass modified laws in order to achieve at least a part of the object of the original Acts. Yet, while the decisions of the Supreme Court gave great comfort to the President's opponents, the majority of the people supported his policies, as was shown in the mid-term Congressional Election of 1934 when the Democrats, in spite of the defection of some of them from the President's ranks, made gains in both Houses.

By 1935 the economic tide began to turn, and when in 1936 Roosevelt ran for a second term he could claim that his policies had succeeded. The result was that he was returned by a much greater majority than in 1932. He thus rightly considered that he had a mandate to proceed with his programme. To do so, however, he had to overcome the obstacle of the Supreme Court. He tried to get a law passed increasing the number of members of the Court from nine to fifteen so that the objectors might be outvoted. The Bill, however, failed to pass Congress, and there was nothing left for the President to do but to wait for time and nature to remove the older members of the Court.

In the mid-term Congressional elections of 1938 the Democrats were returned with a comfortable, though diminished, majority. But Roosevelt's hopes to carry his reforming programme farther were diminished by the very fact that prosperity was returning and hence the need for it was less urgent. Normally, he would have had only two more years in which to continue his plans. But before he had got far, the approach of war in Europe forced him to abandon domestic reform in favour of national security and preparedness. By the time of the next Presidential Election in 1940, not only had war begun but Hitler had overrun most of Western Europe. Only in such circumstances could an event without precedent in American history have occurred as it then did. In that year Roosevelt

was elected for a third term as President, with large Democratic majorities in both Houses of Congress, not so that he
might continue his New Deal policy but because he was felt
to be the best national leader in the crisis of the Second World
War. We shall see later how he carried out that mandate, and
was elected for yet a fourth term.

THE POLICY OF THE "GOOD NEIGHBOUR"

Soon after his first election as President, Roosevelt in 1934
announced that his policy in relation to Latin America would
be that of the "good neighbour". In the age of the New
Imperialism at the end of the nineteenth century and the opening of the twentieth, the United States had tended to treat
Latin American countries with a rather heavy hand. Theodore
Roosevelt, for example, referring to his relations with other
American States, had said: "Speak softly but carry a big stick."
Taft, his successor at the White House, had adopted the policy
of "Dollar Diplomacy", which meant that the way for the
United States to become more influential in world affairs was
to use its money power. These policies had undoubtedly increased the prestige of the United States in the world, but they
had also tended to alienate Latin America.

Nevertheless, the need for co-operation between the United
States and the twenty other American republics had long been
recognised. In fact, at the end of the nineteenth century the
United States had launched a movement known as Pan-
Americanism. In 1899 the first of a series of Pan-American
Conferences met in Washington, and there followed periodical
conferences in various Latin American capitals. The original
motives of the United States were economic rather than political,
and, although the conferences went on, in fact there was a growing suspicion of the United States on the part of the Latin
American republics, some of which, especially Argentina, gave
voice to these fears at the conferences of 1923 and 1928.
F. D. Roosevelt's "good neighbour" policy was intended to
remove these suspicions. His efforts to promote economic

174

development by common action led, for example, to the passing of the Reciprocal Trade Agreements Act of 1934 and to the establishment of the Export-Import Bank. At Buenos Aires (Argentina) in 1936 and again at Lima (Peru) in 1938 special Inter-American Conferences were held to discuss questions of defence. The sense of common interests thus engendered had good results, for in 1942 twelve Latin American states followed the United States into the Second World War, and before the end of the war all the rest had done the same.

The most marked effect of Roosevelt's "good neighbour" policy was the United States' decision to withdraw from active participation in the affairs of the West Indian island of Cuba. Similarly, negotiations were begun with Panama whereby in that country, through which flowed the Panama Canal, the United States relaxed its old policy of interference. Also the United States began to change its policy in the Pacific, and, instead of using the Philippine Islands as a stepping-stone to the enjoyment of what the Americans called "China's illimitable markets", as the American imperialists advocated, granted the islands a constitution in 1935. But shortly afterwards Japan invaded China, a move which was ultimately to have vital consequences for the United States.

Chapter 15

JAPAN AND CHINA

THE CONQUEST OF MANCHURIA

THE depression, which had such striking social and political results in America, spread not only to Europe but to the rest of the world, and particularly to the Far East, where it profoundly affected the relations of Japan and China. Japan, as you will recall, had emerged at the opening of the twentieth century as a great Power, becoming the ally of Britain in 1902 and crushingly defeating Russia in the war of 1904–5. The powerful position she had thus gained in the Pacific was strengthened during the First World War, in which she fought on the side of the Western Allies against the Central Powers. The European Powers, fully occupied in the West, were forced during the war to leave Japan very much to her own devices, and she used this freedom from interference to reinforce her hold on China. Indeed, she presented China with "Twenty-one Demands" which, if fully imposed, would have made that vast country almost a Japanese protectorate.

Under pressure from the Western Powers, Japan withdrew most of these demands, and immediately after the war she seemed to adopt a much more conciliatory attitude towards the Chinese. In Japan, under the influence of pacific politicians, parliamentary institutions were stimulated and a peace movement was encouraged. In external affairs, Japan became an original member of the League of Nations, and in 1922 at the Washington Conference was one of the signatories with the Western Powers to the "nine-power treaties" which affirmed the independence of China and prohibited the making of

THE FIRST INAUGURATION OF F. D. ROOSEVELT AS PRESIDENT, 1933

The new President (centre) is seen taking his oath of office before Chief Justice Hughes (left) in front of the Capitol at Washington. His son James stands behind him and in the right foreground is the retiring President, Herbert Hoover.

THE WATTS BAR DAM, TENNESSEE

One of the projects of the Tennessee Valley Authority (T.V.A.), set up as part of the New Deal Programme in 1933 to develop and control the natural resources of the Tennessee Valley in south-eastern United States.

JAPANESE AIRMEN IN THE WAR WITH CHINA
Parading at Tokyo before setting off for the "Front" in Manchuria, 1932.

CHINESE SOLDIERS IN THE WAR WITH JAPAN
Members of the National Citizen Army, formed under universal conscription to resist the
renewed aggression of the Japanese, 1937.

special agreements to create spheres of influence in Chinese territories. But this pacific policy did not last, because the economic arguments against it proved too strong.

Japan had a rapidly growing population. Indeed, in relation to its area of agricultural cultivation it had the densest population in the world. If, therefore, Japan wished to thrive in accordance with her new position as a world Power, she must develop export markets, and backward China was the natural area for the energetic Japanese to exploit. Such a policy, however, clearly implied not only strong internal government to direct this social urge but also armed power to enforce it against the world. This by itself kept alive, behind the apparent pacific democratic front, a strong party of militarists and warlords. It was the depression which strengthened the hands of this party. The depression in America caused a heavy fall in Japan's export of raw silk, one of its staple products, to the United States, and hence a wave of unemployment. By 1931 the situation seemed propitious for a seizure of power by the military party. A number of parliamentary leaders were assassinated, and by 1932 the military and naval party had gained the upper hand. Having replaced the parliamentary system by a dictatorial régime, the militant party proceeded to adopt an aggressive policy towards China which must eventually involve the repudiation of the Washington naval agreements and the nine-power treaties guaranteeing the integrity of Chinese territory.

An excuse was soon found for a full-scale Japanese attack on the Chinese province of Manchuria in the far north-east of China, with Korea to its south-east and Siberia to its north. Japan had first gained a dominating influence in Korea as a result of her wars with China (1894–5) and Russia (1904–5), and in 1910 had made it, in effect, a Japanese colony. Korea, therefore, was the natural jumping-off ground for the attack on Manchuria, where Japanese troops were already providing police protection for their interests in the South Manchurian Railway. In 1931, charging the Chinese governor with inability to suppress bandits, the Japanese forces, on their own authority, opened hostilities against the Chinese. This provided an excuse for the new Japanese government, which speedily sent reinforcements to the railway troops. Soon the Chinese forces were dispersed and the Japanese overran the whole province. In February 1932 the Japanese set up a native government at Mukden, the capital of Manchuria. Under Japanese orders, this government declared the province independent of China and changed its name to Manchukuo.

In March 1932 the Japanese brought out of his retirement the ex-Emperor of China, P'u Yi, who had lived in Japan since his dethronement in the revolution of 1911, and made him nominal head of Manchukuo. He was, of course, a mere puppet, but in September 1932 the Japanese government went through the farcical formality of signing a treaty with him, recognising the independence of the new state. The Chinese government, under Chiang Kai-shek, offered some resistance, but in May 1933 Chiang was forced to sign a treaty recognising Japan's possession of Manchukuo, to which was added the adjacent Mongolian province of Jehol, and allowing for a demilitarised zone between Manchuria and Peking and Tientsin. In March 1934 the ex-Emperor P'u Yi was declared Emperor, but, although allowed a native ministry, he had to consult a body of Japanese advisers on all vital matters of state. Thus Manchukuo became a dependency of Japan.

THE FAR EAST AND THE LEAGUE OF NATIONS

Both China and Japan were members of the League of Nations, and Japan's aggressive attack on Chinese territory was a formidable test of the League's power to act under the Covenant. The opening paragraph of Article 16 of the Covenant said:

"Should any member of the League resort to war in disregard of its covenants under Articles 12, 13, or 15, it shall, *ipso facto*, be deemed to have committed an act of war against all other members of the League, which hereby undertake immediately to subject it to the severance of all trade or financial relations, the prohibition of all intercourse between persons residing in the territory of the Covenant-breaking State, and the prevention of all financial, commercial or personal intercourse between persons residing in the territory of the Covenant-breaking State and persons residing in the territory of any other State whether a member of the League or not."

Here, in Manchuria, was a clear case of aggression against a member of the League, and China, the victim, quite properly appealed for the help of the League against the aggressor. The League, in reply, sent out a Commission under Lord Lytton to inquire into Japan's "claims and pretexts" on the spot. After an investigation lasting six months the Lytton Commission in its report recommended that Manchuria should become an autonomous, or self-governing, province under Chinese sovereignty. The League accordingly called upon Japan to evacuate Manchuria so that the Lytton Report could be implemented. Japan ignored the demand. At this point the League should have put Article 16 of the Covenant into operation. But it dared not risk a resort to penalties, called sanctions, and it got over the difficulty by a legal quibble, arguing that the Chinese had not specifically invoked Article 16 of the League Covenant.

The Chinese also appealed to the states which had signed the Nine-power Treaties of 1922 in Washington, which were supposed to guarantee the integrity of China, and to the signatories of the Briand-Kellogg Pact of 1928, which was supposed to have outlawed war. But nothing came of these advances either, for no Western Power was prepared at that moment to go to war with Japan. All that happened was that the Assembly of the League and the makers of the Treaties and the Pact refused to give official recognition to Japanese sovereignty in Manchukuo. Japan's answer was to withdraw from membership of the League in 1933 and to denounce her part in the Washington Treaty which, as you will recall, had placed limits on naval armaments. Japan thus at the same time escaped with the ill-gotten gains of her aggression in northern China and freed herself from any restraints on further advances into China, which she soon set on foot.

The ease with which Japan had flouted the League of Nations was the first of a series of blows to its prestige as a preserver of the peace. Not only had Japan carried out her Manchurian aggression with impunity but the League had lost one of its most powerful members. And Japan's example of international lawlessness was soon to be followed by Italy and Germany. In fact, Japan had profited by the growing diplomatic confusion in Europe, which made the Western Powers hesitate to take any decisive action that might involve them in a distant war. At the same time, the European situation was affected, in its turn, by Japanese tactics. Great hopes, for example, had been placed in the prospective World Disarmament Conference which, after many delays, finally assembled at Geneva in February 1932. But when at last it met, it was in a discouraging atmosphere, largely created by Japan's conduct.

From the beginning the discussions at the Disarmament Conference seemed to lack reality, especially after Hitler's assumption of power in Germany, which synchronised with Japan's withdrawal from the League. In that same year Hitler withdrew from the Disarmament Conference and gave notice of Germany's secession from the League of Nations. In the following year the Conference was abandoned, and the various Powers, including Britain, went off to execute their own separate armaments programmes. From that moment the international situation deteriorated; nor did the outbreak of the Spanish Civil War improve it. The cumulative effect of the breakdown of the principle of collective security and the preoccupation of Europe, as we shall soon describe, with the consequences of dictatorship and aggression, encouraged Japan to resume her attack on China.

THE FAR EAST BETWEEN THE TWO WORLD WARS
Showing the growth of Japan's domination of China.

JAPAN'S RENEWED ATTACK ON CHINA

Up to the moment of the outbreak of the Spanish Civil War, the opinion of the Japanese military leaders was divided. There was a group which wanted to concentrate on strengthening Manchuria as an ultimate bulwark against Soviet Russia. There was another faction which wanted to make hay while the sun shone and to proceed at once to the conquest of China. From 1935 there was a sort of unofficial Japanese movement of expansion going on in China. Japanese forces were gradually moving from Manchuria into the northern Provinces, and

181

southward beyond the Great Wall of China. The Japanese government did not openly recognise this movement but secretly sympathised with it. Chiang Kai-shek, the Nationalist leader, at his capital at Nanking, tried to hold off the inevitable struggle by negotiating with the Japanese, but he was kidnapped and visited by Chinese Communist envoys who forced him to end his attempts to appease the Japanese and to join them against the common enemy. Thus a truce was reached between the Nationalists and the Communists and their united forces prepared to resist a renewed Japanese attack.

These events in China saw the end of Japan's hope of achieving the domination of China by "diplomatic methods supported by threats and bribery". Moreover, the European situation created by the Spanish Civil War in 1936 persuaded the Japanese leaders that it was safe to resort openly to arms. In October 1936, as you will read later, Japan signed the Anti-Comintern Pact with Germany as a security against Russian action in China. This brought about a unification of Japanese military policy. In July 1937 main hostilities between Japan and China began in an accidental sort of way. Shots were exchanged between patrols at the Marco Polo bridge in the suburbs of Peking (Peiping), and next day a vast Japanese force of infantry, led by tanks, advanced on Peking itself. Thus a general and long-drawn-out war began without even the formality of a declaration. The Japanese pretended that it never was a formal war and persisted in referring to it as "The China Incident".

In fact, however, it was a most terrible war. The Japanese rapidly overran northern China. Moving southward, they drove Chiang's government out of Nanking, captured Shanghai, and by 1938 had occupied other important centres of population, including Hankow, the chief city in central China. Chiang was forced to retreat far westward into Chungking, and the Communists were driven to the remote Mongolian borderland. Although the Chinese were thus hopelessly overwhelmed by the much superior force and armament of the Japanese, they nevertheless harried the Japanese behind their lines, so that the actual Japanese control of China was largely confined to the chief towns, ports and railways. In these guerrilla attacks the Chinese often used weapons that their irregular forces had captured from the Japanese. But, besides these, they received armaments and supplies from American and other sources by way of the Burma Road, which was constructed at this time by hordes of coolies. It was called the "back-door to China", because the land approach from the west was the only means of entrance into China, which was otherwise completely blockaded by the Japanese.

In this bitter struggle the Japanese lost probably half a million men, but the sufferings of the Chinese people were appalling. Their soldiers were killed on the battlefields and many of those captured were mercilessly massacred by the Japanese. Their cities were bombed, their land laid waste, their homes destroyed by floods, their families decimated by famine and pestilence. It is estimated that in the course of this struggle something like 60 million people were rendered homeless. Nevertheless, there was never a really final surrender to the Japanese. As their lines thinned with their advance, the Japanese, with their best troops left in Manchuria against a possible Russian intervention on China's behalf and their rear constantly harassed by the pockets of guerrillas, found that by 1938 they had still failed to achieve their main military objective of a total conquest of China. Then came the Second World War. The immediate effect of this on the Chinese was disastrous, for they were deprived of even the thin line of supplies which they had been receiving from the Western Powers. But, when the Japanese entered the war, with their attack on the Americans, China, as you will see, became, in effect, part of the Allied Front.

Chapter 16

AGGRESSION: THE PRELUDE TO THE SECOND WORLD WAR

GERMAN RE-ARMAMENT AND THE STRESA FRONT

WHILE militarist Japan was pursuing its policy of aggression with a view to dominating Eastern Asia, Hitlerite Germany was maturing plans for the ultimate domination of Europe. Hitler's immediate objects were to restore Germany's internal prosperity and to recover her external prestige. These two objects were to be achieved by the same means: namely rearmament, which would simultaneously provide the Germans with full employment at home and with bargaining power abroad. German rearmament, of course, involved an open defiance of the disarmament clauses of the Treaty of Versailles. But, in fact, Germany had long been covertly planning to restore her armed strength, and this fact gave Hitler a flying start.

Hitler was emboldened to go forward with his plans by what now happened in the Saar. By the Treaty of Versailles, as you may recall, France was given possession of the Saar coalmines as compensation for the damage caused to her mines in the war, while Saarland was placed under the political control of an international commission, responsible to the League of Nations, for a period of fifteen years, at the end of which time a plebiscite was to be held to decide whether the area should permanently join France or Germany. The plebiscite was duly held in January 1935. The result was an overwhelming vote in favour of reincorporation with Germany, which became effective in the following March. Hitler then announced the repudiation of all limitations on German armaments and the

184

full restoration of conscription, already begun by his predecessors.

Hitler went out of his way to declare that these proposals were solely for defence, but in fact they meant a standing army of more than half a million men and an air force, already being built up by Göring, greater than that of Britain or France. These measures were naturally popular in Germany, but they filled her neighbours with such fears that in the following month a conference was called to discuss the situation. The Conference, held at Stresa, in Italy, was attended by Mussolini and the Prime Ministers of France and Britain. The Stresa Conference issued a declaration stating that the three Powers agreed to oppose any "unilateral repudiation" of the treaties which endangered the peace of Europe and that they would act together to prevent it. Italy, France and Britain thus established what was called the "Stresa Front" against the prospect of German aggression.

But the Stresa Front soon began to crumble. Using Italy as a bridge to Eastern Europe, the French signed a treaty of mutual assistance with Russia, who feared the consequences of a non-aggression pact signed in the previous year between Germany and Poland. Later, Czechoslovakia adhered to this Franco-Russian agreement. Meanwhile, Britain, anxious to secure a limitation of naval strength, made a separate agreement with Germany in June 1935. By it Britain agreed to Germany's repudiation of the naval clauses of the Treaty of Versailles, provided that Germany's shipbuilding did not exceed 35 per cent. of Britain's. So the Stresa Front, far from preventing unilateral agreements, actually encouraged them. Moreover, it emboldened Mussolini to proceed with his aggressive plans in Abyssinia, already maturing at the time of the Stresa Conference.

MUSSOLINI'S ASSAULT ON ABYSSINIA

Colonial expansion was doubtless one of Italy's needs, not only to increase her wealth through trade but to absorb her surplus population. This was Mussolini's professed reason for his attack on Abyssinia, otherwise known as Ethiopia, a Christian land in north-east Africa, ruled by the Emperor (Negus) Haile Selassie. His real reason, however, was to increase his power and prestige. Abyssinia had inflicted a heavy defeat on the Italians at the battle of Adowa in 1896, when they had attacked her, and Mussolini's desire to wipe out the ignominy of that defeat gave added zest to his imperial ambitions. Abyssinia had thus survived the scramble for Africa among the European Powers at the end of the nineteenth century and remained an independent, though land-locked, native kingdom surrounded by British possessions (the Anglo-Egyptian Sudan, Uganda, Kenya and British Somaliland) and two Italian colonies (Italian Somaliland and Eritrea). The Italians, who thus had two bases from which to advance, alleged that it was necessary to suppress disorders on the Abyssinian borderlands. In December 1934, therefore, they crossed the frontier; the Abyssinians resisted and shots were exchanged.

Now, both Italy and Abyssinia were members of the League of Nations; indeed, Italy had originally sponsored Abyssinia's application for admission. Abyssinia, therefore, appealed for the League's protection against Italy's aggression. The League exhausted every expedient to settle the dispute, short of any definitive action which might have deterred Mussolini, who now prepared for an invasion on the grand scale. By bellicose speeches he worked up a warlike spirit among the Italian people and demanded the "annihilation" of Abyssinia. Britain, to safeguard her imperial interests, mobilised the Mediterranean Fleet and pressed the League to take decisive action against Italy. Nevertheless, Mussolini went forward with his plans and in October 1935 invaded Abyssinia in full force.

Then, at length, the League made a definite move. In accordance with Article 16 of the Covenant, quoted earlier, the League denounced Italy as an aggressor, and fifty nations solemnly agreed to apply "economic sanctions", including an embargo on the supply of arms and war materials to Italy, a boycott of her exports, and the withholding of loans and credits to her. This apparently irresistible economic phalanx, however, never got into full operation, and Italy succeeded in spite of it. Pierre Laval, the French Foreign Minister, in a desperate effort to end the struggle, proposed the partition of Abyssinia, and when Samuel Hoare, the British Foreign Secretary, entertained the scheme, he was forced to resign and was succeeded by Anthony Eden.

Hitler, as we shall see in a moment, snatched this opportunity to reoccupy the Rhineland, and this drew the attention of the Western Powers away from Mussolini and Abyssinia. So half a million Italians, armed with the most modern weapons, advanced against the brave but ill-equipped Abyssinian tribesmen. The Italian advance was slowed down by bad roads, but new ones were specially built by the highly skilled Italian engineers. At one point Mussolini even resorted to the use of poison gas to terrorise his primitive opponents. Thus at length, in the middle of 1936, the Italians occupied Addis Ababa, the capital. The Emperor, Haile Selassie, fled to England, and his country was then annexed outright to Italy, while Mussolini added to the titles of the King of Italy that of Emperor of Abyssinia. Within two years the annexation was recognised as an accomplished fact by the Powers of Europe.

The results of Mussolini's flagrant and ruthless aggression were disastrous alike for Italy, Europe and the world. It marked the triumph of violence over public law, of naked nationalism over collective security, and it dealt a mortal blow to the League of Nations. The decision to impose sanctions led Mussolini in 1937 to withdraw Italy from membership of the League of Nations and to join Germany and Japan in the Anti-Comintern Pact. Thus the League was further weakened, in spite of Russia's admission to it in 1934, while the Spanish Civil War heightened the international tension.

HITLER'S ANNEXATION OF AUSTRIA

Hitler had already withdrawn Germany from the League of Nations and abrogated several clauses of the Treaty of Ver-

187

sailles by inaugurating a policy of rearmament and restoring conscription. In March 1936 he took a further bold step in defiance of the Treaty by ordering German troops to march into the demilitarised zone of the Rhineland. It transpired that Hitler had given orders that, if this move should be met by armed resistance, the German troops were to march back without returning fire. But, in fact, no such opposition occurred. Not only did Britain and France dread the prospect of war, but they had their hands full with the complications arising from Mussolini's Abyssinian adventure. So Hitler's gamble came off without a shot being fired. The remilitarisation of the Rhineland was vital to Hitler's aggressive plans. It brought the armed strength of Germany once more up against the French frontier. It liberated great industrial centres like Cologne and Dusseldorf for munition production. And it secured armed protection for the great Ruhr industries.

Hitler's next step was to form with Mussolini a definite alliance that the Dictators called the Rome-Berlin Axis. This entirely changed the situation for Hitler in connection with Austria. As you will remember, when he had tried to interfere in Austria in 1934 he was prevented from reaping the reward of the murder of Dollfuss by the opposition of Mussolini. Now, in 1938, not only was he in a much stronger position of armed preparedness but he could depend, if not on Mussolini's active support, at least on his non-interference. In February 1938, therefore, he forced the Austrian Chancellor, Schuschnigg, under threats, to take certain Austrian Nazis into his Cabinet. Schuschnigg made a desperate attempt to avert the danger of a Nazi domination of Austria by announcing his intention of holding a plebiscite. But he was never allowed to hold it, for two days before the date fixed for the popular vote, Hitler sent a heavily armed German force into Austria, which quickly overran the country without opposition.

Schuschnigg and his colleagues were imprisoned and Hitler entered Vienna in triumph. So Austria, which, according to the treaties ending the First World War, was never to be united to

Germany, became, in Hitler's phrase, "a land of the German *Reich*". Thus did Hitler add, without a shot fired, seven million Germans to the *Reich* and a territory of tremendous strategic importance to his further aggressive plans. Thus, too, did Hitler in respect to Austria reverse the policy of exclusion (*Ausschluss*) pursued by Bismarck and adopt instead that of union (*Anschluss*).

THE DISMEMBERMENT OF CZECHOSLOVAKIA

A glance at the map will show in what a perilous situation Czechoslovakia was placed by the German annexation of Austria. The two most important and highly developed provinces of Czechoslovakia—Bohemia and Moravia, with the capital Prague in the centre—lay in the west of the state, and Germany, by incorporating Austria, now surrounded these Czech provinces on three sides. There were several reasons, political, economic and diplomatic, why Hitler should cast predatory eyes on Czechoslovakia, and why he should choose her as the next victim in his aggressive advance. Czechoslovakia was the most democratic and progressive of the states set up after the First World War. The republic was, on the whole, liberal and enlightened. It had a small but well-trained army, a line of defensive forts along its northern boundary, where it marched with the German frontier, rich resources and large industrial undertakings, such as the great Skoda armament works at Pilsen, some fifty miles south-west of Prague. In Hitler's eyes, therefore, there were political dangers to be removed and economic prizes to be won in Czechoslovakia.

An even more compelling reason for Hitler's intervention was the fact that of the fifteen million inhabitants of Czechoslovakia, formerly within the Austrian Empire, three million were of German blood. They inhabited the north and west borders of Czechoslovakia called the Sudetenland, and were therefore known as Sudeten Germans. Under Czech rule the Sudeten Germans were probably better treated than any minority in any other state in Europe, but this did not reconcile them to their detachment from the Germans of the Fatherland. The problem of government was complicated for the Czechs by the fact that there were also nearly a million Magyars (Hungarians) in the south of the republic and a large number of Poles in the mining district of Teschen on the Czech-Polish border. Hitler realised that the presence of so many different and dissatisfied minorities would make it all the more difficult for the Czech government to resist his demands.

Hitler began his attack by whipping up an agitation among the Sudeten Germans within Czechoslovakia and by urging his Nazi followers on Germany's Czechoslovak frontier to support them. This he did by a ceaseless propaganda of calumny against the Czechs, and especially against Eduard Beneš who had succeeded Masaryk as President. This campaign was intensified after the seizure of Austria. By this time the Sudeten leaders were demanding not merely self-government within the Czechoslovak Republic but outright incorporation with Germany. Hitler openly announced that he would liberate these "oppressed" Germans in Czechoslovakia, if necessary, by force. And his attitude encouraged, as he had expected, a spirit of unrest also among the Magyar and Polish minorities. In May 1938 Czechoslovakia, in a determined effort to resist these attacks aiming at her dismemberment, partially mobilised her army and called upon her allies, France, Russia, Rumania, to come to her assistance.

So disturbed was the British Government at the turn of events that they sent a special mission under an elder Liberal statesman, Lord Runciman, to Czechoslovakia to try to reach a compromise. It failed because Hitler was in no mood for compromise. He knew he was playing with fire, but he was quite prepared to face a general European war, if that price should prove necessary, in this year, 1938. At this point, in September 1938, the British Prime Minister, Neville Chamberlain, took an unprecedented step and, in a desperate effort to prevent a general war, himself flew twice to Germany for personal interviews with Hitler. Having returned with Hitler's demands

and consulted the Cabinet, Chamberlain appealed to Mussolini, who persuaded Hitler to agree to a meeting of the two
Dictators with Chamberlain and Edouard Daladier, the French
Premier. Thus occurred, on September 29, 1938, the famous
conference at Munich, at which it was agreed that the Sudetenland should be annexed to Germany, while the Hungarian and
Polish claims should also be settled. In this way Czechoslovakia
was deprived of over four million inhabitants and of her natural
defences. The four Powers solemnly bound themselves to
respect the new frontiers, and Chamberlain flew home, in what
turned out to be a completely illusory triumph, bearing a
"scrap of paper" containing a worthless undertaking on the
part of Germany never to go to war with Britain on any outstanding issue.

No Czechoslovak envoys had taken part in the Munich
meeting. Nor was Russia consulted. Thus the two Western
Powers, besides suffering a major diplomatic defeat, had at the
same time deserted Czechoslovakia, alienated Russia, and lost
the confidence of all the smaller states of East-central Europe.
No sooner had the revision of territory taken place, as agreed,
than Hitler took steps to carry out the complete destruction of
what remained of Czechoslovakia. He began by encouraging
the Slovaks to declare their independence of the Czechs, and
President Hacha, who had succeeded Beneš in October 1938,
placed in an impossible position, had no alternative but to
accept Hitler's uncompromising demands.

Thus, in March 1939, German troops without resistance
overran the provinces of Bohemia and Moravia, which were
thereupon declared a protectorate of the *Reich*. A few days later
the independent Slovakia was taken over by Hitler and the
remaining section of the republic, Ruthenia, in the east, was,
with German connivance, occupied by Hungarian troops. So
Czechoslovakia, after only twenty-one years of independent
existence, disappeared from the map and Hitler entered Prague
in triumph, as in the previous year he had entered Vienna.

Two more annexations by the Dictators occurred within a

few days of Hitler's entry into Prague. Before the end of March 1939 Hitler sent an ultimatum to Lithuania demanding the surrender of the port of Memel, which the Germans then occupied. In April, Mussolini, feeling the need to make some demonstration in order to share the aggressive triumphs of his Axis partner, ordered Italian troops across the Adriatic to occupy Albania, which he coolly declared annexed to Italy. Mussolini followed this aggression by a violent propaganda attack on France, demanding the restoration of such territories as Savoy and Nice, Corsica and Tunis, which, according to Mussolini, had been filched from Italy when she was weak. Now that Italy was strongly armed and ready to fight for her lost rights, he said, let France beware!

THE END OF THE POLICY OF APPEASEMENT

The years 1938 and 1939 were undoubtedly profitable times for aggressors, as they were indeed unfortunate times for their opponents. Britain and France had hoped that, by making concessions to Hitler's thirst for power, they could bring him to reason. This attitude came to be known as the policy of appeasement. It was a disastrous policy, for, far from checking the aggressor, it merely made him bolder and more exigent. The Western leaders trusted his word as if he were an honourable statesman, which he was not, and for their pains he merely despised them. Yet the British and French Ministers were in a difficult position, because the large majority of people in both countries were strongly averse to any action which might lead to hostilities. Neither country was in a state of preparedness for war, whereas Germany was by then fully armed for a major conflict. Looking back on those disastrous years, British and French critics have blamed Western statesmen for their weakness. Undoubtedly they were weak, and yet, if they had taken strong action, they would merely have precipitated an armed struggle for which they were not prepared.

Up to Easter, 1939, Britain and France continued to hope for an end to the growing trail of aggression. But with the

HITLER'S REOCCUPATION OF THE RHINELAND, 1936

German troops crossing the Hohenzollern Bridge into Cologne to reoccupy the Rhineland which
had been demilitarised by the Treaty of Versailles, 1919.

HITLER'S ANNEXATION OF AUSTRIA, 1938

The Führer responding to the crowd's Nazi salute as he drives into Vienna.

THE MUNICH CONFERENCE, SEPTEMBER, 1938
Chamberlain, Daladier, Hitler and Mussolini at the meeting where they agreed to the dismemberment of Czechoslovakia.

SIGNING THE NAZI-SOVIET NON-AGGRESSION PACT, 1939
A photograph taken in the Kremlin in Moscow. The Russian Foreign Minister, Molotov, is seen signing the Pact, while Stalin and Ribbentrop, the German Foreign Minister (on Stalin's right), stand by.

complete destruction of Czechoslovakia, Italy's annexation of Albania, and her propaganda campaign against France, the Western Powers realised that they must abandon appeasement and take counter-measures. This realisation was strengthened by the action Hitler now took with regard to Poland. In spite of his ten-year pact of 1934 with Poland, by which he had guaranteed to respect her boundaries, he now made two requests of his ally: first, that she should agree to Germany's annexation of Danzig, a city which, though predominantly German in population, was under international control; and secondly, that she should concede land across the Polish Corridor so as to restore to Germany her direct contact with East Prussia.

When the Poles hesitated to respond to Hitler's cajolery, he adopted his customary terrorising tactics. Speeches by the Führer and propaganda organised by the astute Joseph Goebbels denounced the Poles as oppressors and persecutors of Germans in their territory. This new threat removed Chamberlain's lingering doubts, and he gave Britain's guarantee to Poland that if she were attacked Britain would intervene. France joined Britain in this and similar guarantees to Greece and Rumania, both now in danger of assault by the Axis Powers. A little later, Turkey joined in these mutual arrangements to assist in the defence of the Mediterranean. At the same time, the British Parliament passed an Act introducing conscription for the first time in British history during a period of peace. Hitler's reply was to repudiate his peace pact with Poland and his naval agreement with Britain, while in May he and Mussolini signed a ten-year treaty of alliance pledging mutual support in case of war.

With the two sides feverishly preparing for a general war, all seemed to turn on the attitude of Russia. If Russia should come in with the Western Powers, then Hitler would have to face a war on two fronts, and Germany's previous experience of this might make Hitler hesitate to plunge Europe in war. If not, Britain and France had little hope of making good their

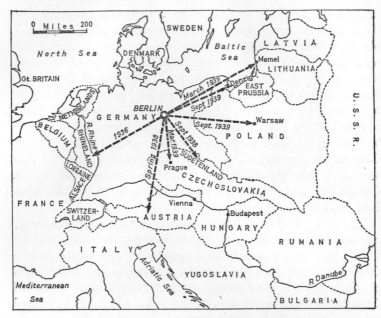

HITLER'S STEPS IN AGGRESSION, 1936–1939
Each step is shown by an arrow from Berlin.

pledges to Poland. In the late spring of 1939, therefore, Britain and France opened negotiations with Russia in Moscow. They made the mistake of supposing that Russia must naturally join them against Germany, who was as much Russia's enemy as theirs. They realised, too late, how subtle that enemy could be. They sent diplomatists of less than top rank, who wrangled interminably about Russia's demands for a treaty which should guarantee the Baltic states against a German attack.

Suddenly, in August, while these negotiations were pursuing their indeterminate and disheartening course, there flashed across the world the staggering news that Germany and Russia had signed a non-aggression pact. It provided that Germany and Russia would not go to war with each other for the next ten years, that neither party would support a third

194

Power attacking either, and that the parties would consult each other on common interests. Russia also promised to export war supplies to Germany. By a secret clause, which was revealed after the war in the German Foreign Office archives captured by the British and American armies, Germany and Russia agreed to divide Poland between them, and Russia was given a free hand to do as she liked with the Baltic states.

Thus Hitler, the supreme master of what the Americans call the double-cross, had again, by his quick-firing diplomacy, left the Western Democracies standing. By this brilliant manœuvre he had at a stroke neutralised Russia and dispelled the nightmare of a war on two fronts. He knew that one further step meant war with Britain and France, but, with Russia out of the way, he regarded such a war as a cheap price to pay for the achievement of his aims. Accordingly on September 1, 1939, after the dispatch of an ultimatum which gave no time for the Polish Government to reply, German armies invaded Poland. The Anglo-French guarantee to Poland became immediately operative. Two days later, after Germany had refused to respond to a demand to withdraw her troops, Britain and France declared war, followed within a week by a similar declaration by the British Self-governing Dominions. So began the Second World War.

Chapter 17

THE SECOND WORLD WAR:
I. HITLER'S CONQUEST OF EUROPE

THE CHARACTER OF THE WAR

THE Second World War was a long and complicated struggle, of which it is possible to give an account here only in the severest outline. The war went through several different phases and the combatants through frequent changes of fortune. Broadly speaking, during the first two years the battles on land, on sea and in the air were confined to Europe and North Africa. Then, with the entry of Japan and the United States as belligerents, the area of the armed conflict widened to include vast battlefields in Asia. This, then, forms a convenient dividing-line between these two chapters, of which the first covers events up to the opening phases of Hitler's Russian campaign in the second half of 1941, and the second follows the story from Japan's attack on the Americans at the end of that year to the final victory of the United Nations in 1945.

Just as the First World War was different from any previous war, so, in many ways, the war of 1939–45 was different from that of 1914–18. It certainly started as a European war, but it afterwards became even more truly a world war than its predecessor, involving battles in the steppes of Russia, in the deserts of Africa, in various parts of Asia, including the jungles of Malaya and Burma, and in the waters of the Far East. There was, besides, a great intensification of aerial warfare which brought the civilian populations into the front line of battle, of submarine warfare which threatened their material existence, and of psychological warfare which played upon their nerves. Methods of "frightfulness", unprecedented in modern times, were employed by the Nazis and the Japanese deliberately to strike terror into the hearts of the conquered peoples. The German crimes against humanity, in particular, included the wholesale deportation and even extermination of whole communities and the imprisonment of tens of thousands in concentration camps.

But it was not everywhere that the Nazis directly controlled the conquered lands. In some they depended on supporters, or collaborators, from among the conquered people, through whom they set up "puppet" governments to do their bidding. This method of seeking the help of collaborators would begin with the invasion of each country when pro-German civilians of the invaded country, ready to act as tools of the Nazis, would work with them in a paralysing combination of sabotage, espionage and treason. Such a body of collaborators was known as a "fifth column", a phrase apparently first used by Franco during the Spanish Civil War, when, before he had taken the capital, he referred to his four columns of armed followers in the country and a civilian "fifth column" inside Madrid.

The counterpart of collaboration with the enemy was what was known as the resistance movement, which was an underground organisation of patriots determined to do everything in their power to embarrass the work of the invaders and their collaborators, including, where circumstances permitted, guerrilla warfare. Such a movement, in a more or less advanced form, appeared in every occupied country; for example, in Poland, Norway, the Netherlands and Greece; in France, where it was later known as the *Maquis*, and in Yugoslavia, where its adherents were known as Partisans (meaning adherents of resistance leaders, such as Tito). When the tide turned against the Germans, the resistance movements in the various countries were of the greatest help to the forces of the liberators.

There were three other ways in which the Second World War

was markedly different from the first war. In the first place, Hitler, by the Nazi-Soviet pact, had removed the danger of a war on two fronts which had proved more than the Germans could tackle in the First World War. When an Eastern Front was opened later, it was because Hitler deliberately created it by his invasion of Russia. Secondly, by the use of heavy armoured weapons, accompanied by intense aerial attack, the Germans ensured such an overwhelming initial success that it was impossible for the opposing forces to recover. This was known as the *Blitzkrieg*, a German word meaning, literally, "lightning war". Thirdly, when it came to the attack on the West the Germans took a much wider sweep than their predecessors in the First World War. In 1940 they included in their attack on France not merely Belgium and Luxemburg but Denmark, Norway and The Netherlands. By these three lines of strategy and tactics—the freedom from eastern preoccupations, the *Blitzkrieg*, and the wider encircling movement in the West—the Germans avoided a repetition of the stalemate reached in the trench warfare of the First World War.

THE PARTITION OF POLAND AND THE "PHONEY WAR"

Munich had given Hitler an easy victory without cost, but it had also granted Britain and France a breathing-space in which to accelerate the process of rearmament which they had already begun. Yet, in September 1939, they were still far from prepared to wage a major war. Hitler knew this as well as they did, and he knew that he was safe to concentrate on Poland before turning on the West. The assault on Poland provided the first example in history of the employment of the *Blitzkrieg* and the "fifth column". The Germans took the Poles unawares. Hopelessly outnumbered and poorly equipped, the Poles had no means of resisting such an onslaught. The attack began with a terrific aerial bombardment of strategic points—fortifications, railways and centres of industry—by the German air force (*Luftwaffe*). This was followed by the advance of the infantry led by armoured tanks. The Germans were much helped by fine weather and dry roads, while the confusion was worse confounded by the activities of pro-German Poles who assisted the physical wreckage by sabotage, and undermined civilian morale by propaganda and terror.

Consequently, within a fortnight the Germans had overrun western Poland, and the Polish Government took refuge in Rumania. On September 17 the Russians, by agreement with the Germans, invaded eastern Poland. The Poles, thus pressed on two sides, after an heroic defence of Warsaw, by then reduced to a shambles, were forced, on September 30, to surrender their capital. Germany and Russia then divided Poland between them. Germany took less than half the total area, but it comprised the more populous and industrialised regions of the west. Hitler divided the Polish area thus acquired into two parts: one, with Warsaw, being incorporated in Germany; the other, with Cracow, being declared a German Protectorate. The inhuman methods of the Gestapo—firing squad, concentration camp and gas chamber—already used in Germany, were applied to Jews and resisting Poles under the ruthless direction of Heinrich Himmler.

Russia, meanwhile, annexed the eastern regions of Poland, and then proceeded to occupy Lithuania, Latvia and Esthonia. These Baltic states offered little resistance, but when Russia made demands on Finland for the cession of certain areas, defensive positions and naval bases, the prospective victim demurred. Negotiations were started, but Russia broke them off and invaded Finland. By March 1940, Finnish resistance was broken down, and the Finns, suing for peace, had to submit to all Russia's original demands, in addition to new ones, including the cession of the whole of the Karelian Peninsula, with the important seaport of Viborg on the Gulf of Finland.

Britain and France, while, of course, deeply sympathising with the Poles, the Finns and the peoples of the Baltic states in their misfortunes, were incapable at that time of relieving them. In the West there was a very different situation from that which had marked the first weeks of the war in 1914. A British Expeditionary Force was safely landed in France, but the British and French were playing for time in which they hoped to build up their strength and to reduce the difference in man-power and armaments between themselves and the enemy. Nor were the Germans anxious to start an attack in the West. Indeed, they hoped that their startling success in Poland and their alliance with Soviet Russia might persuade the Western Powers to come to terms—that is to say, Hitler's terms—rather than risk a general war.

Between the wars the French had built a string of fortresses on their eastern frontier known as the Maginot Line. The Germans similarly had built a line facing the French on their western boundary called the West Wall. In these two great defensive positions the French and the Germans respectively settled themselves, but in very different attitudes. The French thought of the Maginot Line as a complete defence and not as a jumping-off ground for an offensive. This tended to induce an attitude of defeatism. The Germans, on the other hand, while satisfied for the moment to attempt no advance, were actually using the West Wall to cover the marshalling of their forces, as the French were later to learn to their cost. But months went by and outwardly nothing appeared to be happening. The expected *Blitzkrieg*, it seemed, had given place to the *Sitzkrieg*. What was wrong with Germany?, people asked. All sorts of wild rumours and speculations were abroad. It was odd, weird, fantastic, inexplicable. The Americans, with their usual facility for striking the graphic phrase, called it the "phoney war".

There was, however, a certain amount of activity at sea during the opening months. The British Navy, with French help, established a blockade of Germany, as in the First World War, and German surface-ships were driven off the seas. But German submarines again became active as a counter-measure. In September German U-boats sank the liner *Athenia* and the aircraft-carrier *Courageous*, and in October at Scapa Flow the battleship *Royal Oak*. In December, by way of compensation, three British cruisers fought the German pocket-battleship, the *Graf Spee*, and cornered her at the mouth of the River Plate in South America, where, rather than face a further fight, her crew scuttled her. All this time Britain and France were purchasing munitions and supplies from America under the "cash and carry" system. Germany was meanwhile receiving supplies from Russia and feverishly preparing a grand attack on the West, which opened in the spring of 1940 with the invasion of Denmark and Norway.

THE FALL OF FRANCE AND THE BATTLE OF BRITAIN

Norway was strategically important to both Germany and the Western Allies. The long Norwegian coastline, with its creeks and harbours, could furnish excellent bases for German warships and submarines. If, on the other hand, the Western Allies could gain a foothold in Norway, they would be in a position to help the Norwegians if attacked and also secure a line of approach to the Finns. But even more important was the fact that iron ore, imported by Germany from Sweden, was being transported through Norway. Hence on April 8 the British announced the laying of mines along the Norwegian coast near Narvik. On the following day, without warning, the Germans attacked. Denmark succumbed without a blow, although the King of Denmark made a formal protest. Norway offered resistance at first, but was soon overwhelmed by the carefully prepared naval and aerial assault.

In Norway the Germans were helped by a "fifth column" organised by a man named Quisling (which afterwards became a generic term signifying a traitorous collaborator). Quisling, with other Nazi sympathisers, now formed a puppet government under German direction, while the royal family took refuge in England. The Western Allies made some attempt to stay the flood by making two landings in Norway. The troops, which disembarked on either side of the port of Trondheim, were forced to withdraw in a fortnight, and the same fate awaited those landed a little later at Narvik, which could not be held after further disasters in the west.

In Britain vigorous action was taken in face of these set-backs in Norway. On May 10 Winston Churchill replaced Neville Chamberlain as Prime Minister and, with the help of a Coalition Cabinet of Ministers, began to handle British policy much more firmly. It was certainly needed, for on that very day —within a month of the assault on Norway—Hitler let loose a simultaneous offensive on Holland, Belgium and Luxemburg, to all of whom he had sworn everlasting friendship. It was an even more terrific *Blitzkrieg* than the one on Poland in the previous year. The Dutch were helpless before this onslaught. On the first day the Germans captured Rotterdam airfield and followed this by low-level bombing, which reduced the city itself to dust and ashes. Armoured columns, rushing across the land, decimated the Dutch forces and cut the country in half. Within a week Dutch resistance was crushed, the Queen and her family escaped to England, and a Nazi governor was installed.

The fall of Belgium rapidly followed. On May 14 the German armour, moving across the Ardennes, broke through the Allied defences at Sedan, where the Maginot Line ended near the Belgian frontier. By May 20 they reached the sea at Boulogne and so cut the Allied forces in two. The northern army, thus separated from the main French forces and from its supplies, was at the mercy of the Germans, now moving north-ward at alarming speed, in a vast encircling movement. On May 28 the Belgian King, Leopold III, surrendered with his army to the Germans, allowing himself to be taken into "protective custody", while his Cabinet, disapproving his action, escaped to London.

It seemed impossible that the British and French troops, now isolated and deserted, could escape the German pincers. Then occurred a seeming miracle, comparable to that of the Marne in 1914. The scattered troops were concentrated at

Dunkirk, where more than 600 small boats, privately provided in Britain, assisted 200 naval vessels to evacuate the troops. In spite of heavy bombing by the Germans, nearly a quarter of a million British and more than 100,000 French and other Allied troops were brought safely to England. Their equipment and supplies had to be abandoned, but the men were saved. June 3 saw the completion of the evacuation from Dunkirk, whose name will be immortally associated with this superb example of organisation and devotion.

The crushing of the remaining French forces was only a matter of time, for the victorious Germans relentlessly pursued them westward. The chaos in France caused by the military breakdown was increased by hordes of civilian refugees attacked in their flight by the Germans from the air. Despite a change of army command, the French failed to form a line. On June 7 the Germans crossed the Somme and on the 10th the Seine near Rouen. On the following day Italy declared war on France and invaded her south-eastern provinces. The French, meanwhile, agreed to surrender Paris in order to save it from destruction, and on June 14 the Germans entered the French capital. The French Government moved first to Tours and then to Bordeaux, where a majority of the Cabinet decided to abandon the struggle. Paul Reynaud, the Premier, resigned and was replaced by the aged Marshal Pétain, the defender of Verdun in the first war. On June 22 France signed an armistice with the Germans and two days later with the Italians. By the armistice the Germans occupied most of France, including the whole of the Channel and Atlantic coasts. The rest was precariously held by the French as an unoccupied zone.

Pétain set up his headquarters in the unoccupied zone at Vichy, a name which became synonymous with all that is discreditable to French courage and honour. But in England many Frenchmen joined the Free French forces, later called the Fighting French forces, commanded by General de Gaulle, while inside France intrepid patriots began to organise an underground resistance movement which later developed into the *Maquis*. Both de Gaulle's forces and the *Maquis* were later to play an important part in the liberation of France. But, meanwhile, France had indeed fallen, and the British people stood alone on their island facing an enemy in control of an unbroken line of coast stretching from the northern extremity of Norway to the borders of Spain. Only a twenty-one mile strait separated Britain from a foe triumphant from successive victories.

Hitler, like Napoleon before him in a similar situation, prepared to cross those narrow seas. He collected hundreds of barges for an invasion for which the way was to be prepared by an aerial bombardment. He could call on the resources of a continent for men and supplies, while Britain, almost unarmed, prepared to resist the attack. Not only was the Home Guard organised at home but naval action was taken abroad, disabling or interning all French warships, except those in the harbour of Toulon, to prevent them passing into German hands. But, most important of all, the Royal Air Force, although much smaller than the *Luftwaffe*, yet with better built planes and better trained pilots, prepared for action. On August 8 the Germans launched a mass air attack on the south-east coast towns, and so began the Battle of Britain.

Every day through August and September the struggles in the air continued and the trail of destruction spread over the south-east of the island. But the R.A.F. destroyed three times as many planes as they lost, and even made night raids on the waiting barges and other continental targets. Early in September the Germans, having failed in their attacks on airfields and other strategic centres, began the night bombing of London and other cities. In this phase of German air-raids on Britain which continued to the middle of 1941, over 40,000 civilians were killed, but, hideous though it was, the ordeal was bravely borne by the British people because this change of tactics proved that the Germans had lost the Battle of Britain. In this crisis civilian morale was powerfully maintained by the resoluteness of the Prime Minister, Winston Churchill, who spoke truly when he said of the R.A.F. in the Battle of Britain: "Never in the field of human conflict was so much owed by so many to so few". Indeed, it may be said that, by their courage and resource in the summer of 1940, the R.A.F. had saved not only Britain but the world.

AFRICA AND THE BALKANS

Meanwhile, in 1940 the scene of land operations had switched from North-western Europe to the Balkans, Egypt and the Eastern Mediterranean. The British Government boldly decided to send all available forces to Egypt, where they were joined by contingents from Australia, New Zealand and India. As the Germans and Italians dominated the western Mediterranean, this meant for the British forces the long and hazardous journey round the Cape of Good Hope. The Royal Navy, by careful disposition, made this possible. The whole venture was materially helped by the United States, which, though technically neutral, furnished the Western Powers with supplies of all kinds (as explained later).

In the autumn of 1940 Italy undertook two campaigns which proved more than her slender resources could bear. In September she invaded Egypt from her North African colony of Libya, and in October she launched an entirely unprovoked attack on Greece from Albania. But the Greeks, despite their poverty and unpreparedness, forced back the invaders, while the British expelled them with great losses not only from Egypt but from the adjacent Italian province of Cyrenaica. Then the Germans came to the aid of the Italians in both regions and soon transformed the whole situation in the Balkans and the Middle East.

Already the Germans had begun to infiltrate Hungary, Rumania, Bulgaria and Yugoslavia, in all of which Hitler encouraged the Fascist or Nazi minorities and played off one state against another. By the Vienna Award of 1940 he forced Rumania to cede to Hungary northern Transylvania, and in gratitude Hungary joined the Axis Powers. Next he established a virtual protectorate over Rumania, and was thus able to monopolise the vital supplies of Rumanian oil. Similarly, early in 1941, Bulgaria, under King Boris, abandoned her neutrality and threw in her lot with Germany and Italy. In March of the same year Yugoslavia, under the Regent, Prince Paul, joined the Axis, but the move was so unpopular among the majority of Yugoslavs that they deposed the King. The Germans then overwhelmed them by the familiar methods of the *Blitzkrieg*, reducing a large part of Belgrade to ruins. Following this the Germans took the Greeks in the rear from Albania. In spite of the support of a small British contingent, which could ill be spared from the forces engaged in Africa, the Greeks were crushed. The Germans occupied the whole country, including most of the Ægean Islands. The British force was evacuated with considerable loss, and the Germans went on to occupy the island of Crete, where again the British escaped only with severe losses.

In Africa the Germans, using Sicily as a base, landed a powerful and well-equipped army—the *Afrikakorps*—under the command of the remarkable leader, Rommel. By the end of April the British Army under Wavell, weakened by the loss of the men sent to help Greece, was driven back into Egypt, although a detached garrison held out at Tobruk. The situation was extremely ugly, for the British command of the Mediterranean was by no means complete, and the German air forces, based on Sicily, did great damage to British shipping. To add to Britain's difficulties there was in May a rising in Iraq, assisted by Syria, and to secure her eastern flank and the vital oilfields and pipelines of the Middle East, the British, assisted by Free French forces, had to suppress this rising and occupy Syria. It was at this crucial moment that Hitler decided to launch an attack on Russia, and so ultimately sealed his own fate.

THE INVASION OF RUSSIA

In 1940 Hitler had tried to bring Russia in as a full Axis partner with Germany, Italy and Japan. The negotiations,

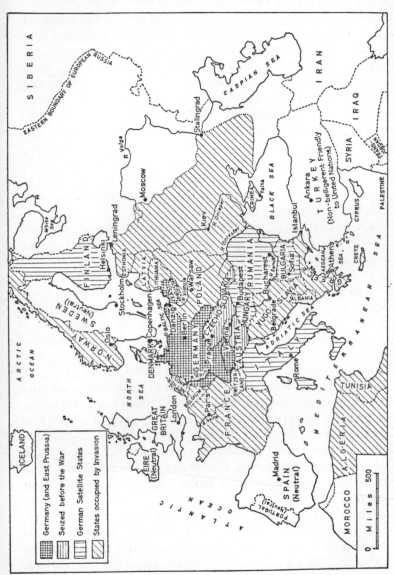

NAZI-OCCUPIED EUROPE AT ITS GREATEST EXTENT DURING THE SECOND WORLD WAR

however, if serious, were not successful, and in the following year, when most of the rest of Europe lay under his heel, Hitler decided to make an undeclared attack on Russia. He considered that the prizes to be gained by the conquest of Russia were worth the hazard. If he succeeded he would acquire power and glory beyond the dreams of any modern European conqueror. He would be in a position to draw on Russia's illimitable resources and also to turn the British flank in the Middle East, overthrow her Eastern Empire, and, in conjunction with Japan, dominate the world. Thus the corollary of Hitler's assault on Russia was Japan's assault on the Pacific bases of the United States, which was to happen in the same unheralded manner before the year was out.

On June 22, 1941, the German Ambassador in Moscow informed the Foreign Commissar, Molotov, that the German forces had crossed the Russian frontier that morning. In fact, the Germans, who were later assisted by contingents from Hungary, Rumania, Finland, Italy, and even by volunteers from Spain, had invaded Russia on a thousand-mile front from the Baltic to the Black Sea. Again Germany profited by the element of surprise, by her greater preparedness, and by her superior equipment in armour and all the engines of the *Blitzkrieg*. The Russians at first could not withstand the attack and had to give ground. They fought heroically in terrific battles amid the most appalling slaughter, but continued to fall back, destroying as they did so everything likely to be of value to the enemy. By the end of November the Germans were encircling Leningrad and threatening Moscow, having meanwhile captured the important cities of Odessa, Rostov and Kharkov. By the end of the year no less than half a million square miles of Russian territory were in German hands.

The *Blitzkrieg* had undoubtedly scored a mighty initial success. But Russia is a vast land, and the Soviet forces were able to retreat into the interior intact. It was during the retreat that the value of Stalin's third five-year plan, which was then current, became evident, for it was mainly concerned with the develop-

GENERAL CHARLES DE GAULLE
(born 1890)
Organiser of the Free French forces in 1940 and
founder of the Fifth Republic in 1958–9.

MARSHAL HENRI PETAIN
(1856–1951)
Defender of Verdun in 1916 and Head of the French state
at Vichy after the fall of France in 1940.

GERMAN SOLDIERS AT THE SIEGE OF STALINGRAD, 1942
A scene in the streets of the devastated city shortly before the successful Russian counter-offensive.

DWIGHT DAVID EISENHOWER
(born 1890)
Supreme Commander of Allied forces in the West
(1944-5). Elected American President 1952.

ERWIN ROMMEL
(1891-1944)
German Commander in North Africa (1941-3)
of an army group in France (1944).

HIROSHIMA AFTER THE EXPLOSION OF THE ATOM BOMB, 1945
An aerial view showing the utter devastation of a city with a population of nearly 350,000.

ment of the "Ural Zone". In spite of the loss of vast agricultural areas, especially the Ukraine, and of invaluable industrial centres, scientific research went on, and a gigantic transfer of technical plant and personnel was made from the west to the safe areas east of the Urals.

The entry of Russia into the war, disastrous for her though its opening stages were, proved a tremendous tonic to the British people. They were now no longer alone and, moreover, Germany's new eastern venture brought them a precious breathing-space. The goodwill of the Western Democracies towards Russia was shown in the most practical way. At this time in Britain and America production began to get level with Germany's, and the two countries were able to supply Russia with those weapons, particularly tanks and aircraft, in which she was deficient. So far as these supplies were carried across the Atlantic, it was often at tremendous cost against German submarine attack. Overland, on the eastward side, they were brought across Persia, which was jointly occupied by Russia and Britain in order to secure their passage.

In these changing circumstances the tactics which had served the Germans so well against much smaller countries no longer held good. As their supply lines in Russia lengthened, the Germans had to stop to build strategic railways and supply depots. Moreover, Hitler, like Napoleon, failed to equip his army to cope with a Russian winter. Thousands of Germans, without adequate clothing, died of frostbite, and the Germans at home began to feel the strain. Nevertheless, in the spring of 1942 the Germans resumed their advance. Striking southward, they occupied the Crimea, and, moving eastward, they reached the River Volga at Stalingrad, which, starting as a small fortified post, had by then grown to be a vast industrial city with half a million inhabitants. Named after the leader who was now the inspirer of the Russian resistance, this city became a sort of rallying-point of Russian national morale. It was to prove to be the limit of the German advance.

Chapter 18

THE SECOND WORLD WAR:

II. ORDEAL AND VICTORY OF THE UNITED NATIONS

PEARL HARBOUR AND THE ENTRY OF AMERICA

As the European crisis developed after Hitler's assumption of power in 1933, the chief anxiety of most Americans was to avoid being embroiled in any European conflict which might arise. To this end Congress passed, between 1935 and 1938, a number of Neutrality Acts designed to prevent the export of arms or the lending of money by Americans to any belligerent. But, as the storm gathered in 1939, President Roosevelt saw that the operation of the Neutrality Acts was actually adding to the difficulties of the victims of aggression in both Europe and China. Hence, when in September the Germans invaded Poland, the President persuaded Congress to revise the Neutrality Acts so as to allow any nation to buy arms in America, provided that it paid cash and carried them away. As Germany's maritime position precluded her from participating in this Cash and Carry system, it worked to the advantage of Britain and France. The success of Hitler's western campaign and the fall of France in 1940 caused Congress to pass the Lend-Lease Act, by which America agreed to lend and lease arms and other war materials to Britain and her allies until the end of the war. As a result, American arms production was speeded up, and the United States became what Roosevelt called the "Arsenal of Democracy".

Isolationism remained strong in America, but Roosevelt,

having been elected for a third Presidential term in 1940, encouraged a growing sympathy with Britain and impressed on the people in his "fireside talks" on the wireless the danger of America's position, emphasising that the Battle of Britain and the Battle of the Atlantic were battles as much for the safety of America as of Britain. It was absurd, he said, that food and arms should be taken from America by British ships only to be sunk by German U-boats, which were by then extending their operations to the western Atlantic. The President's insistence had its effect, for orders were given to American warships to hunt for German submarines. Meanwhile, under an Anglo-American agreement, arrangements were made for the British to lease to the U.S.A. naval bases in Newfoundland and the West Indies in return for fifty destroyers. A further proof of Anglo-American accord was given in their decision to share the defence of Iceland. When the Germans invaded Russia in June 1941, the Americans joined Britain in a Mission to Moscow to discuss ways and means of helping the Soviet people.

The culmination of this growing mutual sympathy was reached in August 1941, when Churchill and Roosevelt met at sea and jointly issued the Atlantic Charter, which stated Democracy's peace aims. These included individual and national liberty, free access of all peoples to the markets of the world, and the realisation of a peace which would remove the danger of aggression. At the time of the publication of the Atlantic Charter, America had not yet become a belligerent, but she became one before the end of the year as a result of what happened on the other side of the world. For some time talks had been going on in Washington between envoys of the United States and Japan in an attempt to settle problems arising from Japan's aggression in China, which had caused America to stop the export of war materials to Japan and to refuse to lift the embargo unless the Japanese withdrew from China. But even while these so-called peace talks were proceeding in Washington, the Japanese were preparing to resort to arms.

On December 7, 1941, the Japanese, without warning, made

a lightning attack, with every engine of modern warfare, on the great American naval base at Pearl Harbour, in Hawaii. Thereby the American Pacific Fleet was put out of action and Japan gained temporary command of the seas in that region. America's consequent declaration of war on Japan was followed by a similar declaration on the part of Britain and the Self-governing Dominions, the Netherlands and some Latin American states, while Germany and Italy, with Rumania, Hungary and Bulgaria, declared war against the United States. The relations of Russia and Japan, however, remained unaffected, for they continued to observe neutrality towards each other. On the other hand, China joined the British and American Commonwealths in active alliance against the Japanese.

The Japanese now moved at incredible speed to exploit their success in the Pacific. They captured the island of Guam and Wake Island from the Americans and confirmed their naval supremacy by sinking two British battleships off eastern Malaya. In a matter of weeks they had gained complete control of the Philippines, conquered the Dutch East Indies, the Andamans, Borneo and Burma, cut the Burma Road, thus isolating China, and captured Hong Kong and Singapore, besides many Pacific Islands, including even the Aleutians off the coast of Alaska. These successes gave the Japanese the vital resources of the East Indies and Malaya, especially in metal and oil, enabled them to eject four great Imperial Powers— Britain, America, France and the Netherlands—from the Pacific, and carried them to positions from which they could threaten both India and Australia.

Thus, by the entry of Japan, the European war became a "global conflict", involving the resources of five continents and of all the great Powers and many of the smaller nations of the world. At the same time, Japan's action galvanised the United States into full war action. Strategically America's position was difficult indeed. Her Pacific Fleet was crippled, her Philippine bases lost, and she was without a plan. Moreover, whichever way she turned she had to face the problem of vast

EXTENT OF JAPANESE CONQUESTS IN THE PACIFIC AND SOUTH-EAST ASIA DURING THE SECOND WORLD WAR

Japan and additions to her Empire by 1914

Chinese mainland under Japanese control by 1939

Areas conquered 1941-42

Miles
0   1000
Equatorial scale

distances. Yet, if she could only hold the position against the Japanese, time was on her side. For this was primarily a mechanised war, and the technological genius of the Americans, harnessing the vast resources of the American continent to war purposes, rapidly proved itself equal to their new situation. An avalanche of weapons of all kinds poured forth from the American factories, particularly of aeroplanes and tanks.

The result was that, as more aeroplanes were brought into action, the Japanese were checked, in May and June 1942, at the battles of the Coral Sea and Midway Island, both fought entirely by carrier-borne aircraft. These successful battles relieved the pressure that the Japanese were exerting on Australia through their recent landing in New Guinea. Also, by July the Americans, based on Britain, were taking part with the British in air raids on Germany. Even more significant was the production of the General Sherman Tank, which proved to be an effective reply to the German Mark IV.

THE TURNING-POINT

In North Africa, in June 1942, Rommel had captured Tobruk, and, racing over the desert, had crossed the Egyptian border and stood within sixty miles of Alexandria. When everything seemed set for a German conquest of Egypt and a German occupation of the Suez Canal, the tide turned. On October 23 the Eighth British Army under General Montgomery fought the famous battle of El Alamein, on the coast, against Rommel with a mixed army of Germans and Italians. It was a battle of tanks and resulted in a spectacular victory for the British. Rommel was driven out of Egypt, and the last pursuit across Africa began.

Meanwhile, in November, at the other side of Africa, mixed Anglo-American forces under General Eisenhower, by tremendous amphibious operations, made landings in French North Africa, on the Atlantic coast near Casablanca and at Oran and Algiers in the Mediterranean. The effect of this was that the Germans immediately occupied the hitherto unoccupied part of France, and this action, combined with the optimism engendered by the new prospects opened up in Africa, encouraged an intensification of the French Resistance movement. In Africa the German-Italian forces were now pressed from east and west. They occupied Bizerta and Tunis, but failed to hold them, and in May 1943 they were squeezed out and the two places fell to the British and Americans. In the succeeding week a quarter of a million prisoners were taken by the Western Allies. Thus Africa was freed from the enemy, the whole length of the Mediterranean was opened to the Allies, and the way was clear for the first assault on Hitler's continental fortress.

These stirring events in Africa were matched by those in Russia. Just as El Alamein proved the turning-point in the west, so the defence of Stalingrad proved the turning-point in the east. On November 19 the Russians started a counter-offensive from the ruins of the city which for two months had been beleaguered and pounded by the Germans. The Russians eventually encircled the huge besieging army in February 1943, destroying much of it and capturing the rest. From that moment the Russians, with only a few occasional set-backs, pushed the invaders slowly but inexorably towards their own borders. In January 1943 the Germans were forced to end the siege of Leningrad, and in March to remove the threat to Moscow. The Russians recaptured Kharkov and Smolensk, and in November the Germans evacuated Kiev, the capital of the Ukraine. By the middle of 1944 the Russians had cleared the original Soviet territory of the enemy.

In January 1943 Roosevelt and Churchill had met at Casablanca and agreed to appoint General Eisenhower as supreme commander of the Anglo-American forces in the west. This excellent appointment soon had its effect. The attack on the European mainland began with the conquest of Sicily which was completed by August 1943. Meanwhile, a curious situation developed in Italy itself, where there was a strong reaction against Mussolini. On July 24 the Fascist

Grand Council asked the King to assume the leadership of the nation. The King agreed, and handed over the government to Marshal Badoglio. Mussolini was imprisoned and, after being rescued by the Germans, was finally caught by the Italians and shot in 1945. Badoglio sought an armistice with the Allies, which was agreed when they actually landed on the Italian mainland in September. The Germans, however, were strong enough to seize the peninsula, and Italy became in effect an enemy-occupied country.

The conquest of Italy was a long and painful process, in spite of the support given to the Allies by the Italians. In October 1943 the Allies captured Naples, but it was not until June 1944 that they entered Rome (the first continental capital to be liberated). Even then the Germans extricated themselves and formed a shorter line farther north. But their expulsion from Italy was really only a matter of time, because not only were the Germans preoccupied with the Russian drive but their supply and transport problem was becoming more and more complicated through the systematic bombing by British and American aircraft of their vital centres of production and lines of communication. This, indeed, became the Allies' chief means of breaking down German resistance. It grew in intensity till the end of the war and it reduced most German cities to heaps of rubble. The Germans, however, were still capable of inflicting great damage at sea. The Russians could never have succeeded in their counter-attack without American supplies, particularly of road vehicles, which were vital as the Russians moved over terrain devoid of railways. But the carriers of these materials, sailing in convoy, had to elude submarine attack across the Atlantic and then face the rigours of the Arctic in order to deliver them in north Russia via the northern coasts of Norway.

The Americans, while carrying so heavy a burden in the Atlantic and Europe, were also successfully attacking the Japanese in the Pacific. By what was called "island-hopping" strategy, the Americans captured one after another of the great

Japanese airfields. In the summer of 1944 they captured Saipan, in the Marianas, and thus secured a base from which to bomb the Philippines and Japan itself. The British had great difficulty against the Japanese in Burma, but in February 1944 they broke the last Japanese offensive and the way was cleared for the reconquest of the country. Meanwhile, in November 1943, Roosevelt and Churchill had met Stalin at Teheran in Persia, where they agreed on the grand combined strategy for the final assault on Germany.

UNCONDITIONAL SURRENDER

On June 6, 1944, the long-awaited D-Day, American and British forces, with some Canadians, Free French and Poles, all under the command of Eisenhower, made successful landings on the French Normandy beaches. Preceded by a vast air offensive, the landings were made from more than 4,000 ships and protected by 11,000 planes. Tremendous preparations had been made. These included the construction of prefabricated harbours and the laying of submarine pipe-lines for the pumping of oil, at first from the Isle of Wight to Cherbourg, later from Dungeness to Boulogne, and finally under the Rhine. Another landing was made near Cannes on the Mediterranean coast, which led to the withdrawal of the Germans from southern France. At first the invasion met with rapid success. On August 23 Paris was liberated, and by the end of September, when Belgium and part of Holland had been freed, the Allies had nearly three million men in France.

In July a group of German army officers, seeing the hopelessness of the position, had plotted to assassinate Hitler by a bomb. The Führer, however, had survived and, having removed the conspirators, determined to fight to a finish. Amazingly, the Germans refused to give up hope. They did much damage and were still able, as late as the first weeks of 1945, to renew U-boat warfare and to drop rocket bombs (V2s) on England. But it was a lost cause. At the end of March the Western Allies crossed the Rhine, while three million

Russians advanced victoriously across Germany from the east. By the end of April the Russians had captured Vienna and were investing Berlin, where the Germans continued their resistance in the very streets. Only then did Hitler give up the hopeless struggle, and on the last day of April shot himself in his bunker in the capital. At the same time the Germans in Italy surrendered, and on May 2 Berlin capitulated. On May 7 the German commanders met the Allied leaders at Rheims and surrendered unconditionally. On May 8, European Victory (V.E.) Day was celebrated throughout the western world.

Thus ended the war in the west. But Japan remained to be finally overthrown. It was expected that it would be a long and bitter struggle, although by then shattering blows were being delivered against the Japanese. By the middle of 1944 the Americans, moving by island-hops from New Guinea and with Australian help, were making landings in the Philippines. In October they defeated the Japanese at the battle of Leyte Gulf, the biggest naval engagement in history, which paved the way for the complete recovery of the Philippines. The conquest of islands farther north, especially Okinawa, only 320 miles from the Japanese mainland, provided bases from which Japan itself could be bombed and prepared the way for landings on Japanese territory. Japanese centres, including the great cities of Tokyo and Yokohama, were bombed, while the coasts were incessantly shelled by American and British warships, and British submarines were taking a heavy toll of Japanese shipping in the South China Sea. British land forces, advancing through Burma, captured Mandalay in March and Rangoon in May, while plans were prepared for the final assault on Malaya. In July a terrific air bombardment of Japanese naval bases destroyed most of their warships.

By August 1945 a vast plan for the invasion of Japan, with the help of what the strategists rightly described as "the most powerful armada in air history", was ready to be put into action. But it turned out to be unnecessary, for in August occurred the most startling events of the whole war. On August 6 an

American plane dropped an atomic bomb on the Japanese city
of Hiroshima, destroying it utterly with about 60,000 people.
On the following day Russia (as secretly agreed at the Yalta
Conference in the previous February) declared war on Japan
and began an advance into Manchuria and Korea. Two days
later a second atomic bomb on Nagasaki reduced that city to
ruins and killed 40,000 people. The onrush of these events,
following the German capitulation, was too much for the
Japanese imperialists, and on August 10 they surrendered unconditionally. So hostilities in the Far East came to an unex-
pectedly abrupt end, and the Second World War was over.

THE PRICE OF WAR

The havoc wrought by the six years of the Second World
War was much more widespread and disruptive than that
caused by the four years of the first. This was inevitable, since
many more parts of the world became actual scenes of battle
and technological advances had made the engines of war much
more devastating. Again, civilian populations were much more
directly involved, both because of the increased drain on man-
power for non-belligerent purposes and because of the use of
air power to weaken civilian morale. Moreover, some nations,
such as the French and the Dutch, suffered a double agony of
loss and destruction: first through the initial German invasion
and secondly through the process of liberation.

It is impossible to calculate the cost of the war in wealth
and human life. Even if we could compute the direct expenditure, whether in terms of money poured out or of capital funds
permanently lost by realisation, there remain the incalculable
losses due to the destruction of property and physical resources. In human terms, too, it is estimated that more than
twenty million people, combatants and civilians, were killed and
more than thirty million wounded and maimed, and this within a
few years of the tremendous losses sustained in the First World
War. But these figures, again, take no account of the permanent
ill-health and shortening of life caused to millions by years of

under-nourishment or captivity. Nor do they bring into consideration the sapping of the energy of survivors by anxiety and bereavement.

In many countries the war left farmers short of agricultural implements, fertilisers and livestock. Industry lacked both sufficient coal to work its machines and raw materials with which to feed them. Railways and other means of transport were disrupted. External trade had been brought almost to a standstill, and foreign exchange, on which its restoration depended, was almost non-existent, while in each country prices rose through the inflation of currencies. Vast populations were deprived, through war damage and poverty, of adequate shelter, food and clothing. The problem of employment was complicated by the return of demobilised Service men and women and of prisoners of war, who increased the pressure on the labour market.

In some countries, besides, there were millions of homeless people, officially described as "displaced persons". They included Jews and other political refugees returning from exile or concentration camps, and large bodies of people expelled from their homes by their new political masters, including Poles ejected by the Russians, and Germans forced to leave East Prussia, Silesia and the Sudetenland. Also there was the difficulty of restoring order after the fall of the Fascist and Nazi régimes, which involved a complete reorganisation of the civil services and the police forces.

These social difficulties complicated the political problems created by the overthrow of the armed might of Hitlerite Germany and Imperialist Japan, which upset the balance of world forces far more profoundly than it had been disturbed by Germany's defeat in the First World War. In 1918 Germany remained physically unscathed and politically intact; Russia was in the birth-throes of the Bolshevik Revolution; and Japan was on the victorious side. In 1945 Germany was a physical ruin, an economic desert and a political chaos; Soviet Russia, her revolution triumphant, dominated Eastern Europe and a large part of Asia; and Japan lay at the mercy of the American power. Britain emerged victorious from the Second, as from the First, World War, but with her material and imperial power much more fundamentally weakened. France, crushed and broken, first by the German occupation and then by the Anglo-American invasion of Hitler's fortress, had begun to recover only in the last months of the war. Italy, having rid herself of the Fascist poison, was "working her passage" back to a respectable place among the democratic nations.

Altogether, then, the peacemakers in 1945 had to cope with a situation far more formidable than that which had confronted their predecessors in 1918. Their task was not merely to tackle immediate questions left by the war but to try once again to lay the foundations of a lasting settlement. The victory had been won by an alliance of many peoples which came to be known as the United Nations. It was the function of true statesmanship to mould this war-time coalition into a permanent instrument for the maintenance of world peace and security. How far the statesmen succeeded in accomplishing this end we shall see in the remaining part of this book.

A. SUMMARY OF PART TWO

Chapter 10. The Russian Revolution passed through two phases in 1917. In March the Czar abdicated, and in October the Provisional Government was forcibly overthrown by Lenin, who declared Russia a Republic of Soviets. The land was distributed among the peasants, the factories were run by workers' committees, and the banks and principal industries were nationalised. Two years of civil war followed the Treaty of Brest-Litovsk with Germany (March 1918), but the Bolshevik power triumphed in 1920. After Lenin's death in 1924, Stalin "liquidated" the Trotskyists and introduced the policy of "Socialism in one country". Stalin revolutionised industry through his first two Five-year Plans (1928–37) and agriculture by extending the policy of collectivisation. The third Five-year Plan, beginning in 1939 and developing the Ural area, helped Russia to defeat the Germans in the Second World War. The Union of Soviet Socialist Republics (U.S.S.R.) was formed in 1923. Stalin promulgated a new constitution in 1936, although this did not diminish his personal power.

Chapter 11. Mussolini, originally a Syndicalist, became an ardent nationalist during the war and in 1919 founded the Fascist Fighting Groups (Blackshirts), with himself as leader (*Duce*). The movement rapidly spread and in 1922 the Fascists marched on Rome. At the King's invitation, Mussolini formed a government, and Parliament granted him unrestricted powers for a year, which Mussolini extended indefinitely. Working through the Fascist Grand Council, Mussolini established a totalitarian dictatorship. He banned all non-Fascist parties and associations, destroyed central and local democracy and the jury system, instituted a complete press censorship, and denied all liberty in education. From 1924 Mussolini gradually built up the Corporate State, based on National Syndicalism, which was completed in 1939 when the Chamber of Fascios and Corporations was opened.

Chapter 12. Hitler's political career seriously began in 1920, when the German Workers' Party, of which he had become the leader, was renamed the National Socialist (Nazi) Party and adopted Hitler's programme. After the failure of the raid (*Putsch*) in Munich in 1923 and his release from prison in 1924, he re-formed the Nazi Party and determined to gain power first by constitutional means. By 1932 the Nazis had become the largest single party in the Reichstag, and in January 1933 President Hindenburg appointed Hitler Chancellor of the Reich, with special powers for a year. Next, the *Reichstag* granted him, for a period of four years, personal power to issue and enforce new laws, under which he dissolved all parties but the Nazis, and destroyed the federal element in the German state. In June 1934 he "purged" the Party of difficult elements, and when Hindenburg died in August, he combined the offices of President and Chancellor in his own hands. Hitler abolished all trade unions and replaced them by the state-controlled Labour Front. The secret police (*Gestapo*) interfered in every aspect of life, all youths were forced to join the *Hitler-Jugend*, and the curriculum of schools reshaped in a Nazi mould. By the end of the four years Hitler had completely transformed the federal democracy of the Weimar Republic into a centralised autocracy.

Chapter 13. Authoritarianism, in one form or another, spread to many other European states. In France the Popular Front (of Radicals, Socialists and Communists) was formed against the Fascist threat, which also appeared in Belgium. In Austria, when Chancellor Dollfuss tried to counter the growing pro-German Nazi movement, he was assassinated (1934) and succeeded by Schuschnigg. In Hungary a Nazi Party grew in strength, while in Czechoslovakia the democratic régime was weakened by the growth of Nazism among the Sudeten Germans. In the 1930's every Balkan state experienced a change of a Fascist or Nazist kind, and the democratic systems in Poland and the Baltic States were modified in an authoritarian direction. In Portugal the Prime Minister, Salazar, set up in 1933 a sort of benevolent despotism through the constitution of his Corporate State, and in Spain, Franco, after his victory in the civil war (1936–9), established a personal dictatorship.

Chapter 14. When F. D. Roosevelt became President of the United States in 1933, the depression was at its worst. Industrial production and farm income dropped by half, the banking system collapsed, unemployment figures reached 15 millions, and many citizens faced starvation. Roosevelt's remedy, the New Deal, included measures connected with finance (e.g. stabilisation of banking), agriculture (e.g. government loans to farmers), industry (e.g. National Industrial Recovery Act), public utilities (e.g. Tennessee Valley Authority), labour (e.g. regulation of conditions, hours and wages), and social security (unemployment insurance and old age pensions). Opposition to the New Deal led to decisions against it in the Supreme Court, which Roosevelt attempted, but failed, to reconstitute. Re-elected in 1936 and 1940, Roosevelt had to abandon his domestic reform programme to concentrate on the war situation in Europe. He pursued a "Good Neighbour" policy towards the republics of Latin America.

Chapter 15. The position of Japan as a Great Power was strengthened by her alliance with Britain (1902), her defeat of Russia (1904–5), and her freedom from European interference in the Far East during the First World War. After the war the militarist party in Japan gained in strength and, taking advantage of the world depression, seized power in 1932, set up a dictatorial régime, conquered Manchuria and made it a Japanese dependency under the name of Manchukuo. China appealed to the League of Nations, which merely refused to recognise Japanese sovereignty in Manchukuo, while Japan withdrew from the League and denounced her part in the decisions of the Washington Conference of 1922. In 1936 Japan joined Germany in the Anti-Comintern Pact, as a security against Russia, and in 1937 resumed her attack on China. The Japanese soon overran northern China, driving the Nationalists and Communists (who had joined forces against the invader) into remote corners of the land. This devastating war continued until the Second World War, when China became, in effect, a part of the United Nations front against Japan.

Chapter 16. Following the plebiscite which restored the Saar to Germany in 1935, Hitler began openly to rearm and reintroduced conscription. The Stresa Front, formed by the West against these moves, did not last, and in 1936 the Germans reoccupied the demilitarised Rhineland without opposition. Meanwhile, Mussolini invaded Abyssinia in 1935 and, in spite of economic sanctions applied against him by the League of Nations, conquered and annexed it in 1936. In 1937 Italy withdrew from the League of Nations and joined Germany and Japan in the Anti-Comintern

Pact. In April 1938 Hitler annexed Austria, and in September, after the Munich Conference had agreed to the step, he occupied the Sudetenland of Czechoslovakia and completed the dismemberment of that country in March 1939, following it by the seizure of Memel in Lithuania; while in April Mussolini annexed Albania. When Hitler then approached Poland to agree to his occupation of Danzig and to grant a passage across the Polish Corridor, Britain and France gave Poland guarantees of their support. The West's negotiations with Russia were abruptly ended by the Russo-German Non-aggression Pact. On September 1 the Germans invaded Poland, and two days later Britain and France declared war.

Chapter 17. By the end of September 1939 Poland was conquered and Germany and Russia shared the spoils. The "Phoney War" in the West ended in April 1940 with the German invasion of Denmark and Norway, and of Holland, Belgium, Luxemburg and France (in May), leading to evacuation at Dunkirk (June 3). Before the end of June the Germans were in Paris and the French signed an armistice with the Germans and Italians, who had meanwhile declared war. In August the Germans began an aerial assault on Britain, but by September had lost the Battle of Britain. In autumn 1940 the Germans reinforced the Italians in the Balkans and Africa and soon dominated both regions, driving the British back into Egypt (by April 1941). In June 1941 the Germans invaded Russia without warning, and by the end of the year occupied half-a-million square miles of Russian territory. In the spring of 1942 they conquered the Crimea and began the siege of Stalingrad, which was to prove the limit of their advance.

Chapter 18. The unheralded Japanese attack on Pearl Harbour in December 1941 brought America into the war, which then became a "global conflict". The Japanese soon occupied the Philippines, Burma, the East Indies, and Malaya, thus threatening India and Australia. But by autumn 1942 the Americans were checking the Japanese and taking part with the British in air raids on Germany. After the victory at El Alamein (October 1942) and Anglo-American landings in North-west Africa, the Germans and Italians were driven back into Europe. Meanwhile, the Russians, starting with a counter-attack at Stalingrad, had by the middle of 1944 cleared the Germans from Soviet territory, while the Americans were island-hopping against the Japanese. On D-Day (June 6, 1944) the invasion of France began and was soon followed by the liberation of Paris and the clearance of Belgium and part of Holland. For nearly another year the Germans resisted, while their country, invaded from west and east, was reduced to rubble by air raids. But in May 1945, after Hitler's suicide, they surrendered unconditionally, as did the Japanese in August, to the United Nations.

B. FURTHER STUDY

1. IMPORTANT WORDS

Absolutism, acquisition, ægis, afforestation, amalgam, annexation, appeasement, authoritarianism, *bourgeoisie*, censorship, cession, chaos, collaborator, commission, community, compromise, corollary, corporation, counter-attack, counterpart, *coup d'etat*, débâcle, defeatism, defection, demilitarisation, dependency, despotism, diatribe, directive, dismemberment, embargo, envoy, espionage, expropriation, famine, fertilisation, foreclosure, formality, ideology, infiltration, innovation, integrity, intervention, isolationism, guerrilla, liquidation, livestock, magistrate, malnutrition, mandate, manifesto, metallurgy, militia, morale, mortgage, objective, pestilence, pipeline, prefabrication, proletariat, protectorate, psychology, puppet, purge, rearmament, refugee, repercussion, repudiation, role, sabotage, safe-conduct, sanction, secession, serfdom, soviet, steppes, strategy, subjugation, superman, syndicate, tactics, terrain, terrorisation, totalitarianism, treason, tyranny.

2. IMPORTANT TECHNICAL TERMS

Afrikakorps, amphibious operations, *Anschluss*, Anti-Comintern Pact, anti-Semitism, Atlantic Charter, *Ausschluss*, Autarky, Axis, *Blitzkrieg*, Bolshevik, "Cash and Carry", *Caudillo*, collective security, collectivisation, Cominform, Comintern, Commissar, Communism, concentration camp, consumer goods, Corporate State, *Cortes*, D-Day, Dictatorship of the Proletariat, Directory (Spanish), Displaced Persons, *Duce*, *Falange*, Fascism, "fifth column", Five-year Plan, *Führer*, *Gestapo*, *Herrenvolk*, *Hitler-Jugend*, Home Guard, Inaugural Address, *Kulaks*, Labour Front, labour market, *Lebensraum*, Lend-Lease, *Luftwaffe*, Maginot Line, *Maquis*, Marxism, mechanised warfare, Menshevik, Middle East, Nazism, New Deal, non-aggression pact, Pan-Americanism,

Partisans, "phoney war", Polish Corridor, Popular Front, Provisional Government, public utilities, Red Army, resistance movement, S.A., S.S., Sudetenland, supply line, Supreme Court, Syndicalism, Tennessee Valley Authority, Trotskyist, unconditional surrender, unilateral agreement, unitary state, Ural Zone, Wall Street, West Wall.

3. IMPORTANT PERSONS

Alexander (King of Yugoslavia), Alphonso XIII (of Spain), Antonescu, Azana, Badoglio, Beneš, Blum, Boris II (of Bulgaria), Carmona, Carol II (of Rumania), Chiang Kai-shek, Churchill, Daladier, de Gaulle, Degrelle, Dollfuss, Eden, Eisenhower, Fan Noli, Franco, George II (of Greece), Giolitti, Goebbels, Göring, Haile Selassie (of Abyssinia), Himmler, Hindenburg, Hitler, Hoare, Horthy, Kerensky, Laval, Lenin, Leopold III (of Belgium), Lytton (Lord), Marx, Metaxas, Molotov, Montgomery, Mussolini, Perkins (Frances), Peter II (of Yugoslavia), Pilsudski, P'u Yi, Quisling, Rivera, Reynaud, Rommel, Roosevelt (F. D.), Runciman (Lord), Salazar, Schuschnigg, Seipel, Smetona, Stalin, Taft, Tito, Trotsky, Venizelos, Wavell, Zamora, Zog (King of Albania).

4. IMPORTANT DEVELOPMENTS (in chronological order)

Lenin and the Bolshevik Revolution; Stalin and "Socialism in one Country"; Mussolini and the Corporate State; background and rise of Nazism; Hitler's "revolution of destruction"; effects of spread of authoritarianism; causes, course and results of Spanish Civil War; Roosevelt and the New Deal; Pan-Americanism and the "Good Neighbour" policy; growth of Japanese domination of China; rise and decline of influence of League of Nations; Hitler's steps in aggression; policy of appeasement: its pursuit and abandonment; significance of Russo-German Non-aggression Pact; opening phases of the Second World War; change from a European war to a "global conflict"; the changing situation causing Germany's defeat; unconditional surrender of Germany and Japan.

5. NOTES ON SPECIAL POINTS

(a) *Marx and the Russian Revolution*

Marx had argued that capitalism grows by the accumulation of what he called "surplus value", by which he meant the amount by which the fruits of the workers' labour exceeds the wages paid to them. The more a community becomes industrialised, the greater becomes the wealth of the capitalists by this accumulation. Moreover, said Marx, as capital grows, the smaller the body of capitalists becomes, because the big capitalists tend to absorb the smaller. Thus the capitalist class gets smaller, wealthier and more powerful, while the proletariat gets larger, poorer and more depressed. When capitalist growth has reached an advanced stage, the extremes of wealth and power on the one side and of poverty and subjection on the other, create inequalities which become so manifest that the revolution is inevitable. Now, this stage of capitalism had by no means been reached in Russia, which was still an essentially agrarian country when Lenin, the disciple of Marx, led the Bolshevik Revolution. In fact, it was precisely the absence of Marx's prerequisite conditions in Russia which ensured the success of the Revolution there.

(b) *Syndicalism*

The term Syndicalism comes from the French word *syndicat*, meaning originally a local trade union. In the early years of the twentieth century in France and some other countries, trade unionism assumed a militant form which became generally known as Syndicalism. It took many of its ideas from Marx, and was backed by French intellectuals, such as Georges Sorel, who wrote a book about it called *Reflexions on Violence*. Syndicalists repudiated both nationalism and political democracy. They thus aimed at the replacement of the territorial constituency, the normal democratic electoral unit, by an occupational or functional constituency. Their weapon was the general strike, by which they hoped to end the capitalist system and to usher in the new free society. The movement declined after the First World War, when the more militant Left Wing went over to the Communists, while the rest concentrated on a more moderate type of trade unionism.

(c) *The Third Reich*

Hitler called Nazi Germany the Third *Reich* to give it a sort of historical glamour. The First *Reich* was the Holy Roman Empire (962–1806), and the Second *Reich* was the German Empire created by Bismarck (1871–1918).

6. READING AND REFERENCE

(a) *General* (in addition to the titles under this heading at the end of Part One).—Carr: *Twenty Years' Crisis*; Hampden-Jackson: *The Between-War World*; Reynolds: *British Foreign Policy in the Inter-War Years*; Seton-Watson: *Eastern Europe between the Wars*.

(b) *Biography*.—Hill: *Lenin and the Russian Revolution*; Deutscher: *Stalin*; Bullock: *Hitler, A Study in Tyranny*; Pini: *Mussolini*; Lockhart: *Winston Churchill*; Frances Perkins: *The Roosevelt I Knew*; Brogan: *Roosevelt and the New Deal*.

(c) *Communism, Fascism and Nazism*.—Dobb: *U.S.S.R., her Life and People*; Seton-Watson: *The Pattern of Communist Revolution*; Schneider: *Making the Fascist State*; Rossi: *The Rise of Italian Fascism*; Salvemini: *Under the Axe of Fascism*; Ciano's *War Diary*; Roberts: *The House that Hitler Built*; Trevor-Roper: *The Last Days of Hitler*; Hitler's Autobiography, *Mein Kampf* (translated by James Murphy); Goebbels' *Diaries*.

(d) *America*.—Consult the books named in Part One (for U.S.A.). Humphreys: *The Evolution of Modern Latin America*.

(e) *The Far East*.—Peffer: *Japan and the Pacific*; Fitzgerald: *China*.

(f) *The Second World War*.—Ensor: *Miniature History of the Second World War*; Falls: *The Second World War*; Fuller: *The Second World War*; Hasluck: *The Second World War*; Joubert: *The Third Service (R.A.F.)*; Eisenhower: *Crusade in Europe*; Horrabin: *Atlas of the Second World War*; Wilmot: *The Struggle for Europe*.

(g) *Fiction*.—Hemingway: *For Whom the Bell Tolls* (about the Spanish Civil War); Storm Jameson: *Cloudless May* (fall of France); Steinbeck: *The Moon is Down* (invasion of Norway); MacLean: *H.M.S. Ulysses* (Arctic convoy to Russia); Pearl Buck: *The Good Earth* (China).

C. TOPICS FOR ESSAYS AND DISCUSSIONS

1. Describe the background and course of the Bolshevik Revolution and compare the parts played in it respectively by Lenin, Trotsky and Stalin.

2. How did Mussolini destroy the traditional parliamentary democracy of Italy, and what did he put in its place?

3. Name some of the significant influences on Hitler's early life and account for his rise to supreme power in Germany.

4. Imagine yourself at a Fascist or Nazi rally in Italy or Germany in the 1930's, and write your impressions.

5. Write a general account of the spread of Fascism and Nazism to other countries beyond Italy and Germany, and describe in some detail the effects in any one country.

6. In what circumstances did civil war break out in Spain in 1936, and what were the results of Franco's victory?

7. Imagine yourself in America at the time of F. D. Roosevelt's inauguration as President in 1933 and explain (in a letter to a friend at home) the situation which faced him.

8. Account for the success of Japan's aggressive campaigns against China from 1931.

9. Trace Hitler's steps in aggression which led to the outbreak of the Second World War.

10. Explain the circumstances in which (a) Russia and (b) the United States entered the Second World War as belligerents.

11. How did the Second World War differ from the First in respect of its causes, course, conclusion and consequences?

12. Debate the following propositions:

(a) That soviet government is less democratic than parliamentary government.

(b) That Hitler was unworthy of the support of the German people.

(c) That the formation of the International Brigade to serve in Spain against Franco was a praiseworthy undertaking.

(d) That Roosevelt's New Deal was justified as a means of coping with the American situation at the time.

(e) That the League of Nations should have intervened in arms against Japan in 1931 and against Italy in 1935.

(f) That the policy of appeasing Hitler was bound to fail.

(g) That the decision to end the Second World War only on the basis of unconditional surrender was a mistake.

(h) That the dropping of bombs on Japanese cities in 1945 was (i) immoral and (ii) unnecessary.

PART THREE

THE UNITED NATIONS AND THE PROBLEM OF WORLD PEACE

Chapter 19

THE ORGANISATION OF THE UNITED NATIONS

THE CHARTER

THE term United Nations was first officially used in January 1942, when twenty-six nations, allied in the war, signed a joint declaration at Washington, agreeing to support the principles laid down in the Atlantic Charter. A further step was taken at the Conference held in Moscow in October 1943, when the representatives of Russia, the United States, Britain and China signed a convention known as the Moscow Declaration. Article 4 of that Declaration stated that "the four Powers recognise the necessity of establishing at the earliest practical date a general international organisation based on the principle of the sovereign equality of all peace-loving states, and open to membership by all such states, for the maintenance of international peace and security".

In November 1944, at a conference held at Dumbarton Oaks, in the United States, the representatives of the same four Powers approved the framework of the proposed organisation. They agreed that their proposals should be cast in the form of a treaty, to be known as the Charter, and that the organisation should be called the United Nations. The principles enunciated at Dumbarton Oaks were endorsed, with some modifications, at the meeting of Churchill, Roosevelt and Stalin at Yalta in February 1945. They were finally formulated in the Charter which was signed by the representatives of fifty nations sitting in conference at San Francisco from April to June in the same year. Poland's signature was added shortly afterwards, so that there were fifty-one originating members of the United Nations Organisation. The Charter thus signed, went into effect in October 1945.

The Charter of the United Nations Organisation is a long document, with a Preamble and 111 Articles contained in 19 Chapters. The Preamble begins with the significant words: "We, the peoples of the United Nations . . .", as the American Constitution opens with the words: "We, the people of the United States . . ." It was the intention of the people of the United States, through their Constitution, to "establish justice, insure domestic tranquillity, provide for the common defence, promote the general welfare, and secure the blessings of liberty". So it was the genuine hope of the peoples of the United Nations, through the Charter, "to save succeeding generations from the scourge of war", "to promote social progress", "to practise tolerance and live together in peace with one another as good neighbours", "to maintain international peace and security" and "to secure . . . that armed force shall not be used, save in the common interest".

THE ORGANS OF THE UNITED NATIONS

The purposes of the Organisation, then, as stated in Article 1, were chiefly two: to maintain international peace and security, and to achieve international co-operation in the treatment of economic, social, cultural and humanitarian questions. To realise these purposes, six principal organs were established: (1) the General Assembly, (2) the Security Council, (3) the Economic and Social Council, (4) the Trusteeship Council, (5) the International Court of Justice, (6) the Secretariat. It is clear that this set-up owed much to the League of Nations which the United Nations replaced. For the League had an Assembly, a Council, an International Court, and a Secretariat. The Economic and Social Council and the Trusteeship Council were not part of the machinery of the League, but even these were elaborations of special bodies of the League;

namely the International Labour Organisation (which continued in existence) and the Commission on Mandates (for the supervision of backward areas).

The General Assembly of the United Nations (Articles 9–22) is similar in function to, but different in composition from, the Assembly of the League. Any member-state may send up to five representatives, though only one may vote. It normally meets once a year, but may be summoned specially between ordinary meetings. It may discuss, and make recommendations to the Security Council on, questions relating to the maintenance of peace. It has exclusive control over the finances of the Organisation and approves its annual Budget. It has general supervisory authority over the work of the Social and Economic Council and of the Trusteeship Council, but shares with the Security Council responsibility for filling vacancies on the Bench of the International Court of Justice and for appointing the Secretary-General.

The Security Council (Articles 23–54) is different in both function and status from the Council of the old League. It is composed of eleven state members each with one representative and one vote. Of these, five are original permanent members —namely the United States, the U.S.S.R., Great Britain, France and China—and six are non-permanent members elected by the General Assembly from among the other states in membership for a period of two years. Its duty is to deal with any dispute "likely to endanger the maintenance of international peace and security". It functions continuously, and the delegates on it have a full-time job. It may call on the United Nations to take armed action against an aggressor. It is assisted by commissions and committees, as, for example, the Military Staffs Committee, composed of the Chiefs-of-Staffs of the great Powers. Originally it had also two separate Commissions to deal respectively with conventional armaments and with atomic energy, but in 1952 they were brought together in one Disarmament Commission. On any important issue all five permanent members must agree; if they are not unanimously in favour, the proposal cannot pass.

The Economic and Social Council (Articles 61–72), as its name implies and as the Charter says, "is responsible, under the authority of the Assembly, for all the economic, social, cultural, educational, health and related activities of the United Nations". Eighteen state-members are elected by the General Assembly to serve for three years, each with one vote. The Council works through various commissions, including transport, communications, human rights, population, status of women, traffic in drugs, and several others. The Trusteeship Council consists of members from countries administering Trust Territories (known as Mandated Territories under the old League). The objects of the council are to promote the welfare and advancement of the inhabitants of Trust Territories, and their progressive development towards self-government. The Council also arranges periodical inspections of Trust Territories.

The International Court of Justice is the successor of the Permanent Court under the League. The Court has its seat, as before, at The Hague. There are fifteen judges drawn from various countries and representing the various systems of law. Nothing in the Charter obliges any member state of the United Nations to use the Court, but any states appealing to it undertake to accept its decision. If its judgment is not accepted, the Court may appeal to the Security Council to take appropriate measures to enforce it.

Finally there is the Secretariat. The chief administrative officer, as in the former League, is called the Secretary-General, appointed by Council and Assembly, and assisted by an international staff appointed by him. The Secretary-General acts as Secretary at all meetings of the General Assembly and the various Councils, and has to submit an annual report to the General Assembly on the work of the whole Organisation. The Secretariat is constantly at work preparing documents, drafting reports and collating information over the vast field of the work of the United Nations.

U.N. SPECIALISED AGENCIES

The United Nations, then, while its main functions are political, is concerned also with economic and social questions. But in this great field of international social work there were already in being other bodies, known as Specialised Agencies. It was to these that the U.N. Charter referred in its statement that the Economic and Social Council "will make agreements with the various Agencies already established by international conventions for economic and social purposes, so that they may be brought into relationship with, and be co-ordinated by, the United Nations". There are several of these Agencies, and it is important to understand the place and function of the chief of them.

First, there is the United Nations Educational, Scientific and Cultural Organisation (U.N.E.S.C.O.). Its purpose and functions are "to contribute to peace and security by promoting collaboration among the nations through education, science and culture in order to further universal respect for justice, for the rule of law, and for the human rights and fundamental freedoms which are affirmed for the peoples of the world, without distinction of race, sex, language, or religion, by the Charter of the United Nations". On this high note U.N.E.S.C.O. set off on its great post-war mission. It held its first full conference in Paris in 1946, and by the end of 1958 there were eighty-one nations in membership. These states contribute to the cost of the Organisation, which has its headquarters and a large staff of international officers, under its Director-General, in Paris. Delegates from member-states meet in conferences, originally held annually but more recently once every two years, in various cities of the world. The programme of U.N.E.S.C.O.'s activities is worked out as a result of the decisions of the conference.

Next there is the Food and Agriculture Organisation of the United Nations (F.A.O.). Its objects are the raising of levels of nutrition and standards of living of the peoples of the world;

securing improvements in the efficiency of production and distribution of all foods and agricultural products; and improving the condition of rural populations. The F.A.O., which, in 1958, had seventy-six nations in membership, has its headquarters in Rome. It holds periodical conferences to discuss policies, and has a Council of twenty-four members to act for the Conference between its meetings.

Next comes the World Health Organisation (W.H.O.), with its headquarters in Geneva and a total membership in 1958 of 88 nations. Its main objects are "the supply of technical aid in fighting epidemics, such as cholera, malaria and tuberculosis, and the support of backward and financially weak countries in improving their medical services". Two other Agencies with a humanitarian purpose were the United Nations Relief and Rehabilitation Administration (U.N.R.R.A.) and the International Refugee Organisation (I.R.O.), but these, having completed their post-war tasks, were dissolved, respectively, in 1948 and 1951. Here we may mention (though not actually a Specialised Agency) the United Nations International Children's Emergency Fund (U.N.I.C.E.F.), founded in 1946 to help children in war-devastated areas.

The World Meteorological Organisation (W.M.O.) became a Specialised Agency in 1951. Its object is to facilitate the exchange of weather information, and its centre is at Geneva. There, too, is the head office of the International Labour Organisation (I.L.O.), which has existed since the foundation of the League of Nations. Its purpose is to undertake research on international labour and economic questions, to act as an advisory service to governments on these matters, and to formulate international standards of labour conditions. There is, further, at Geneva the International Trade Organisation (I.T.O.), whose object is to encourage the expansion of world trade and to remove trade barriers between countries. Other institutions with purposes complementary to those of the I.T.O. are the International Monetary Fund and the International Bank for Reconstruction and Development, set up in

UNITED NATIONS

GENERAL ASSEMBLY

Composition: All member-nations.
Function: To discuss international questions in general and to control U.N. finances and approve the annual Budget.

SECURITY COUNCIL

Composition: 5 Permanent and 6 Non-permanent member-nations.
Function: To maintain peace and to order collective armed action against aggression.

INTERNATIONAL COURT OF JUSTICE

Composition: 15 judges from various nations.
Function: To judge cases submitted and to advise on international law and such matters as the interpretation of treaties.

ECONOMIC AND SOCIAL COUNCIL

Composition: 18 member-nations (3 years each).
Function: To promote international collaboration and co-ordinate work of specialised Agencies (which are detailed below).

TRUSTEESHIP COUNCIL

Composition: Permanent members of Security Council, plus states with Trust Territories and equal number of others.
Function: To promote advancement of inhabitants of Trust Territories.

THE SECRETARIAT

Permanent administrative staff under Secretary-General, who is appointed by General Assembly on recommendation of Security Council and whose colleagues are selected from various member-nations.

SPECIALISED AGENCIES

UNITED NATIONS EDUCATIONAL, SCIENTIFIC AND CULTURAL ORGANISATION (U.N.E.S.C.O.)
   To promote universal respect for justice, the Rule of Law, and human rights.

FOOD AND AGRICULTURE ORGANISATION (F.A.O.)
   To raise standards of living, increase agricultural production, and facilitate food distribution among peoples under the jurisdiction of member-nations.

WORLD HEALTH ORGANISATION (W.H.O.)
   To help underdeveloped countries to fight epidemics and improve their medical services.

WORLD METEOROLOGICAL ORGANISATION (W.M.O.)
   To facilitate international exchange of weather information, promote application of meteorology to agriculture, aviation, etc., and encourage research.

INTERNATIONAL LABOUR ORGANISATION (I.L.O.)
   To give advice on international labour questions and to formulate standards of labour conditions and promote economic and social stability.

INTERNATIONAL TRADE ORGANISATION (I.T.O.)
   To encourage the expansion of world trade and the removal of trade barriers between countries all over the world.

INTERNATIONAL MONETARY FUND AND INTERNATIONAL BANK
   To promote international monetary co-operation, balanced trade and exchange stability.

INTERNATIONAL CIVIL AVIATION ORGANISATION (I.C.A.O.)
   To ensure that international air transport is developed on a safe and fair basis.

UNIVERSAL POSTAL UNION (U.P.U.)
   To unite its members in a single postal territory for the reciprocal exchange of mail.

INTERNATIONAL TELECOMMUNICATIONS UNION (I.T.U.)
   To organise and regulate international communication by telegraph, telephone, cable and radio, and to promote the development of technical facilities.

THE UNITED NATIONS AND ITS SPECIALISED AGENCIES

1944 at Bretton Woods in New Hampshire, U.S.A. The objects of these institutions were stated to be "to promote international monetary co-operation . . . to facilitate the expansion and balanced growth of international trade . . . and to promote exchange stability".

Three other interesting Specialised Agencies may be mentioned. First, there is the International Civil Aviation Organisation (I.C.A.O.), which, in 1958, had seventy-two members. It has its headquarters in Montreal, and it is governed by an Assembly and Council. Its object is to ensure that international civil aviation is developed "in a safe and orderly manner" and international air transport established on the basis of "equality of opportunity". Secondly, there is the Universal Postal Union (U.P.U.), founded in 1874 at Berne, Switzerland, where it still has its central bureau, and first brought into relationship with the United Nations in 1948. Every country in the world, except Nepal, now belongs to the U.P.U., and this ensures the achievement of its object, which is "to alleviate the uncertainty, confusion and excessive cost of international postal communications by uniting its members in a single postal territory for the reciprocal exchange of mail". The third of these Agencies is the International Telecommunications Union (I.T.U.). This grew out of the International Telegraph Union, which was founded in 1865 and which in 1932 amalgamated with the Radio Telegraph Convention of 1906. The object of the I.T.U., whose central office is now in Geneva, is to organise and regulate exchanges of international communication by telegraph, telephone, cable and radio. By 1947, when it came into association with the United Nations, there were seventy-eight countries in membership, a number since increased to ninety-seven.

THE UNITED NATIONS AT WORK

Here, then, was a vast scheme designed to encourage the growth of international understanding and co-operation in almost every field of human endeavour. The outlook for the success of the United Nations Organisation in 1945 seemed much more promising than that of the League of Nations in 1920. For in 1945 America welcomed the opportunity of reversing the decision she had made a quarter of a century earlier not to become a member of the League. Indeed, the United States not only worked wholeheartedly for the establishment of the United Nations but offered a site for the headquarters of the Organisation in Manhattan, New York, where it is now housed in a magnificent building specially erected for the purpose. Moreover, Russia was no longer a political outcast, as she had been when the League was established, but a dominant force in world affairs. She, too, appeared to be an ardent supporter of the new Organisation at its inception.

It was soon evident, however, that there could be no permanent sympathy between Soviet Russia and the nations of the West. With the removal of the common enemy, whom the United Nations had overthrown, mutual doubts and fears rapidly developed in the Organisation which they set up to maintain the peace achieved by their common sacrifices. The high hopes originally entertained for the success of the new enterprise began to be dashed at the early meetings of the Security Council. The General Assembly held its first meeting in London during January and February 1946. It carried through a great deal of preparatory work and chose the non-permanent members of the Security Council, which held its first meeting in London before the end of January.

Now, as we have shown, it is not the General Assembly, a large body ordinarily meeting once a year, but the Security Council, a small body, functioning continuously, which must take the vital decisions. But, as we have already seen, no resolution on any major issue can be carried in the Council if one of its five permanent members votes against, or vetoes, it. In other words, a decision on a vital question of policy and action can be reached only by a unanimous vote of the permanent members of the Council. Hence any member of the Council exercising the veto, as Russia did, could cause a deadlock. In 1950, therefore, it was decided that a question thus blocked in the Council could be referred to the General Assembly for settlement by a two-thirds majority.

But, indeed, during the early days of its existence immediately following the war, the work of the United Nations was administrative and social rather than political and diplomatic. There was much organising work to be done before the new body could get into its stride, and the Secretariat, under the first Secretary-General, a Norwegian named Trygve Lie, was heavily engaged in preparing surveys of the post-war situation and collating reports from the various Specialised Agencies, particularly from U.N.R.R.A. and F.A.O., for submission to the various committees of the General Assembly. Moreover, the Organisation was not in a position to play a directing part in the settlement of the questions which required immediate military and political handling on the spot in the defeated countries. Such questions were inevitably left mainly in the hands of the three Great Powers on the victorious side: Great Britain, the United States and the U.S.S.R., with France playing a slightly subordinate role.

One most important provision in the Charter is that which allows for the making of separate regional agreements between state members of the Organisation, so long as any such agreements are consistent with the principles and purposes of the United Nations, and the Security Council is kept fully informed of them. Indeed, the Charter says that "the Security Council shall encourage the settlement of disputes through such regional arrangements, and shall, wherever appropriate, use regional arrangements for enforcement action". This provision, as will be seen later, has had an important bearing on the maintenance of international security, and, far from weakening the authority of the Organisation during the first decade of its existence, has actually enhanced it by vindicating its fundamental aim. Moreover, the membership of the United Nations has grown. Thus, starting in 1945 with fifty-one members, by 1950 the number had increased to sixty, and by 1960 the total membership was ninety-nine.

THE YALTA CONFERENCE, 1945

Here, in this Crimean resort, Churchill, Roosevelt and Stalin (clearly recognisable), among other decisions, endorsed the principles for the establishment of the United Nations Organisation.

THE SAN FRANCISCO CONFERENCE, 1945

Some of the delegates of fifty nations which signed the Charter of the United Nations, in session in the Opera House, where Mackenzie King, Prime Minister of Canada, is speaking at the rostrum.

TRIAL OF WAR CRIMINALS AT NUREMBERG, 1946
In the dock are some of the leading Nazis, including Göring, Hess, Ribbentrop and Keitel (first four, front row, left to right).

AIR FORCES MEMORIAL AT COOPER'S HILL, RUNNYMEDE
The shrine of the Memorial, opened by the Queen in 1953. The sculptured figures represent Justice, Victory and Courage. Surmounting the building is a crown of stars and wings.

Chapter 20

THE AFTERMATH OF THE
SECOND WORLD WAR

THE OCCUPATION OF GERMANY, AUSTRIA AND JAPAN

THE immediate question in Europe was what to do with Germany. Already at Yalta in February 1945, Churchill, Roosevelt and Stalin had reached a provisional agreement as to how Germany should be divided and occupied. When the final arrangements came to be made at the Potsdam Conference in the summer of 1945, only Stalin of the original Big Three remained in office. Clement Attlee had succeeded Winston Churchill as Prime Minister, following the Labour victory at the General Election held in July, while the conference was in progress, and Harry Truman had become President of the United States on the death of Franklin Roosevelt in April. These changes, however, made no immediate difference to British and American foreign policy.

The three Powers agreed that, pending a final peace treaty, the eastern boundary of Germany should be tentatively drawn along the line of the Rivers Oder and Neisse, Russia taking the northern half of East Prussia, and Poland gaining Danzig, Upper and Lower Silesia, eastern Brandenburg, most of Pomerania, and the southern half of East Prussia. Also the Sudetenland went back to Czechoslovakia, which was, of course, restored. In the west, Alsace and Lorraine were, naturally, restored to France, and Malmédy and Eupen to Belgium. The Saar was made politically independent as the Republic of Saarland (although later, in 1947, its people voted for economic union with France).

For purposes of the occupation, Germany was divided into four zones, broadly corresponding to the areas in which the four Powers had respectively fought. Thus the British took the north, the Americans the south, the Russians the east, and the French the west. The city of Berlin, in the heart of the Russian Zone, was similarly divided into four sectors. Power was to be exercised by the four Commanders-in-Chief, forming what was called the Allied Control Council, which met in Berlin to discuss common interests. Similarly, Berlin had a four-power council of commandants, or *Kommandatura*, for the discussion of questions common to the four sectors. In theory the Allied Control Council was to maintain the unity of Germany; in practice Germany was divided into four separate parts, and, as time went on, the opposition between Russia and the other three became more and more marked.

The four main purposes of the occupation, as laid down at Potsdam, were: to disarm and demilitarise Germany; to convince the German people of their responsibility for the sufferings caused by the war; to destroy Nazism utterly; and "to prepare for the eventual reconstructon of German political life on a democratic basis and for eventual peaceful co-operation in international life by Germany". It was a vast programme to be carried out in the chaotic conditions of Germany following the war. The Occupying Powers had the double task of uprooting Nazism and militarism, and helping Germany, at the same time, to stand on her own feet once more.

A similar four-Power division was made in the case of Austria, where Vienna, like Berlin, was divided and placed under a *Kommandatura* of the four Powers. But the attitude of the Powers towards Austria was different from that towards Germany. They had already agreed at Moscow in 1943 that Austria, having been forcibly annexed to Germany in 1938, should be re-established as a "free and independent state". In April 1945, the Russians, who were by then in occupation of Vienna, allowed the Austrians to set up a Provisional Government, which was later recognised by the other three Powers.

ALLIED ZONES OF OCCUPATION OF GERMANY AND AUSTRIA
FOLLOWING THE SECOND WORLD WAR

But the prospect of a treaty faded before the conflicting views of the Occupying Powers as to the form it should take. In fact, Austria remained under the shadow of a foreign occupation for ten years, and it was not until May 1955 that the four Powers at last signed a treaty which made Austria once again a "sovereign, independant and democratic state."

As to Japan, the Allies had agreed at Yalta to deprive her of all the territories which she had gained by her policy of imperial expansion since 1895. Theoretically, Japan was placed under the control of a Far Eastern Committee, composed of the delegates of eleven Powers. In practice, however, the occupation was undertaken exclusively by United States forces under the command of General MacArthur, who exercised great personal power. Under a new constitution first promulgated in 1946, the Emperor (Mikado) was deprived of his traditional

243

divinity and became a mere figurehead. All titles of nobility were abolished and ministers were made responsible to a parliament elected by all adult citizens, including women. A far-reaching measure of land-redistribution was begun and conscription abolished. At length, in 1951, Japanese independence was restored by a treaty signed by forty-eight nations, although Russia refused to recognise it.

One important decision made by the victorious Powers at the Potsdam Conference was to bring to trial war criminals; that is to say, those charged with "plotting aggressive warfare", "committing atrocities against any civilian group", and, in general, with "crimes against humanity". In accordance with this decision, an international tribunal, composed of judges and prosecutors from the four major Powers (U.S., U.K., U.S.S.R. and France) was set up at Nuremberg in November 1945. Individuals, including Göring and Ribbentrop, and certain groups or organisations, were indicted, tried and convicted. In 1946 some of these were hanged, and others were given prison sentences of varying length. In 1946–7 similar trials took place of twenty-eight Japanese war criminals, and several were executed. Local and national courts in both Germany and Japan continued during the next two or three years to try others charged with war crimes, and by 1950 about 8,000 had been tried, 2,000 being executed.

SOME MINOR PEACE TREATIES

There was no general Peace Conference to settle the world's affairs after the Second World War as there had been after the First World War. At the Potsdam Conference in 1945 arrangements were made to prepare a general settlement. This was placed in the hands of the Council of Foreign Ministers of five Powers: Britain, U.S.A., U.S.S.R., France and China. They were to proceed at once to the drafting of treaties for Italy, Rumania, Bulgaria, Hungary and Finland. It was also intended to prepare a draft treaty for Germany, to be ready to come into operation as soon as a recognisable government should be established there. But the differences between East and West proved too strong for the two sides to reach agreement on this last proposal.

In February 1947, treaties were signed for Italy, the Balkan states, Hungary and Finland. Each of the treaties provided for the payment of reparations, enforced a strict limitation on armed forces, and prohibited Fascist and Nazi organisations. Italy was forced to cede certain territories to France, Yugoslavia, Albania and Greece, while Trieste, in dispute between Italy and Yugoslavia, was placed under an international régime, and the Italian colonies in Africa were handed over to the trusteeship of the United Nations. Britain and America, however, renounced their claims to a share in Italian reparations. Hungary was obliged to restore Transylvania to Rumania, who, in her turn, had to give up Bessarabia and Bukovina to Russia, and South Dobrudja to Bulgaria. Finland was forced to return to her frontiers of 1940 and to grant Russia a naval base on the Gulf of Finland. The Paris Conference which settled all these comparatively minor treaties, however, got no farther with the more thorny question of a treaty for Germany.

Meanwhile, each state tried to find a method of government suited to its post-war needs. In France a new constitution was promulgated in 1946, when the Fourth Republic was established. It restored most of the features of the Third Republic. The former Chamber of Deputies was renamed the National Assembly and the former Senate renamed the Council of the Republic, while there was set up a third assembly, known as the French Union (*L'Union Française*), comprising two Chambers, concerned with the affairs of the French Empire as a whole. But governments under the Fourth Republic were no more stable than under the Third. An added difficulty was that General de Gaulle, with a strong popular backing, stood for a more powerful executive, while complications were caused by the growth of a considerable French Communist Party. In Italy a plebiscite was held in 1946 to decide whether the monarchy should be abolished. A narrow majority voted in favour of a Republic, for which the present constitution became effective in 1947.

In Norway, Belgium and The Netherlands the exiled royal families returned, while in Denmark the monarchy resumed its former status. In most of these states the pre-war constitution was restored, but in Belgium, while it remained a monarchy, there developed strong opposition to King Leopold, who had surrendered to the Germans and remained their captive. In the end he was forced to abdicate in favour of his son, Baudouin. These states, while having to face tremendous post-war problems of reconstruction and restoration of normal life, managed to retain the general principles of Western democracy. In Eastern Europe, however, the fate of the restored governments was very different. The treaties, signed in Paris in 1947, promised them the enjoyment of "human rights and fundamental freedoms". But, detached from Western influences, they found their rights and freedoms cut to a Communist pattern.

THE IRON CURTAIN AND THE COLD WAR

By 1947 it was evident that there was no hope of a world settlement based on agreement between the Democratic West and the Communist East, and any further attempts to formulate a treaty for a united Germany were tacitly abandoned. By this time the disruptive effects of Germany's unconditional surrender were beginning to be appreciated in their full significance. The fact was that the foundations of the traditional balance of power in Europe, shaken by the First World War and undermined by Hitler's aggression, were completely pulverised by the Second World War. Germany, which had formerly been so full of vital diplomatic air, was now a political vacuum. Into this vacuum had moved two sets of alien forces, one from the East, the other from the West, hopelessly at variance in the aftermath of the victory which they had gained by their joint efforts in war.

On the one side stood Soviet Russia, dominating not only the eastern third of Germany and the part of Austria which she occupied by right of conquest, but all the states on her western borders which had been liberated from Nazi occupation as a result of Germany's defeat (not to mention the Baltic States which had been actually incorporated in the Soviet Union). These states were Poland, Czechoslovakia, Hungary, Rumania, Bulgaria, Yugoslavia and Albania. All of them, as we shall see later, established, under Russian influence, a régime on the Soviet model, and all, except Yugoslavia, became Russian satellites, which formed, with Eastern Germany, a complete Communist *bloc*.

On the other side stood the three allied Powers—the United States, Britain and France—which occupied their several zones of western Germany. The three Powers not only worked together in broad sympathy with one another in Germany but held a common view about the occupation, which was to end it at the earliest practicable moment. By far the most powerful and influential member of the alliance, as we shall see in greater detail later, was the United States. At first, the Americans and their European partners believed that their Russian allies in the war would prove their companions in peace. But vital and creative contact between the two sides became increasingly difficult. In fact, Soviet Russia, with her satellites, set up between Eastern and Western Europe a barrier so impenetrable that it became known as the Iron Curtain.

The decline of Western Europe as the centre of world power and the rise to pre-eminence of America and Russia had been foretold in the first half of the nineteenth century. In the 1830's and 1840's two writers in particular—the French political philosopher Alexis de Tocqueville and the Russian thinker Alexander Herzen—had made this discerning prophecy. But they had supposed that it would materialise much earlier than, in fact, it did, for they had failed to appreciate the delaying effect of the Industrial Revolution and its consequences. That revolution carried Britain in the second half of the nineteenth century and the opening years of the twentieth into a period of economic and imperial supremacy without precedent in the history of the world. The two world wars brought that supremacy to an end and left the field of directive power at last to America and Russia, as the prophets had foretold.

As the nineteenth century has been called "Britain's century", so the twentieth has been called the "American century". And just as Britain's supremacy arose from the Industrial Revolution, so do the later manifestations of that revolution explain America's present leadership of the Western World. Her man-power has sprung mainly from European emigration which was one of the consequences of the Industrial Revolution, while her enormous wealth has come from the exploitation of her vast resources in the Machine Age. The United States, therefore, may be regarded as having taken over the torch from Britain. The American economic situation to-day, in fact, closely resembles that of Britain in the later nineteenth century. That is to say, she is still enjoying an expanding economy, whereas Britain and the countries of continental Europe are burdened with a contracting economy. The United States has much surplus wealth which enables her to be strong in arms without diminishing the social amenities the American people enjoy, while the peoples of Europe cannot have a full measure simultaneously of both "guns and butter".

The present position of Russia, again, is a consequence of the Industrial Revolution, but in a different sense. The Russian Revolution could not have occurred—indeed, Karl Marx could not have developed the Communist theory on which that revolution was based—without the Industrial Revolution. Yet it was precisely because the industrial revolution in Russia was only in its early stages of development that the Bolshevik Revolution succeeded, whereas in highly industrialised countries similar Communist revolutions did not take place. In other words, Lenin and his successors adapted Marxist doctrine to a situation quite different from that which Marx had envisaged as a prerequisite of the proletarian revolt. While this made the Russian break with the past all the more complete, it is nevertheless true that Soviet Russia has inherited from Czarist Russia both the habit of an authoritarian régime and an imperialising policy. Soviet imperial ideas now take the form of offering to the rest of the post-war world a Communist panacea for all the social ills from which it suffers. The United States, with its long tradition of free enterprise, is naturally opposed to such an ideology, and offers in its place help to those who may thereby resist the Communist virus.

Neither the U.S.A. nor the U.S.S.R. is a national state in the ordinary sense. The United States is a federation of fifty states which have emerged, through a process of immigration and assimilation in what has been called the "melting-pot", out of many nationalities. Russia is a Union of Soviet Socialist Republics, a federation of many states formed by several different nationalities in Europe and Asia. It is significant that the only other Great Power, besides these two, remaining after the war is Britain, which, although itself a national state, is the centre of a vast Commonwealth of Nations still spread across the world. But Britain's economic strength is much diminished, and her influence in world affairs, therefore, is now moral rather than material.

Britain and the other former Great Powers of Europe are overshadowed by the two Powers which the Second World War has left in a dominant position. The American Union is supreme in the West, the Soviet Union all-powerful in the East, and the dividing line between them lies across the heart of Germany. From 1947 there developed between these two pivotal Powers a tense, though temporarily bloodless, conflict which came to be known as the Cold War. It was in this atmosphere of mutual hostility between America and Russia that the United Nations, to which both belong, had to carry on its work for the maintenance of world peace and security.

Chapter 21

BRITAIN AND A PLANNED SOCIETY

POST-WAR VICTORY OF LABOUR

BRITAIN emerged from the Second World War, in which her part had been crucial to the ultimate victory of the United Nations, deeply scarred and weakened. She was still a leading Power, but her material and imperial strength was radically sapped. The British people displayed a remarkable spirit of national solidarity in the war, and nowhere was that spirit more manifest than in Parliament. Indeed, Parliament shared, in an intimate way, the physical sufferings of the country, for in 1941 the House of Commons was completely destroyed in an air raid, so that Parliament had to carry on with makeshift arrangements until 1950, when the new House of Commons was opened.

The war Government under Winston Churchill's Premiership was a coalition of all parties. Next to the Conservatives, the strongest party was Labour, which, in the election of 1935, had recovered much of the ground it had lost through the break with Ramsay MacDonald in 1931, and raised its membership to 163. Several Labour leaders were in the War Cabinet, in which Clement Attlee was the Deputy Prime Minister. With the end of the war in Europe in May 1945, Parliament was dissolved and a general election on party lines held in July. The result was a surprise to many. Labour won 392 seats and the Conservatives only 189, the rest going to a few Liberals and Independents. For the first time Labour had an absolute majority over all other parties combined, and Clement Attlee was called upon to form a Cabinet.

The Labour Party, which thus came into power to direct Britain's affairs after the war, was, as it still is, a Socialist party, but unique in its growth and character among the Socialist parties of the world. Although it emerged mainly from the trade unions, where its greatest strength still lies, it was never a purely manual workers' party, or even a party of workers in the wider sense which embraces the so-called "white collar" or "black-coated" workers. From the beginning it included, and was strongly influenced by, members of various Socialist organisations outside the normal ranks of Labour, such as the Fabian Society. In fact, it contains among its adherents not only public school and university men and women but even members of the aristocracy. It is not a revolutionary party, like the Communists and Syndicalists abroad, but a constitutional party, believing in the use of Parliament for the widest possible diffusion of social welfare.

Hence, when Clement Attlee became Prime Minister in 1945, no fundamental revolution was involved. Indeed, much of Labour's programme foreshadowed only a rapid expansion of the social services introduced by the Liberals in the early years of the century and endorsed and extended by succeeding Coalition and Conservative Governments.

The policy of the party was set out in a pamphlet issued shortly before the election, entitled *Let Us Face the Future* and containing what was called Labour's "five-year plan" (five years being the statutory maximum length of the life of a Parliament). It committed the Party to a policy of full employment, declared for the public ownership of certain large industries and undertakings, demanded a continuance, during a post-war transition period, of the public supervision of monopolies, price controls and priorities, and promised active measures to stimulate exports, to pursue a vigorous agricultural policy, and to carry out a large housing programme. It further promised to improve the social insurance and national health services and to see that the Education Act of 1944 was fully implemented. At the general election of 1945 the Labour

251

Party undoubtedly received a strong mandate from the nation to carry this programme into effect.

SOCIAL INSURANCE

The idea of social insurance first became effective in Britain after the Liberal victory of 1906. The first National Health Insurance Act, passed in 1911, instituted state insurance against both sickness and unemployment. Only those earning less than a certain maximum amount were obliged to come under the sickness scheme, though in this case there were arrangements for voluntary contributors. As to unemployment insurance, all manual workers had to be insured as well as all others earning less than £420 a year. Although old age pensions for the needy over seventy had been introduced in 1908, it was not until 1925 that an Act was passed to provide old age pensions insurance for those insurable under the National Health Insurance Act, as well as for voluntary contributors to the scheme.

In spite of these provisions, there was still the difficulty of meeting the needs of the long-term unemployed who had run out of benefit. This became specially acute in the 1930's when the depression caused widespread unemployment, which in certain distressed areas became almost permanent. In 1934, therefore, Parliament set up the Unemployment Assistance Board, now called the National Assistance Board, whose function is to assist those without resources or even when still in benefit if without sufficient income to maintain a reasonable standard of life. But payments are made only on proof of need; in other words, by a means test, much resented by those impoverished through no fault of their own.

By the outbreak of the Second World War national insurance had become an accepted social plan, supported, though in varying degrees, by all parties. In 1941, the government appointed Sir William (afterwards Lord) Beveridge, a great economist and educational administrator, to advise it on the future of social insurance and allied services. In his report, made in November 1942, Beveridge proposed a comprehensive scheme available to the whole population, still to be based on the tri-partite contributions of state, employers and employed. There was to be a full range of benefits, including free medical service available to all, children's allowances, a new method of dealing with industrial injuries, and training schemes for the unemployed, all to be administered by a proposed Ministry of Social Security. As a first step towards implementing the Beveridge Plan, the Coalition Government established the Ministry of National Insurance in 1944. But before anything more decisive was done, the general election supervened.

The Labour Government introduced a number of Bills to broaden the basis of social insurance, largely on the lines of the Beveridge Plan. First, and most important, was the National Insurance Act of 1946. By it every citizen in receipt of a personal income became compulsorily insured, the state contributing about one-quarter of the citizens' contributions (employers' and employees' together). It was thus much wider than any previous Act. The Act, which came into operation in 1948, covered unemployment, sickness and maternity benefit, widows' and old age pensions, and (by an Act of 1945) children's allowances. Going with it was the National Health Service Act, which also came into operation in 1948. This established a nation-wide medical, dental, optical, hospital and specialist service, and made the hospitals the property of the state.

THE NATIONALISATION OF FUEL, POWER AND TRANSPORT

As to nationalisation, the Labour Party had said in their election manifesto that, while they wished to leave a place for private enterprise, they intended to secure, "by suitable public control or by an extension of public ownership", that "certain basic industries and services, such as fuel and power, transport and the iron and steel industries, should make their maximum contribution to the national well-being". Although much of this policy was new, in a sense it was only an extension of existing practice. Services like posts, telegraph and telephone, for example, had long been under public ownership, while Broadcasting was controlled by a nationally financed Corporation. Also there were already existing such publicly constituted bodies as the Marketing Boards for hops, bacon, milk and potatoes.

The Ministry of Fuel and Power had been set up in 1942 as one of a number of new war-time central government departments. But it had permanent functions which continued in peace-time, for it dealt, among other things, with policy affecting coal, electricity and gas. As to coal, the Sankey Commission, as has been said, recommended nationalisation as early as 1919. Although nationalisation was not then adopted, a partial step towards it was taken in 1938 when by a special Coal Act all privately owned mines no longer being worked were acquired by the state at a cost of over £66 million. Again, in the case of electricity a series of Acts had brought the service more and more under government direction. In 1919 Commissioners were appointed with the duty of "promoting, regulating and supervising the supply of electricity", and another Act in 1926 set up the Central Electricity Board to carry out a scheme of electricity generation and transmission for the whole country. It was this Board which was responsible for the grid system, a triumph of electrical engineering. Gas, too, was subject to growing legislative restriction. Acts passed in 1920, 1929, 1932 and 1934 regulated the gas undertakings, which by 1945 were almost all under the ægis of a nation-wide organisation known as the Incorporated British Gas Council.

The same growth of statutory restriction and control may be traced in the case of transport. In 1919 the Ministry of Transport was established, but the Minister's powers became much wider during and after the Second World War, and now cover most forms of inland transport, as well as civil aviation. Parallel with the growth of the Ministry was considerable reorganisation of the railways under statutory enforcement. An extremely important statute was the Railways Act of 1921, by which, in 1923, 120 different railways were merged into four regional groups, while in 1933 another Act established the London Passenger Transport Board to administer the services of the Metropolis. Similar government restrictions had been placed on air transport. In 1939 the British Overseas Airways Act established the British Overseas Airways Corporation (B.O.A.C.) to secure the economic development of overseas air transport services and their operation at reasonable charges.

By 1939, then, state control, although not state ownership, of these vital services had been well developed. The Second World War made the final step towards nationalisation much easier, for during the war the direction of these services had been taken over by the government in order to concentrate the resources and energies of the nation on the war effort. The nationalising legislation introduced by the Labour Government began in 1946 with the Coal Industry Nationalisation Act, which brought the entire industry into the possession of the nation at a cost of £164 million. The assets and responsibilities of the industry were transferred to the National Coal Board, a public corporation composed of nine members, appointed by the Minister of Fuel and Power. The Board is responsible for production, welfare, labour relations, finance, marketing and scientific development. The coalfields of the country were divided into eight regions, which were subdivided into forty-eight areas, each under a general manager.

The Electricity Nationalisation Act of 1947 established the British Electricity Authority, which was made responsible for generation and supply, while distribution was placed in the hands of fourteen Area Boards. The total capital of the industry was then about £840 million. The Gas Act of 1948 nationalised the gas industry, and thus superseded all the previous Acts, mentioned earlier. It established twelve Area Boards which took over all rights and liabilities of previously existing undertakings. The Boards were to be responsible for generating gas, while the functions of the Gas Council, set up by the same Act, were mainly advisory, financial and educational.

The railways were nationalised by the Transport Act of 1947. By this Act the railways were vested, from January 1, 1948, in the British Transport Commission which was made responsible also for the main forms of land transport, including road haulage. The Act established five Executives, which were to operate under the Commission. The five Executives were Railway, Road Haulage, Docks and Inland Waterways, Hotels, and London Transport. Aviation, too, was nationalised by the Civil Aviation Act of 1946, whose object was "to secure the development of air transport services by corporations operating under national control". Added to the B.O.A.C. were two others—British European Airways Corporation (B.E.A.C.) and British South American Airways Corporation (though this latter was later discontinued as a separate organisation).

IRON AND STEEL AND THE BANK OF ENGLAND

In spite of a good deal of natural dissatisfaction in various quarters, the Labour Government successfully established the nationalisation of the fuel, power and transport services. But when it came to an attempt to nationalise the iron and steel industry, the government ran into a storm of opposition so violent that it was forced to compromise on the date originally proposed for its introduction. The Nationalisation Bill was introduced in 1948. It proposed the establishment of an Iron and Steel Corporation, which was to acquire all the shares in the industry and operate it from May 1, 1950. This date was later postponed to January 1, 1951, and on this basis the government proceeded to the appointment of a Chairman and six members of the Corporation. But in October 1951 there was a General Election which gave the Conservatives a majority. The new Conservative Government at once directed the Iron and Steel Corporation "to suspend its reorganisation of the publicly owned companies, pending legislation to restore the industry to private ownership".

In 1952 a new Bill was introduced to denationalise the

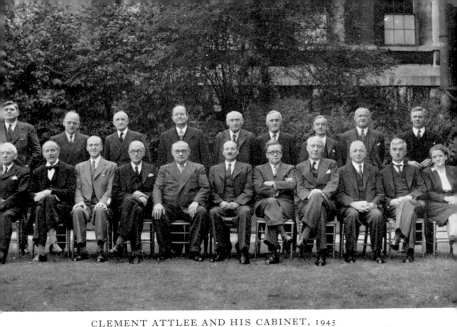

CLEMENT ATTLEE AND HIS CABINET, 1945

The first Labour Government to hold an absolute majority over all other Parties. Photograph
taken in the garden of No. 10 Downing Street.

THE NEW HOUSE OF COMMONS, OPENED 1950

M.P.s claiming seats on the day of the opening of the new Chamber built to replace the one
destroyed in an air raid in 1941.

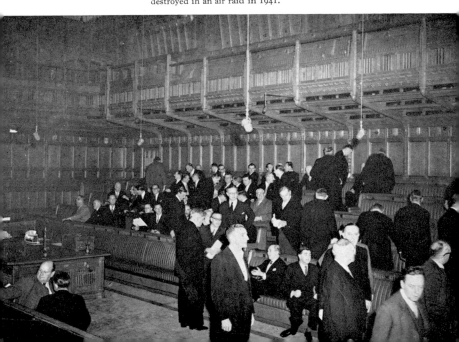

FIRST MEETING OF THE NATIONAL COAL BOARD, 1946

In preparation for January 1, 1947, the vesting day for the nationalisation of the mines. The Chairman, Lord Hyndley, is in the centre.

VALE OF LEVEN HOSPITAL, DUNBARTONSHIRE, SCOTLAND

A ward in the first entirely new hospital to be built since the National Health Service Act of 1946 nationalised the hospitals in 1948 and placed them under Regional Boards, such as that for the Western Region of Scotland which is responsible for this one.

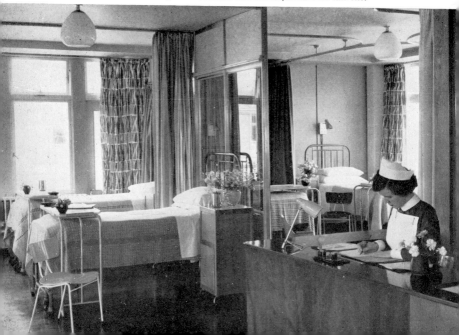

industry. The Iron and Steel Corporation was to be dissolved, and a Board to be set up to supervise the industry, distribute raw material, encourage capital development, and fix maximum selling prices. On this Board were to sit representatives of the various interests concerned, including trade unions and steel workers. At the same time there was to be established a Holding and Realisation Agency to sell the nationalised companies to private owners. In 1953 this new Iron and Steel Act became operative. In the same year Parliament passed an Act instructing the Transport Commission to dispose of property held, under the Act of 1947, by the Road Haulage Executive. From October 1 of that year, moreover, the Transport Commission was reconstituted, and all the Executives originally under it. except London Transport, were abolished.

One important statute of these years was that which revised the conditions of the Parliament Act of 1911. The Bill was introduced in 1947 with the object of reducing the period of the Lords' Suspensive Veto from two years to one, because the Labour Government feared that the Lords might use the veto to the full to hold up further legislation. But the Labour Party had no mandate for this measure, as they had for extending the social services and for nationalising public undertakings. The occasion of the introduction of the new Parliament Bill was the timing of the passage of the Iron and Steel Act. The passing of the Parliament Bill of 1947 was an interesting illustration of the working of the Parliament Act of 1911. In 1949 the Commons passed the Bill in the third successive session. In November 1949 the Lords rejected it a third time, but, two years having elapsed, the Bill became law in spite of the Lords' objection. Thus the machinery of the original Act was used to amend it. The Parliament Act of 1949 shortened the period of the suspensive veto of the House of Lords, but in no other respect affected its powers.

The other measure of nationalisation was concerned with the Bank of England, but here it was almost an inevitable change, which could not have been long delayed even if

Labour had not come to power. During the twentieth century the relations between the Treasury and the Bank of England grew closer. Indeed, as one writer has recently reminded us, up to the time of the First World War, "the treasury was known as the West End branch of the Bank; thereafter the Bank became the City branch of the Treasury". Between the wars the Treasury more and more assumed the dominant role. It was responsible for financial policy and the borrowing operations of the government. Hence it had a decisive voice in the note issue of the Bank and in controlling the value of sterling. The Bank, in fact, became the servant of the government, and by the Bank of England Act of 1946 its capital was acquired by the state and its Directors appointed by the Crown. Thus the Act merely gave statutory force to a situation which had already grown up during the two preceding decades.

Another important Act passed in 1946 repealed the Trade Disputes Act of 1927, which, following the General Strike of 1926, had, among other things, declared a general strike illegal and forced the trade unions to adopt the method of "contracting-in" instead of "contracting-out" in connection with the collection of a political levy. It was natural that a Labour Government should wish to restore these lost powers to the unions, and the result was that the law with respect to trade unions broadly reverted to the position existing before the Act of 1927 was passed.

In February 1952, shortly after the General Election, King George VI died and was succeeded by his daughter, Elizabeth, who was crowned, amid popular rejoicing, on June 2, 1953.

THE EDUCATION ACT OF 1944

Just as, towards the close of the First World War, the important Education Bill of 1918 became law, so, towards the close of the Second World War, Parliament passed the even more important Education Act of 1944, perhaps the most significant measure of social reform carried in Britain in the first half of the twentieth century. The Bill was introduced under the Coalition Government, and both a Conservative and a Labour Minister piloted it through the House of Commons, for the President of the Board of Education was the Conservative member, R. A. Butler, later Chancellor of the Exchequer, and the Parliamentary Secretary to the Board was the Labour member, Chuter Ede, later Home Secretary. The Act, however, had to be first applied during the six years of the Labour Government (1945–51), and afterwards under the Conservative Government. And both parties were anxious to make the Act work. Some time before the Bill was first laid before the House of Commons in January 1944, the Board of Education had discussed plans of educational reform with Local Education Authorities, teachers' associations and other educational societies, including the Churches. These discussions showed that the war had profoundly affected educational opinion and brought about a realisation that Britain's place in the post-war world would depend on how her future citizens were educated. Acts of Parliament, however, cannot of themselves achieve such social changes: they can only lay out the ground for their development. And this is what the Act of 1944 did for education more than any of the previous Acts passed in 1870, 1902, 1918 and 1936.

In one sense, the Act of 1944 continued and extended the provisions of those earlier laws and gave statutory force to a number of proposals which had appeared in reports and memoranda published both before and during the Second World War. The Act abolished the Board of Education and replaced it by the Ministry of Education, so that the President of the Board became the Minister of Education. But this was really little more than a change in name, because in practice the former Board never met. In other ways the Act introduced some quite new, and even revolutionary, plans. The general aim of the Act was to offer to all children in school equality of opportunity. Thus it said that every child should be educated according to its "age, ability and aptitude", whereas all the earlier Acts had said that the duty of the parent was merely to see that his child

259

received efficient instruction in reading, writing and arithmetic.

The Act of 1944 laid down that there are three stages of education—primary, secondary and further. This meant that every child must pass at the age of 11 plus from the primary to the secondary stage, although there were to be different types of secondary education according to the abilities and needs of the pupils. The Act also abolished all fees in all kinds of schools under Local Education Authorities so that no child should be handicapped by the economic difficulties of its parents. It did not abolish private schools, although it arranged for their inspection. It safeguarded the rights of those parents who wished to send their children to schools of various religious denominations, and it obliged all Education Authorities to see that the school day in all schools under them should start with an act of corporate worship.

The Act also said that the school-leaving age should be raised to 15 on a date to be decided, and eventually to 16. The Labour Government carried out the first of these proposals in 1947, but nothing has yet been done about the second. The Act further proposed that compulsory part-time day continuation schools, to be known as County Colleges, should be provided for young people between the ages of 15 and 18 who have left school and entered employment, but this provision had still not been carried into effect sixteen years after the passing of the Act.

There were many other important provisions in the Act designed to improve the educational system in its many different aspects outside the ordinary day schools. These included the provision of nursery schools and classes, the compulsory extension of the number of special schools for physically and mentally handicapped children, and the establishment of boarding schools for children whose home circumstances might make it difficult or inappropriate for them to be educated in day schools. Among other important provisions of the Act were those concerned with school meals and the school medical service, which was greatly extended and which takes on a new significance when considered in relation to the new National Health Service.

The Act applied to England and Wales, but similar Acts were passed for Northern Ireland, whose educational system is broadly like that in England and Wales, and for Scotland whose traditions in education are somewhat different from the rest. In all cases, the Acts imposed on every Local Education Authority the duty to prepare and submit to the appropriate Minister for his (or her) approval a Development Plan designed to implement the proposals contained in the relevant Act. This was an important aspect of the proposed reforms, whose success must ultimately depend on the spirit in which all those concerned with them endeavour to carry them into effect.

Footnote on the Welfare State outside Britain

Such, then, was the Welfare State, as it developed in Britain after the Second World War. This conception of the state, in which social welfare is diffused by means of legislation, has by no means been confined to Britain. Indeed, it is characteristic of most advanced communities to-day. This truth is well illustrated in a report prepared by the United Nations in 1955 entitled *An International Survey of Programmes of Social Development.* The report describes the extraordinary expansion in many countries all over the world of "governmental measures designed to raise standards of living, provide social security, and improve public health, education, housing and conditions of work". Since 1945, the report adds, "forty-five nations have adopted new constitutions or made major constitutional changes, the effect of which is to lay upon the state basic responsibility for social welfare".

Chapter 22

THE COLONIAL REVOLUTION AND
THE RETREAT FROM ASIA

THE NATURE OF THE COLONIAL REVOLUTION

FOR three centuries Britain had been building her Empire. She had emerged supreme from her struggles with Spain and Portugal, Holland and France. In her imperial career she had planted colonies in North America which had become independent as the United States. She had made other settlements in America, Australia, New Zealand and South Africa, from which developed the Self-governing Dominions of to-day. She also held the great Dependency of India (with Burma) and Crown Colonies in every continent.

Then, towards the end of the nineteenth century, under the incentive of the New Imperialism, hitherto unknown regions of Africa were opened up and divided among the European Powers, while in Asia these same Powers sought spheres of influence for trade and investment. The non-European peoples both in Africa and in Asia were forced to adapt themselves to European usages, or perish. But the very dominance of the European Powers encouraged among these non-European peoples the growth of nationalist ideas and economic aims similar to those caused in Europe by the effects of the French and Industrial Revolutions. These movements, already under way in Asia, from the Near to the Far East, by the end of the First World War, made great strides between the two wars.

Japan's achievements in the Second World War, despite her ultimate overthrow, had shown what a vigorous Asiatic nation, properly equipped and trained, could do against the Imperial

Powers of the West. It had also shattered beyond recovery the prestige of Western European nations, impoverished and enfeebled by two world wars. The cry "Asia for the Asiatics" was a demand not only for the political independence of Asiatic nations but also for economic power, produced, so to speak, under their own steam, as well as for higher standards of living and a more widely diffused native culture. These demands implied nothing less than a colonial revolution which was destined to involve the liquidation of most of Western Europe's imperial enterprises in Asia. Among the first Powers to recognise the character and force of this revolution was Britain.

INDIA AND PAKISTAN

The most striking example of this change was seen in India. Immediately after the war an attempt to resume provincial powers under the Act of 1935 was only partially successful. It was soon evident that that Act was obsolete, and the policy of the Indian leaders was to get rid of British control as soon as possible. The British Government agreed that "India must decide her own destiny", and in March 1946 sent a mission of three Cabinet Ministers to India to discuss with the Indian leaders plans for an independent, united India. The discussions broke down owing to the conflict of views between the Hindu and Moslem communities. The Moslem League, under the leadership of Mohammed Ali Jinnah, refused to co-operate with the Congress Party, under Pandit Nehru, and would accept nothing short of partition so as to secure a separate Moslem state, to be formed by a union of those areas where the majority of the inhabitants were Mohammedans.

In June 1947, the party leaders in India agreed on a scheme of partition as the only possible solution, and in August Parliament at Westminster passed the Indian Independence Act, which divided British India into two Self-governing Dominions, to be known respectively as India and Pakistan. Lord Mountbatten was appointed Governor-General of India, with its capital at Delhi, and Nehru Prime Minister, while

Jinnah became Governor-General of Pakistan, with its capital at Karachi, and Liaquat Ali Khan Prime Minister. British soldiers and civilians were to leave India in two months. The words "Emperor of India" were eliminated from the royal title and any remaining functions of the old India Office were transferred to the Secretary of State for Commonwealth Relations, whose department had been established in that year. Meanwhile, the Native States, of which there were 570 with a total population of some ninety millions, had the option of remaining independent or joining one or other of the new Dominions.

There followed a period of civil strife and bloodshed over boundary-making between the two Dominions. The boundaries having been settled, each Dominion began to hammer out its own constitution through the Assembly which it had elected. As a tentative measure, the appropriate parts of the Act of 1935 were adopted as a basis of government in each state, supplemented by temporary orders approved by each Assembly. In the course of these debates. India announced its intention of becoming a republic, although wishing to remain within the British Commonwealth. Britain raised no objection. So, when the new constitution came into effect in January 1950, it applied not to a Self-governing Dominion with a Governor-General representing the King but to an independent republic with an elected President. All the native states agreed to join the republic except thirteen which joined Pakistan, and Kashmir which remained in dispute between them.

The Republic of the Union of India is a federation of twenty-eight states, nineteen of which are former provinces and the remainder grouped native states. Each of these units has a Governor appointed by the President of the Republic and a legislature, of either one or two Chambers, whose powers are defined in the constitution. The federal legislature at Delhi has two Houses: the Council of States, elected proportionately by the various state legislatures, and the House of the People with 500 members elected by an electorate of 170 million men and women of twenty-one or over. The life of the lower House is five years, subject to earlier dissolution. The President and Vice-President of the Republic are elected by an Electoral College composed of all members of state legislatures.

The Dominion of Pakistan found constitution-making more difficult. Geographically, Pakistan is cut in two by the area of the Indian Republic. The larger part of it (chiefly Baluchistan, West Punjab and Sind) is on the west, and the rest (mainly East Bengal) on the east. Politically, therefore, it is less homogeneous than India, and economically less rich in resources. Like India, however, it is a federation. By the new constitution, as finally approved in 1956, the Dominion became the "Islamic Republic of Pakistan", although, like the Republic of India, it wished to remain within the British Commonwealth.

Britain's achievement during her period of supremacy in India was remarkable, but even more remarkable was what it left behind. The new India is exerting a growing influence on the politics of Asia. This is largely due to the statesmanship of Nehru, whose strength derives from a combination of Eastern and Western civilisations, for he is a Kashmiri Brahman, a caste famous for its Hindu culture, and also a distinguished graduate of Cambridge University.

CEYLON, BURMA AND MALAYA

A similar British withdrawal took place after the Second World War from Ceylon and Burma, while in the case of Malaya there were several modifications in the system of colonial control. The island of Ceylon, which had become a British Crown Colony in 1815, offers an excellent example, which may well be followed in other parts of the Empire, of political growth from Colonial to Dominion status. Its population, mixed in race and religion, the great majority being Buddhists, has more than doubled itself in the present century, being, according to the census of 1953, slightly more than eight millions. In 1909 an elective element was introduced into the Legislative Council and native representation was extended in 1920 and 1923. In 1947 a new constitution, granting Ceylon responsible government, came into operation, but the Ceylonese made such good use of the political opportunities thus offered that in the same year the British Parliament passed the Ceylon Independence Act, under which Ceylon became a Self-governing Dominion. In 1948 the new Ceylon Parliament was officially opened.

In 1950 Colombo, the capital of Ceylon, became famous as the meeting-place of a conference of Commonwealth Foreign Ministers, which formulated a scheme for Co-operative Economic Development in South and South-east Asia, known as the Colombo Plan. It envisaged a long-term programme of development in former British territories and existing colonial areas, as well as those of France and the Netherlands. Later such states as Japan and Siam were included in the Plan. A budget of nearly £2,000 million was to be financed partly by the Asian territories themselves and partly by interested governments, including those of Great Britain, Australia, New Zealand, Canada and the United States. It was a novel and interesting experiment in "joint planning and mutual self-help", and, although it has not produced rapid results, it continues to encourage in the lands concerned progress in irrigation and agriculture, transport and communications, mining and manufacture, health and education.

The British had acquired political control of Burma piecemeal during the nineteenth century, and up to 1935 governed Burma as a province of British India. In 1935, however, Burma was detached from India, and, under an Act passed at the same time as that for India, it was given a large measure of responsible government. During the war the Japanese invaded Burma and were ejected only after three arduous campaigns fought between 1943 and 1945. After the liberation British administration was provisionally restored, on the understanding that the Burmese should be entirely free to decide their own future. In 1947 a Constituent Assembly declared for an independent republic, which was established in 1948 when the British Parliament passed the Burma Independence Act.

The early political passage of republican Burma was made difficult by the growth of an armed Communist Party. A general election in 1952 gave the Socialists, who formed the so-called Anti-Fascist People's Freedom League, a majority, and in the following year the Communists were disarmed. Yet the fact that, for half its length, Burma's eastern frontier marches with that of Communist China constitutes a standing menace to the political stability of the new state. It has been helped to resist that menace first by a large loan jointly subscribed by Britain, India, Pakistan, Ceylon and Australia, and later by being brought into the Colombo Plan.

In the Malay Peninsula were several British or British-controlled territories, including nine sovereign Malay states, the two British settlements of Penang and Malacca, the three colonies of Singapore, Sarawak and North Borneo, and the British-protected state of Brunei. After the Second World War, when, following the withdrawal of the Japanese, anarchy prevailed, efforts were made to unite the nine Malay states with Penang and Malacca, and in 1948 they were joined in the Federation of Malaya. Each unit had its own constitution and its own local government, but over the whole federation there was a Legislative Council as well as a British High Commissioner. There was also a Commissioner-General for the United Kingdom in South-east Asia, whose general supervision included that of the separate colonies of North Borneo, Sarawak and Singapore, besides Brunei.

Thus, whereas the British imperial power had ceased in India, Pakistan, Ceylon and Burma, it remained in South-east Asia. The position was doubly difficult. First, the whole area was in the strategic control of the United States as part of its general responsibilities in the Pacific. Secondly, there had grown up in Malaya considerable Communist parties under Russian influence. In 1952 the British Colonial Office issued to the High Commissioner of Malaya a directive which said that the Malayans "should, in due course, become a fully self-governing nation". Meanwhile it was feared that Communist activity was retarding the country's development. But during the next three or four years much progress was made towards political stability. The result was that in 1957 the Federation of Malaya became an independent state and a fully-fledged member of the British Commonwealth of Nations.

THE FRENCH AND DUTCH IN ASIA

French Indo-China originally consisted of five countries: Cochin-China, Annam, Tonking, Laos and Cambodia. During the Second World War France, of course, lost control of these areas, which then came under the powerful influence of the Japanese who supported a revolutionary movement known as Viet Minh. In 1945 Viet Minh dethroned the pro-French Emperor Bao Dai of Annam, and put in his place a candidate of their own, Ho Chi Minh, whom they proclaimed President of an independent republic which they called Viet Nam. In the autumn of 1945 the French restored their protectorate over Cambodia and Laos, and persuaded Ho Chi Minh to bring under French protection his Viet Nam Republic, which included the other three original French territories. But, before long, Ho Chi Minh, a Communist of long standing, proved distasteful to the French, who later disowned him and restored their original protégé, Bao Dai. There were thus rival régimes in Viet Nam, and between the two a civil war followed. Ho Chi Minh was helped by Chinese Communist troops and recognised by Soviet Russia, while Bao Dai had the support of French arms and was recognised by Britain and America.

Under pressure of these events, the French National Assembly abandoned its old colonial policy in Indo-China and in 1949 decided to recognise Viet Nam as an independent state within the French Union of Overseas Territories. The independence of Viet Nam was recognised by Britain and America, but Russia and China continued to support the "Viet Minh Communist Front". So the civil war went on, to the great detriment of France whose resources were overtaxed in keeping up the fight. At last an armistice was arranged, but at the cost of sur-

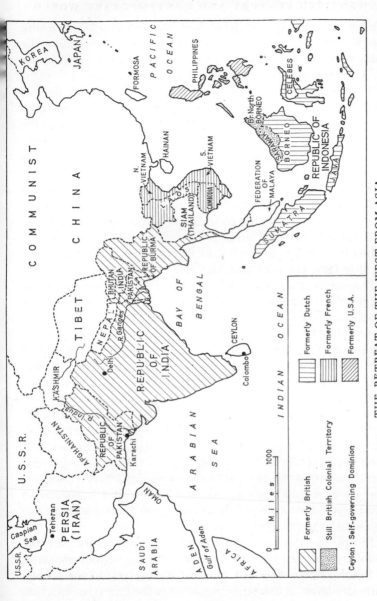

THE RETREAT OF THE WEST FROM ASIA

Showing the changes in the political map brought about by the withdrawal of the Western Powers and the unbroken stretch of Communist territory across the north.

rendering Hanoi, the capital of Viet Nam, to Viet Minh, whose troops entered that city on October 9, 1954. Since then the country has been politically divided into two: the north under the Communists and the south under their opponents.

The Dutch interest in the East Indies dates back to the beginning of the seventeenth century when the Dutch East India Company was formed and when the Dutch began to drive the Portuguese from the islands. They thus built up a prosperous commercial empire which came to be known as Netherlands India. This region is now known as Indonesia, meaning literally "Island India", a name coined in the middle of the nineteenth century to cover all the islands of the Malay Archipelago. The term was adopted by nationalists in the Dutch East Indies as a suitable one to "suggest the unity of all the native inhabitants", and now applies to a large group of islands, including Java, Sumatra and Madura.

During the Second World War the Japanese, then in occupation of the islands, encouraged the nationalists, who in 1945 proclaimed the Republic of Indonesia. The Dutch Government refused to recognise the republic and took military action against it. The situation, however, got beyond the control of the Dutch. Consequently, in 1948 the Security Council of the United Nations entered the dispute and in 1949 persuaded the Netherlands Government to recognise the Indonesian Republic as a sovereign independent state, which was to include the whole of the Dutch East Indian Empire, except the Dutch part of New Guinea. At the end of 1949 The Netherlands formally surrendered its sovereignty, and a provisional government was set up. In 1950, after the promulgation of a constitution which created an elected Presidency and a legislature of two Houses, the new republic was recognised by most states and admitted to the United Nations.

In this way the former European Imperial Powers retreated from Asia. The nationalist movements of the various countries of South-eastern Asia had thus rid themselves, in some cases without a blow, of what they regarded as the European incubus, and nearly 600 million Asiatics—Indians, Pakistani, Ceylonese, Burmese, Indo-Chinese and Indonesians—had established new independent states which they were now free to run as they themselves desired. But they had formidable obstacles to overcome. Internally, each had to build up a government which could establish authority and command respect, an economic organisation which would ensure tolerable living standards, and a social system which could find a way of reducing illiteracy. Externally they stood between two pressures: on the one hand, that of American and European financial and technical aid, and, on the other, that of Communist propaganda designed to lure them into the Russo-Chinese orbit as an insurance against a recrudescence of Western Imperialism.

DEVELOPMENTS IN AFRICA AND WEST INDIES

We may refer here to some interesting colonial developments in Africa and the West Indies which have come about since the war and which illustrate certain aspects of the colonial revolution. The Gold Coast may be taken as a good example of progress towards responsible government which is fully encouraged by Britain. Most of the colonial territories in Africa have made advances of this sort in varying degrees, but in 1957 the Gold Coast achieved the distinction of being the first native colony in Africa to become a fully independent state, under its new name of Ghana. But sometimes the growing native political consciousness expresses itself in the most violent form, as it has done in Kenya. There, in 1952, occurred the first of a series of outrages by gangs of terrorists who became notorious as Mau Mau, a secret society of Kikuyu tribesmen whose object was to drive out all Europeans. It was described as "an unholy union of ancient superstition and modern gangsterism", and must be suppressed before any true political progress can be made in Kenya.

Another project, recently introduced in Central Africa, is the bringing into closer political association of three adjacent areas: namely the self-governing colony of Southern Rhodesia and the Protectorates of Northern Rhodesia and Nyasaland. These three regions are in very different stages of political advancement, yet they contain economic resources which ought to be jointly exploited, while political union should enable the less advanced people to be helped by the more fully developed. Hence, in 1954, after much discussion, the three areas were joined in a Federation. But the plan did not work smoothly, and in 1960 a special Commission, sent out to study the situation on the spot, recommended in its report that the scheme should be radically revised. In West Africa, on the other hand, the Federation of Nigeria, formed, also in 1954, among the three Regions of the Territory, was so successful that in 1960 it gained its independence.

Another significant change has occurred in the status of the Sudan. In 1953 an Anglo-Egyptian agreement "guaranteed to the Sudanese the right to determine their own future", and provided for "early free and secret elections to a Sudanese Parliament and for a transitional period of self-government during which the sovereignty of the country should be kept in reserve until self-determination had been achieved". On this basis elections were held, and in 1954 the first full Sudanese Parliament was opened at Khartoum. In 1956 the Sudan was proclaimed an independent republic.

Similarly in the West Indies, British policy is one of "progressive devolution towards self-government". The various colonies have reached different stages of growth. In the Leeward Islands and in the Windward Islands, for example, there is a legislature of a single chamber in which the majority of members are elected by the people, the others being nominated by the Governor. But in four colonies—Jamaica, Barbados, Bermuda and the Bahamas—greater progress has been made. Each of these has a two-Chamber legislature, the lower of which is wholly elected by the people, though the qualification for the franchise varies from one colony to another.

One promising plan, proposed in 1953 and approved in 1956, was the ultimate formation of a West Indian Federation,

CONFERENCE OF COMMONWEALTH PRIME MINISTERS AT
No. 10 DOWNING STREET, 1955

Those present are (left to right): standing: C. R. Swart (Deputising for Prime Minister of South Africa), Mohammed Ali (Pakistan), Sir John Kotelawala (Ceylon), Godfrey Huggins (Central Africa); sitting: S. C. Holland (New Zealand), L. St. Laurent (Canada), Winston Churchill (Britain), R. G. Menzies (Australia), Pandit Nehru (India).

A MODEL VILLAGE IN THE REPUBLIC OF PAKISTAN

Built to house 250 families of Moslem refugees displaced by the partition of India.

POLITICS IN NORTHERN NIGERIA, 1955

Sir James Robertson, Governor-General of the Federation of Nigeria, with three of the native Ministers on the Executive Council of the Northern Region.

A NEW ENGINEERING COLLEGE IN THE REPUBLIC OF INDIA

Recently built in the city of Chandigarh, the new capital of the part of the Punjab within the Indian Republic.

to include all the British colonies in the Caribbean, except British Honduras and British Guiana which are on the Central and South American mainland. The proposed federation, with its capital at Port of Spain, in Trinidad, was to have a bicameral legislature with a nominated Senate and an elected House of Assembly, the members to be nominated or elected by the federating colonies in proportion to their size and importance. Federal powers were to include external affairs, defence and exchange control; but many important functions, such as agriculture and education, would continue to be discharged by each colony separately. The plan, when it came into force, was to be tried out for an experimental period of five years. It materialised in 1958 when the Parliament of the Federation of the British West Indies was officially opened.

But, in under-developed colonial areas, as in more advanced communities, the enjoyment of mere political rights is not by itself enough. The British Parliament, realising this, has passed a number of statutes, the most recent in 1949, called Colonial Development and Welfare Acts and designed to encourage, by means of financial aid, the social and economic development of British Colonial Territories in various parts of the world. The result has been that most colonies have prepared comprehensive development programmes for the exploitation of their economic resources and the improvement of social conditions. A further Act, passed in 1948, established in London the Colonial Development Corporation, charged with the duty of encouraging the increase of productive capacity and trade in colonial territories. The Corporation, which is authorised to borrow up to £110 million, operates on commercial principles in close consultation with Colonial Governments "in order to ensure that its activities will be conducted in the best possible way to promote the welfare of Colonial peoples".

Chapter 23

BRITAIN, EGYPT AND THE ARAB LEAGUE

THE MIDDLE EAST

SOUTH-EAST Asia was not the only part of that vast continent in which political and economic nationalism asserted itself after the Second World War. It also took a vigorous, and even violent, form in Western Asia and in Egypt. The region stretching eastward and south-eastward from the Levant and bounded by the Red Sea and Egypt on one side and by Persia on the other is a region of Arab lands. They formed part of the original Ottoman Empire and were freed from subjection to the Turks when that Empire broke up as a result of the First World War. They have since gained complete independence and are now sovereign states. These Arab states are Saudi Arabia, Iraq, Syria, Lebanon, Jordan and Yemen. Israel, a non-Arab state in the same region, is, as we shall see, in a special position in relation to the Arab lands which surround it.

Egypt is not strictly an Arab state, though often regarded as one, since Arabs form the second largest element in its mixed population. Still less is Persia an Arab state, although most Persians are Moslems. Yet in recent years both countries—and especially Egypt—have been much affected by the policies of the purely Arab states which lie between them. All these lands, which in the past played a highly creative part in the making of our culture, are full of historical associations, being the homes of old civilisations and the cradles of Judaism, Christianity and Islam. They are not what they were, but situated as they are between the West and the East, and grouped as most of them are to-day, they hold a key position in the contemporary world in its search for peace and security.

The area stretching from the Levant to Persia is properly described as the Near East, to distinguish it from the Middle East (Baluchistan to Burma) and the Far East (Siam to Japan). But during the Second World War the British and Americans made Cairo the co-ordinating centre of a vast system of supplies to the whole Arab region, which, for this purpose, was loosely referred to as the Middle East. The label has stuck for general usage ever since. It is in this looser sense, therefore, that we use the term here.

ANTI-BRITISH MOVEMENTS IN EGYPT AND PERSIA

Egypt, as you may recall, became a constitutional monarchy in 1922, when a descendant of the original Khedive was proclaimed King, and a sovereign state in 1936 under the terms of the Anglo-Egyptian Treaty of that year. The British military occupation then came to an end. subject to certain safeguards concerning the Suez Canal Zone and the Sudan, and on the understanding that the situation should be reviewed in 1946. The Second World War delayed further action, but after the war the Egyptians, like so many other peoples, developed a highly militant nationalism, which had a double purpose: first to create a strong government within the country and secondly to drive out foreigners, which meant the British.

In Egypt popular feeling grew against King Farouk, who had come to the throne in 1936 and whose extravagance and incompetence caused a revolt against him. In 1952 a military *coup d'état* under General Neguib brought about Farouk's abdication in favour of his infant son, but in 1953 Neguib deposed the baby king, proclaimed Egypt a republic, and appointed himself President. Throughout these months anti-British feeling was running high among the Egyptians, and there were loud demands for Britain's unconditional withdrawal from the Sudan and the Canal Zone. Neguib's government, however, in spite of outrages against British troops in the Canal Zone, seemed willing to negotiate, and a more reasonable atmosphere surrounded the resumption of talks. As we have seen, agreement was reached on the future self-government of the Sudan. A settlement of the problem of the Canal Zone soon followed. By the Suez Canal agreement, signed in October 1954, all British troops were to leave the Zone within twenty months. In July 1956, the British withdrawal having been duly completed, Colonel Nasser, who had meanwhile replaced General Neguib, precipitated an international crisis by declaring "the Suez Canal Company to be an Egyptian Company."

So ended Britain's official connection with Egypt which had begun in 1882. Having lost this vital strategic centre in the Middle East, the British decided to use the island of Cyprus as an alternative base, which aroused the violent opposition of nationalist Cypriots. Meanwhile, Nasser's maltreatment of former Canal-users drove the British and French into an attempt to assert their rights by force. In 1956 they attacked Egypt by land and air, but later withdrew when the United Nations intervened. In January, 1957, Anthony Eden, who had succeeded Winston Churchill as Prime Minister in 1955, resigned on grounds of health, and Harold Macmillan took his place, while the triumphant Nasser aspired to the leadership of the Arab world.

Britain's influence in Egypt had been mainly political; in Persia it was mainly economic, being chiefly concerned with Persian oil. In the twentieth century Persia was discovered to be one of the world's richest sources of petroleum, a vital need for modern transport. In 1901 the Persian Government had granted to an Englishman named D'Arcy a concession of 400,000 square miles in southern Persia for the exploitation of petroleum mines. Oil was struck in large quantities in 1908, and in 1909 the Anglo-Iranian Oil Company was formed to take over D'Arcy's concession. The British Government itself became closely interested and, in 1914, in order to ensure supplies of oil fuel to the Navy, bought £2 million worth of the Anglo-Iranian Oil Company's shares. The Company's oil-fields in south-west Persia, which produced practically the whole of Persia's oil for export, were so successfully exploited that between 1938 and 1948 their output was doubled, rising from ten million to twenty million tons.

Simultaneously with this exploitation of Persia's natural resources by an alien company there grew up a nationalist movement which took a progressively militant form. Persia was traditionally governed by an autocratic ruler called the Shah. In 1906 he was forced to grant a constitution, establishing a Parliament of two Houses: the Senate and an elected Assembly called the *Majlis*, and a Ministry responsible to it. After the First World War there was a revolution in Persia rather like that in Turkey. In 1925 the Persian Prime Minister, a soldier named Reza Khan, dethroned the Shah, had himself proclaimed Shah, gave his dynasty the name of Pahlavi, carried out several reforms, and restored the ancient name of Iran, as already recounted in Chapter 6.

During the Second World War Persia, which became one of the principal routes for Anglo-American supplies to Russia, was jointly occupied by British, Russian and American troops. At a conference held at Teheran, the Persian capital, in 1943, Churchill, Roosevelt and Stalin issued a declaration guaranteeing Persia's independence. The Americans withdrew their forces in 1945, the British theirs in 1946, and the Russians theirs a little later. After the war Persian nationalism took the form of a determination to nationalise the oil industry, and hence became violently anti-British. Inspired by the fiery leadership of the aged Prime Minister, Mussadiq, the Persian Parliament in 1951 passed a law to nationalise the oil industry and carried a resolution recommending the immediate taking over of all installations, including those of what they called "the *late* Anglo-Iranian Oil Company". The company offered to carry the claim to arbitration and the British Government to take the dispute to the International Court at The Hague. But Mussadiq, with his strong backing of fanatical nationalists, refused all compromise.

Deprived of the expert organisation of the company, the oil supplies virtually ceased and exports with them. As the nation lived mainly on the labour and profits of the oil-fields (in which, of course, the Persian Government shared), this deprivation led first to economic distress and then to political demonstrations against those responsible for it. Consequently, in 1953 the Shah appointed a new Prime Minister and arrested Mussadiq and several of his Ministers, who were tried and imprisoned. After further disorder and discussion, wiser counsels prevailed, and in October 1954 the *Majlis* ratified an agreement partially restoring British rights in the Persian oil-fields. On October 29 it was signed by the Shah and on the same day there steamed out of Abadan the first loaded British oil-tanker to leave that port since June 1951.

THE ARAB LEAGUE AND ISRAEL

The Arab League is an association of the Arab states mentioned above, together with Egypt, Libya, Morocco, Tunisia and Sudan. It originated during the Second World War when the area covered by these states was of vital strategic importance. The supplies from the Middle East depot in Cairo, to which we have referred, were carried through this region, which vital air routes also crossed. The Arab peoples were thus brought into closer contact with one another, and this contact made them realise that many of their problems were common and might be helpfully dealt with on a regional basis. An even stronger binding force was supplied by their common hostility to the state of Israel, which we shall discuss in a moment. The League has a Council and a Secretariat, but, although some enthusiasts think it might be extended to include the whole Moslem world in Africa and India, it is never likely to be more than a loose localised confederation.

Of the Arab states the Kingdom of Saudi Arabia, formed by a union of Nejd and the Hejaz effected in 1932, is geographically the largest, but, as most of it is desert, its population is no more than six millions. The Kingdom of Iraq (formerly Mesopotamia),

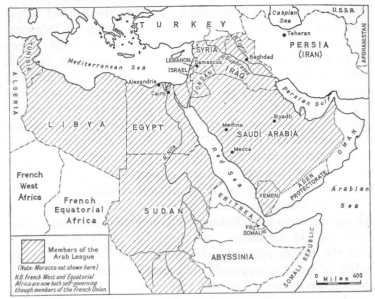

THE ARAB STATES AND ISRAEL

with its capital at Baghdad, has a population of about three and a
half millions. It was recognised by the Turks in 1932, but did not
gain its complete independence until 1935. Syria and Lebanon
gained their independence with the end of the French Mandate in 1943, while Jordan (originally Transjordania) and
Yemen gained theirs in 1946. In 1958, however, Syria joined
Egypt to form the United Arab Republic, which Yemen joined
later in the year. Libya, a late-comer to the Arab League, is
a constitutional monarchy. A former Italian colony, it became
independent in 1951. The kingdom of Morocco and the Republic of Tunisia are the newest League members.

Palestine, conquered from the Turks by British forces in
1917–18, was placed under British mandate after the First
World War. In population the Arabs far outnumbered the
Jews, so that when the British Government decided to create a
Jewish national home there, conflicts arose between the two

279

peoples. The situation became worse after the Second World War, when many displaced Jews sought refuge in Palestine. For twenty-five years, under the mandate, Britain tried to keep the peace and laid the foundations of self-government. In 1948, however, Britain decided to give up the mandate and left Palestine. Immediately the Jews, who were more advanced and better equipped than their neighbours, helped as they were by Zionist organisations all over the world, proclaimed an independent state of Israel at Tel Aviv. It was then that the Arab League attack began. Hostilities continued until January 1949, when, under the auspices of the United Nations, an armistice was signed and a number of agreements reached.

Troops of the Arab state of Jordan were left in occupation of the eastern strip of Palestine, including what is known as the "old city" of Jerusalem, and Egyptian forces continued to hold the "Gaza strip" in the south-west. This left the Republic of Israel in possession of most of Palestine—an area of about 8,000 square miles, with a population of about 1,600,000, of whom 1,450,000 were Jews. The republic was then constituted with an elected President and a Prime Minister responsible to an elected Assembly (*Knesset Israel*). The government removed its capital from Tel Aviv to the new city of Jerusalem. The *Knesset* passed a law in 1950 stating that "an immigrant visa shall be granted to every Jew who expresses his desire to settle in Israel". The result was that, from the establishment of the independent state and up to the end of January 1952, no fewer than 687,801 immigrants had entered Israel from forty different countries. But, notwithstanding the armistice agreements, Arab hostility to Israel continued, and, in spite of the continued efforts of the United Nations, by the end of 1960 still no permanent treaties had been signed between Jewish Israel and her Arab neighbours.

PROGRESS OF THE TURKISH REPUBLIC

It is appropriate to add here a final note on the progress of the Turkish remnant of the original Ottoman Empire in West

Asia and North Africa, on whose ruins the states of the Arab League had risen. The Turkish Republic, which was so solidly founded by Ataturk, has continued its advance under his successors since his death in 1938. For a time it was the most stable state in the Middle East, and, because of this, it exercised a sobering influence on the international politics of that region. Eighty per cent. of the population follow agricultural and pastoral pursuits. Agricultural methods are still largely primitive there, but in some parts they are being rapidly mechanised. Again, although Turkey's considerable mineral resources remain largely unexploited, great strides have been made in industry, particularly in the production of steel, cement, textiles, artificial silk, paper, leather and glass. In education, too, much progress has been made. There has been a great increase in the provision of primary schools, and higher education flourishes in the university founded by Ataturk in 1934 at Ankara.

But it is in the political field that the most striking things have happened. After the death of Ataturk one-party government continued for a time under his successor, President Inönü. But the system led to such electoral apathy that it was agreed to allow an official opposition in the Assembly, at first with limited numbers but later unrestricted in strength. This had a vitalising effect on Turkish political life, and the opposition, formed by a party called Democrats, made an increasingly powerful appeal to the electorate. The result was that in the general election of 1950 the Democrats scored a resounding victory, gaining 408 seats against 69 won by the Republican Party, which Ataturk had founded. Thereupon Inönü resigned in favour of the Democratic leader. Thus it was left for the Asiatic Turks to provide the first example in modern history of a dictatorship voluntarily surrendering its power in response to the popular will. But more recently there has been increasingly bitter strife between the two political parties.

Chapter 24

THE SOVIET POWER IN EUROPE AND ASIA

THE COMMUNIST WORLD

WHILE Britain was constitutionally creating her Welfare State, peacefully withdrawing from most of her Eastern Empire, and encouraging the development of representative institutions in her Colonial Territories, Soviet Russia was sponsoring and directing the spread of revolutionary Communism in Europe and Asia. As we have seen, Russia's gains from the Second World War placed her in a strong position to execute these plans. In fact, she reaped from the war a treble harvest of territorial aggrandisement. As we have seen, first, in accordance with her Peace Pact with Germany in 1939, Russia annexed the Baltic States, eastern Poland, and parts of Rumania. Next, she snatched territories from Finland following a war made possible by Germany's preoccupation with the general conflict. Then, as a result of the war with Germany and Japan, she gained in Europe most of East Prussia from Germany, Ruthenia from Czechoslovakia, and Bukovina from Rumania, and in the Far East certain regions from Japan and in Manchuria. Finally, she shared the post-war occupation of Germany and Austria.

When Soviet Russia, with Britain and America, sponsored the foundation of the United Nations, she gave her implied support to the principles of the Atlantic Charter and thus pledged herself to renounce "territorial aggrandisement" and to restore liberty to the peoples deprived of it by the aggressors. Her conduct in Europe and Asia following the war was scarcely in keeping with these undertakings, at least as they were understood in the West. She had seemed ready enough to support these ideals when she was hard pressed by a ruthless invader and in dire need of help, but when the time came to give them effect, she was in a position to flout her wartime allies.

Moreover, Russia maintained her armed strength to the full when the war was over, while Britain and America rapidly demobilised their forces and largely disarmed themselves. Thus, since Russia was in possession and since America and Britain were in no position to oust her, there was nothing they could do to prevent her having her own way in Eastern Europe. Indeed, the Western Powers hoped that, by raising no objection to Russia's conduct in Eastern Europe, they would gain her co-operation in the urgent task of resettling the world in peace. In spite of all their efforts, they were at last driven to realise that they had destroyed one authoritarian régime and one form of aggression only to have it replaced by another.

The differences between Russia and the West arose from historical causes. The Russian Revolution was ultimately due to the same industrial, social and political ferment as conditioned the radical changes which had already taken place in Western Europe. The difference lay in the fact that in the advanced industrial countries of Western and Central Europe the changes had come gradually or by evolution, whereas in Russia they had come suddenly or by revolution. The Communist Revolution which Karl Marx had envisaged could, according to him, occur only in a state of advanced capitalist development. What Lenin and his colleagues and successors did was to prove that such a revolution could be carried out in an industrially backward country, in which the people had always been accustomed to government under an "unenlightened feudal autocracy". So the Communists imposed on the country a government no less autocratic than that to which it had been used, although it was much more efficient and ruthless.

Two other considerations have to be borne in mind. First, the Russian leaders may be Communists but they are still Russians, and, as such, they have inherited the imperial ideas of the Czarist régime which they overthrew. So, while they have imposed the "Dictatorship of the Proletariat" on the state and society, they have incorporated with it an imperialistic policy of expansion. Secondly, the Communist régime in Russia is based on Marx's theory of international revolution. It was believed by the early Bolshevik revolutionaries, as you may recall, that the Russian Revolution would be followed by revolutions in all other countries. When this did not happen, Stalin adopted the plan of "Socialism in one country" and destroyed the Trotskyists who wished actively to pursue the aim of the universal revolution. But this did not mean that Stalin had abandoned the policy of sponsoring a general revolution. It merely meant that for the moment he saw the wisdom of putting that policy into cold storage, to be brought out again when circumstances were more propitious.

It was the Second World War which presented Stalin with a new opportunity. Since the fortunes of war had made him military master of so many countries, he, as a Communist and a Russian, was bound to behave as he did. That was to incorporate in the Soviet Union the countries he annexed, to set up Communist régimes under local Communist leaders in the countries he occupied, to encourage the growth of Communist parties and the employment of Communist tactics in more westerly countries, and finally to inflame any Communist revolution wherever it might occur.

Let us summarise the position following the Second World War. In Europe Russia incorporated into the Soviet Union Lithuania, Latvia, Esthonia, East Prussia, Ruthenia, the eastern half of Poland, and parts of Finland and Rumania. In Europe, too, she set up or sponsored Communist régimes in Poland, Czechoslovakia, Hungary, Rumania, Bulgaria and Albania, as well as in Yugoslavia and in the Russian Occupied Zone of East Germany. In Asia, where the whole of Siberia eastward to the Pacific coast had been part of the Soviet Union since the earlier years of the Bolshevik Revolution, Russia incorporated Sakhalin and the Kurile Islands in the north of

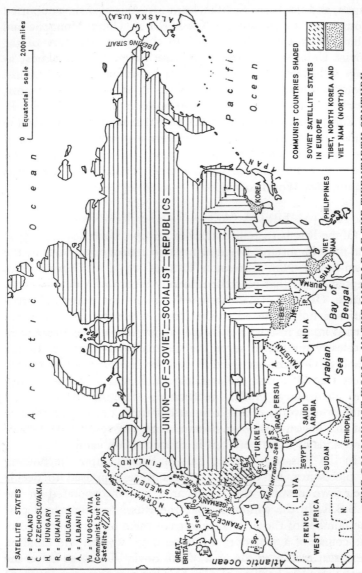

THE COMMUNIST WORLD IN THE MIDDLE OF THE TWENTIETH CENTURY

SATELLITE STATES

P = POLAND
C = CZECHOSLOVAKIA
H = HUNGARY
R = RUMANIA
B = BULGARIA
A. = ALBANIA
Yu = YUGOSLAVIA
(Communist, but not
Satellite (!?))

COMMUNIST COUNTRIES SHADED

SOVIET SATELLITE STATES
IN EUROPE

TIBET, NORTH KOREA AND
VIET NAM (NORTH)

UNION—OF—SOVIET—SOCIALIST—REPUBLICS

ALASKA (U.S.A)

BERING STRAIT

Pacific
Ocean

Arctic Ocean

Equatorial scale

0   2000 miles

JAPAN

KOREA

CHINA

PHILIPPINES

VIET
NAM

BURMA SIAM

TIBET

Nepal

INDIA

Bay of
Bengal

PAKISTAN

A.

PERSIA

Arabian
Sea

TURKEY

S. IRAQ

SAUDI
ARABIA

EGYPT

SUDAN

ETHIOPIA

LIBYA

FRENCH
WEST AFRICA

N.

Mediterranean Sea

FINLAND

SWEDEN

NORWAY

North
Sea

Baltic Sea

GREAT
BRITAIN

FRANCE

GERMANY

Sp.

Sp.

E.

Atlantic Ocean

Japan, and the bases in Manchuria. In Asia also she supported Communist revolutions in North Korea, Outer Mongolia and China. Russia has thus added to the actual territory of the Soviet Union nearly 200,000 square miles, an area almost as large as France, and brought under her influence an additional 500,000 square miles in Europe, and, if we include China, nearly 4 million square miles in Asia. With the original U.S.S.R. in Europe and Asia, this makes a total area of some 13 million square miles, which is approximately a quarter of the area of the globe, and a total population exceeding 900 millions, which is about a third of the world's total population. That is the Communist World to-day.

SOVIET SATELLITES IN EUROPE

Of the Russian satellite states in Europe, Poland is the largest and most important. Divided into two almost equal parts by the Nazi-Soviet Non-aggression Pact of 1939, it became from September of that year the unhappy victim of a double occupation. Of the German-occupied portion, the heavy industrial half was fully annexed to the *Reich*, while the other half was turned into a reservoir of forced labour, and its resources were ruthlessly pirated to serve the German war-machine. In the whole of German-occupied Poland the Nazis set out to destroy every trace of Polish life and culture, closing all schools above the elementary grade, confiscating printing presses, and plundering works of art. They also started a campaign to wipe out the Jewish people in Poland, with the result that tens of thousands of Poles perished in concentration camps.

In the Russian-occupied half of Poland, after the holding of plebiscites, by which the Poles were supposed to decide their own destiny, the whole area was incorporated in the U.S.S.R. In the winter of 1940 the Russians began to deport the families of those Poles who gave them any trouble, and in the course of a year over a million men, women and children were scattered over the area of the Soviet Union as far as the Arctic and the borders of China. That was the situation until the German invasion in June 1941, when the Russians were driven out of Polish territory and Poland became Germany's chief base of operations in the eastern campaign.

Meanwhile, the Polish Government, which had escaped, remained in exile, first in France until her collapse in 1940, and afterwards in London. This government for a time restored friendly relations with Russia, who promised to restore Polish sovereignty in full after the war. But in 1943, as Russia was rapidly recovering, Moscow recognised a "League of Patriots" formed by Communist Poles who had escaped to Russia. Later, Polish Communist sympathisers formed a "People's National Council" in Warsaw. As soon as the Russian armies crossed the River Bug in July 1944, the League of Patriots and the National Council united to set up a provisional administration in Lublin. There were thus two rival bodies claiming authority in Poland: the exiled Polish Government in London, supported by a majority of Poles, and the Soviet-sponsored Lublin administration on the spot, backed by Russian arms.

Russia meanwhile had reclaimed eastern Poland, which she had originally gained by the Nazi-Soviet Pact of 1939, and at Teheran (December 1943) the Western Allies had agreed to this on the understanding that the Poles should be compensated with parts of the eastern German borderland. At Yalta, in February 1945, the Allies agreed to recognise the Lublin administration, on condition that its basis was broadened to include non-Communists, and on this understanding the London Polish Government-in-exile was dissolved. In fact, only four non-Communist members were included in the Lublin Government, and they were incapable of preventing the economic and social revolution which followed.

In January 1946 a government decree abolished the capitalist system, and nationalised basic industries. In January 1947 an election was held for a Constituent Assembly. The election was dominated by the pro-Russian (Communist) minority which was supported by troops and police, and it is not surprising, therefore, that it resulted in "an overwhelming majority for the new régime". The Assembly which thus came into being adopted a constitution on the Soviet model. All anti-Communist organisations were dissolved and all institutions were "brought into line with Marxist principles". Poland thus became a Russian satellite, cut off from the West, although some concessions were later made to popular feeling.

Similar régimes were established in Albania, Bulgaria, Rumania, Hungary, Czechoslovakia and Yugoslavia. In Albania, in 1945, a Russian protégé set up a provisional government, deposed King Zog, and established a "People's Republic". In Bulgaria, George Dimitrov, who had been trained in Russia, formed a Communist Party which dethroned King Simeon II and established a "People's Republic", with a constitution on the Russian model. In Rumania a combined government of Communists and non-Communists was set up, but non-Communists were soon excluded. King Michael was forced to abdicate in 1947, when the monarchy was replaced by a "People's Republic", in which all non-Communist parties were banned and their leaders imprisoned or executed.

In Hungary an election in 1945 produced a large majority of democratic elements in the National Assembly, with the result that a republican constitution was promulgated. But the Communists, supported by Russian police and military forces, carried a *coup d'état* in 1947 and established a Communist Ministry. Two years later a new constitution inaugurated a "People's Republic" on the Soviet plan. When in 1956 the Hungarian people rose against the Communist régime, the Russians stepped in and ruthlessly crushed them.

But it was Czechoslovakia which experienced the bitterest defeat of democratic institutions. In 1945 the pre-war republic was restored, and Beneš, who became President once more, tried to maintain good relations with both Soviet Russia and the Western Democracies. In the election of 1946 there were some Communist gains, but the majority of the people were clearly in favour of the maintenance of the democratic republic which Thomas Masaryk had founded. In February 1948, however, a

TOWN PLANNING IN THE SOVIET UNION

Pushkin Avenue in the new city of Magnitogorsk in the Urals whose population is now probably a quarter of a million.

FORESTRY IN THE DESERT

Russian workers planting a tree belt near the Kara Kum Desert in Turkmenistan, a Soviet Republic in Asia.

CHIANG KAI-SHEK (born 1887)
Leader of Nationalist China, now confined to Formosa.

MAO TSE-TUNG (born 1893)
Chairman of the People's (Communist) Repu of China (1949–1959).

A NEW RAILWAY IN COMMUNIST CHINA
The Minister of Railways cutting the ribbon at the opening ceremony of the new Chengtu-Chungking Railway at Chungking Station, in central China.

coup d'état was carried by a Communist named Gottwald, and President Beneš, for the sake of peace, invited him to form a Cabinet. In fact, Gottwald established a dictatorship. Jan Masaryk, son of the founder, committed suicide, and in June 1948, Beneš, who could not bring himself to approve the new constitution, resigned the Presidency, retired to his country house, and died in the following September. The new constitution established what was called a "Democratic People's Republic", but it soon became an instrument of Communist coercion which sent thousands of "sympathisers with the West" into forced labour camps in Russia.

The most interesting developments of all took place in Yugoslavia, where rival resistance movements had formed guerrilla detachments against the Nazi occupiers. One of these groups, led by Mikhailovich, was loyal to King Peter II, who, with his government, was in exile in London. The other was organised by a Russian-trained Communist named Joseph Broz, who later changed his name to Tito. After 1941 these two leaders became bitter enemies, but in June 1944, under pressure from the Allies, Tito came to terms with the royal government and the King appointed him Prime Minister. Then Tito, still supported by the Western Powers, gained sole control. In November 1945 an Assembly, convened by an engineered election, deposed King Peter, and Marshal Tito assumed the powers of a Dictator under a new Soviet-type constitution. Thus was established in 1946 a Federal People's Republic, of which the federating units were Serbia, Croatia, Slovenia, Bosnia-Herzegovina, Macedonia and Montenegro.

Tito was an original Bolshevik supporter, having actually taken part in the civil war following the Revolution of 1917 in Russia, where he remained until 1923. The Russians naturally supposed, therefore, that they had in him a subservient tool. But from 1948 he began to display remarkable nationalist tendencies. The régime remained Communist, but the Yugoslav Marshal refused to take orders from Moscow and began to look to some extent towards the Western Powers. The Russians

289

started a vendetta against him, but he stood his ground, and remained in a sort of limbo on the western edge of the Communist world.

COMMUNIST PARTIES IN NON-COMMUNIST STATES

The interesting thing about Tito's refusal to submit to the dominance of Moscow is that it places Yugoslavia in an intermediate position politically between the Soviet satellites and the states of western continental Europe. The states to the east of Yugoslavia are in the immediate Russian orbit. In those to the west, Moscow influence is exerted mainly through Communist Parties in Parliament. The one important democratic state in Western Europe which has not produced a parliamentary Communist Party is Britain, where Communist influence is felt, if anywhere, rather in the industrial field of trade union activity. But in France and Italy powerful Parliamentary Communist Parties grew up, especially after the Second World War. In both countries during the war the Communists had played an important part in the resistance movements, particularly after the German invasion of Russia had begun. They, therefore, seemed to have a claim to take part in post-war governments whose business was to restore the national prosperity.

In France, when the constitution of the Fourth Republic was adopted after a plebiscite in 1946, a general election was held. In that election the Communists gained nearly 200 seats, or about one-third of the total, in the National Assembly. It was impossible for any other group to find the basis of a coalition with them, and hence they formed the main opposition to a coalition of Christian Democrats (*Mouvement Républicain Populaire* = M.R.P.), Radicals and Socialists. The only thing that held this coalition together was a common fear of a triumph of either the extreme Right under General de Gaulle or the extreme Left under the Communists, for either, if victorious, threatened to establish an authoritarian régime. Yet it was Parliament itself which, by its inability to govern, finally destroyed the Fourth Republic. In 1958 de Gaulle was called in to preserve France from anarchy. He drew up a new constitution granting the President wide powers of control over Parliament. The people voted in favour and elected de Gaulle, who in January 1959 was thus installed as the first President of the Fifth Republic.

In Italy, when the plebiscite of 1946 narrowly declared for a republic and the monarchy was abolished, an election was held for an assembly to draw up a Republican Constitution. At that moment Italy was in serious danger of becoming a Communist state. The strong Communist movement in Italy was largely due to the violent reaction from Fascism. Besides the actual Communist Party, there was in Italy a large body of extreme Socialists, under Pietro Nenni, who veered towards Communism, taking the line of those who have come to be called "fellow-travellers". The Communists and Nenni Socialists together gained 219 out of the 556 seats in the Chamber of Deputies. The Christian Democrats, under the leadership of Alcide de Gasperi, gained 207 seats, but, by uniting with a few Liberals and some Socialists who broke away from Nenni, they just managed to form a coalition government, which established the republican constitution on a parliamentary basis. In the election of 1948 de Gasperi gained an absolute majority. So, with American financial aid, the Communist threat was resisted and the Republic saved for Western constitutionalism.

RUSSIA AND CHINA

As we have seen earlier, the intellectual appeal of Communism in China was as old as the Bolshevik Revolution itself. Sun Yat-sen, the founder of the Chinese Republic, took a Russian adviser, and a strong Communist section of the Kuomintang developed. It was this section that Chiang Kai-shek resisted, and from this split developed the conflict between Nationalist and Communist China. The cleavage, concealed to some extent during the Second World War, became more marked as the war closed. The Communist leader, Mao Tse-tung, had learned his Marxism in Russia, and it was inevitable that, as soon as Russia was freed from the pressure of war and China from the pressure of Japan, Communist Russia should take a big-brotherly interest in the movement in China. Moreover, apart from their community of ideological interests, Russia and China have a common frontier of 4,000 miles.

At Yalta, in February 1945, Russia had promised, in return for the advantages she gained in Manchuria, to support the Nationalist Government of Chiang Kai-shek, and she actually made a treaty with him. But this did not prevent Russia supplying the Chinese Communists with the arms that she had captured from the Japanese in the last days of the war. With this equipment Mao's armies were able to launch an offensive against Chiang. During the next two or three years Chiang lost ground, and in 1949, when he appealed for help to the Western Powers, he was advised to take the Communists into political partnership. This he consistently refused to do. The Communists captured many Nationalist strongholds, including Tientsin, Peking and Nanking. By the end of 1949 Chiang was driven off the Chinese mainland and forced to seek refuge in the island of Formosa.

Thus the year 1949 saw the end of the supremacy of the Kuomintang under Chiang Kai-shek and the dawn of the era of "Red China" under Mao Tse-tung. In September 1949 Mao promulgated a constitution modelled on that of Moscow and christened the state the "People's Republic of China". So it seemed that China, a country with a population exceeding 600 millions, had become the "far eastern wing of the Communist Revolution". Undoubtedly, this was a big ideological victory for Moscow in Asia, but it by no means implies that Communist China is a Russian satellite. On the contrary, if Mao's vast programme of agricultural and industrial development, through the regimentation of these teeming millions in "People's Communes", should fully succeed, China might well one day dominate not only Soviet Russia but the world at large.

Chapter 25

AMERICA AND THE WESTERN WORLD

THE UNITED STATES AFTER THE WAR

FRANKLIN ROOSEVELT, as we have seen, died in April 1945, and was succeeded by his Vice-President, Harry S. Truman. Of the long line of Presidents of the United States, Franklin Roosevelt must be counted among the select few, which includes Washington, Jefferson, Jackson, Lincoln and Wilson, who have shaped the destinies of the American people in the most critical periods of their history. Even among these he was unique, for his Presidency lasted longer than that of any of them, and, moreover, covered an epoch more dynamic and eventful than any since the birth of the republic.

In the New Deal Roosevelt had had a vision of a new America which he had only just begun to realise by the time of the outbreak of the Second World War. Even so, the New Deal, as pointed out earlier, was bitterly opposed not only by Republicans but by some members of his own Democratic Party, and when Truman determined to continue that policy, which he called the Fair Deal, he met a generally hostile Congress. Truman had been a Senator from the state of Missouri when Roosevelt chose him as his "running-mate" in the Presidential Election of 1944. By the inviolable law of the American constitution, as Vice-President he automatically went to the White House on the President's death for the remainder of his four-year term of office. He was derisively referred to as "the farm boy from Missouri" and was generally considered to be "too small for Roosevelt's shoes". In fact, however, he showed a stubborn strength and a moral courage which surprised even his friends.

In the autumn of 1945 Truman submitted to Congress a "21-point programme" of social and economic legislation in continuation of Roosevelt's New Deal, but, as a result of the mid-term Congressional elections of 1946, the Republicans gained majorities in both the House of Representatives and the Senate. So the President found himself faced with the kind of political stalemate which can occur in the United States where the executive works in isolation from the legislative department of government and thus makes it possible for a majority in Congress to nullify the President's policies.

The Constitution, however, grants the President a tremendous power in the right to veto, or refuse to sign, any Bill passed by Congress. If the President does so veto a Bill, it must go back to Congress, and only if it is passed by a two-thirds majority in each House is the President forced to sign it. Truman showed great courage in vetoing certain measures, particularly one, called the Taft-Hartley Bill, to restrict the powers of the trade unions. It is true that it ultimately gained the necessary two-thirds majority and therefore became law. But, in fact, Truman's courage and shrewdness in this matter afterwards stood him in good stead, for in the next Presidential Election he had the strong backing of organised Labour.

This election of 1948 was perhaps the most extraordinary in American history. It had always been regarded as certain that the party which lost the mid-term elections would lose the next Presidential Election. Hence it was thought to be the turn of the Republicans to gain the Presidency. Truman had some difficulty in getting himself selected by the Democrats as the Presidential candidate, and, although he was eventually chosen, he had to fight an almost lone battle against the Republican candidate, Thomas Dewey, the Governor of the State of New York, with all the omens against him. In fact, everyone prophesied a Republican victory except the President himself. He toured the country in support of his Fair Deal programme and proceeded to confound all the prophets by being elected and thus performing what the Americans called the "miracle of the century". So Truman stayed at the White House for a further four years, and continued to lead the American people through a most critical post-war period.

In his Inaugural Address on taking office in January 1949, Truman outlined his proposed Four-point Programme of American action in world affairs. The first point emphasised the importance of America's continuing to support the United Nations. The second insisted that the United States must continue its programmes to assist world economic recovery. The third stated that America must do all in her power to "strengthen freedom-loving nations against the dangers of aggression". Point Four, which was of vital world importance, declared that the United States must "make available for the improvement of under-developed areas the benefits of American scientific and industrial advances". "On the basis of these four major courses of action," the President concluded, "we hope to help create the conditions that will eventually lead to personal freedom and happiness for all mankind."

THE MARSHALL PLAN

The question now was whether the United States, which had emerged from the Second World War, as from the First, materially the richest of all countries, could, by distributing those riches, preserve the peace of the world. At first, as we have seen, the Americans had shared with the rest of the Western World the hope that the war-time alliance with Russia would continue into the peace for the reconstruction of what they called "one world". Gradually, however, they were forced to abandon this hope and to realise that there were, in fact, two worlds, one of which they must strengthen to save it from being overwhelmed by the other. The general turning-point in the relations of West and East, as we have indicated, had been reached in 1947, and it was in that year also that

President Truman made a significant move by appointing General George Marshall as Secretary of State.

In the war General Marshall had been Chief of Staff of the United States Army, and immediately after it had gone to China as a special envoy. His experience in fostering war-time co-operation among the Allies, combined with his qualities as a strategist, fitted him admirably for the post he now took up. He realised that the only way to resist the spread of Russian power was by true co-operation among the democratic nations, and, if this were to be done, the democratic nations must be helped economically. In June 1947 Marshall made a speech at Harvard University, in which he elaborated an idea already mooted in America and summed up in the proposition that "enduring political harmony rests upon economic stability", which implied the granting of aid to other nations to help them to recover from the ravages of war.

Out of this idea grew the scheme of help known as the Marshall Plan. The notion at the back of what came to be known as Marshall Aid was that the various nations who wished to share in it should decide for themselves what they proposed in a programme of recovery. "When," said General Marshall, "the European countries have agreed on their requirements and on the part they themselves will play, then and then only can the United States take supporting action." President Truman gave the Marshall Plan his unqualified support and appointed three Committees, drawn from both parties (for this was what the Americans call a bi-partisan undertaking): one to study America's resources for the purpose of the Plan, a second to explore the likely effect of the Plan on the American economy, and the third to examine and report on the findings of the other two. Meanwhile, the Foreign Secretaries of Britain, France and Russia met to discuss the American offer. Within five days, however, the Russian delegate, Molotov, withdrew, and Russia declined to have any further contact with it.

In July a larger conference of delegates from most states in Western Europe met in Paris, where for the next two months they discussed European Economic Recovery (E.E.R.) in order to work out the bases of an Economic Recovery Programme (E.R.P.). At last an agreed figure was reached, namely 22,400 million dollars, to be spread over four years. Early in 1948 the Marshall Plan was debated in Congress, where its opponents were heavily defeated, and in April the President signed the Foreign Assistance Act, which granted to sixteen European states, as well as to Turkey and Nationalist China, financial aid amounting in the first year to 6,000 million dollars.

These sixteen European nations set up in Paris an Organisation for European Economic Co-operation (O.E.E.C.) for the continuous discussion of how best to use American aid so as eventually, through co-operative planning, to live without it. In 1949 the report of this body proved how stimulating was the effect of Marshall Aid on European recovery. It led also to a closer integration of policies among the European democratic nations which tended to be drawn together in special pacts. Moreover, in 1949 the pound sterling and other currencies were devalued in relation to the dollar, in order to stimulate European exports to the United States.

RUSSIAN REACTION TO THE MARSHALL PLAN

While America and Western Europe saw in the Marshall Plan a hopeful approach to European recovery, Russia denounced it as a piece of capitalist propaganda. Her reply to it was to revive a pre-war international Communist organisation in another form and under a new name. This was what was originally known as the Comintern, founded in 1919. The Comintern was a "general staff of world revolution", created with the object of "establishing the Dictatorship of the Proletariat and the International Soviet Republic". In deference to the views of her allies in 1943, Russia had dissolved the Comintern.

In September 1947, realising the menace of the unifying effect of the proposed American aid, the Russians called a meeting at Warsaw of Communist Party representatives from her own satellites and from France and Italy. The Warsaw Conference agreed to establish a Communist International Bureau called the Cominform, which was, in effect, a revival of the old Comintern. Its immediate object was to strengthen the link between Soviet Russia and other Communist states and parties, and to do everything possible to intensify propaganda in and against states receiving American aid. A flood of propaganda followed, denouncing the Marshall Plan as a capitalist, imperialist and war-mongering stratagem. Thus the events of 1948–9 only widened the gulf which divided the two sides, as each move towards greater security on the part of the one led to counter-measures on the part of the other.

Towards the end of 1947, Belgium, The Netherlands and Luxemburg had formed a customs union, called, from the initial letters of the signatories, Benelux. By this the three states agreed to abolish all tariff barriers between them. It was when Britain and France announced their intention to open discussions with the Benelux countries with the object of forming a Western Union, that the opponents of parliamentary government in Czechoslovakia, with the open support of the Soviet Union, carried out their *coup d'état* and established a Communist régime. The shock to the Western world of this act of violence to democratic institutions hastened the conclusion, in March 1948, of the Treaty of Brussels between Britain, France and the Benelux countries.

By this treaty the contracting parties pledged themselves for fifty years to the closest economic, social and cultural co-operation and to collective self-defence. To secure these objects the parties set up a joint organisation and a consultative council. Another significant step in the same month was that taken by France and Italy, who signed the protocol of a proposed customs union, while in September a congress of French and Italian Chambers of Commerce met in Turin. The United States welcomed these signs of West European collaboration and recognised the Brussels Treaty as a regional pact within the framework of the United Nations. At the same time, Con-

gress approved a plan for American rearmament, agreed to a
limited measure of conscription, and authorised heavy additional expenditure for defence.

During these years the United States also pursued its "good
neighbour" policy toward Latin America, despite the obstacles
which it had to surmount. The post-war years were marked by
great political instability in almost all the Latin American
states. There were, on the one hand, popular revolts of varying strength, and, on the other, military dictatorships to counter
them, as, for example, in Venezuela, Bolivia, Paraguay and
Peru. In Argentina a dictatorial régime was set up in 1946 by
Colonel Perón, whose policy was a curious mixture of nationalism and socialism. Perón's régime, however, was destined to
last only until the autumn of 1955, when he was overthrown by
a counter-revolution and forced to seek asylum in Paraguay.
Meanwhile, in Brazil and Chile, for example, ding-dong
struggles for political power went on between Right and Left
coalitions. In certain other states Communism gained some
ground, especially in Colombia, where in 1948 a Pan-American
Conference meeting in Bogotá, the Colombian capital, was held
up for several days by serious riots, fanned by Communist propaganda. When the Conference was able to resume its meetings,
it discussed a "Charter for the Organisation of American States",
and finally agreed to set up a Council, with its headquarters at
Washington, and an advisory committee. It also arranged for
periodical meetings of the Foreign Ministers of the states in
membership.

No sooner had the prospect of peace in Latin America been
secured than Russian action in Berlin focused American attention once more on Europe. In April 1948 Russia suddenly
repudiated her agreement with the Western Occupying Powers
for the quadripartite control of Berlin. As you will remember,
Berlin was in the heart of the Russian zone of German occupation, and the Americans, British and French, who shared the
government of the capital, had to cross the Russian zone to
keep contact with, and transport supplies to, their several sec-

tors of Berlin. Russia now declared a Berlin blockade, denying to the other three Powers the use of roads and railways in the Russian zone of Germany. Such an embargo might easily have turned the Cold War into a hot one, but that dreadful consummation was averted by the decision of the Western Powers in June to carry their supplies by air. For nearly a year this Berlin Air Lift, as it was familiarly called, continued successfully to counter the Berlin blockade, and during that time over 2 million tons of food and fuel were transported from the West to Berlin over Russian-occupied territory. The blockade had failed, and in May 1949 the Russians abandoned it.

THE NORTH ATLANTIC TREATY ORGANISATION

The Berlin Blockade marked the culminating point in the gradual process of enlightening the Democratic West as to Communist Russia's hostile attitude. They now saw that, if they wished successfully to resist the menace of the spread of Communism, they must do so from strength. It was this realisation that led in 1949 to the establishment of the North Atlantic Treaty Organisation (N.A.T.O.). The North Atlantic Pact, which founded the Organisation, was signed in Washington by the United States, Canada, Britain, France, Italy, The Netherlands, Belgium, Luxemburg, Norway, Denmark, Iceland and Portugal. It was a defensive alliance, to last, in the first instance, for twenty years. It set up a North Atlantic Council, which has been in continuous session since 1952. It also established an Executive Committee of Foreign Ministers, who were to meet at least once a year, a defence Council of War Ministers, and a Committee of Chiefs of Staffs. It established its headquarters at the Palais de Chaillot (later removed to the Porte Dauphine) in Paris, with a Secretary-General and an international staff.

The United States made an initial grant of a thousand million dollars to members of N.A.T.O. to help them to set about the immediate business of rearmament. The first Supreme Commander to be appointed was General Eisenhower, who held the post until 1952 when he ran as Republican candidate for the

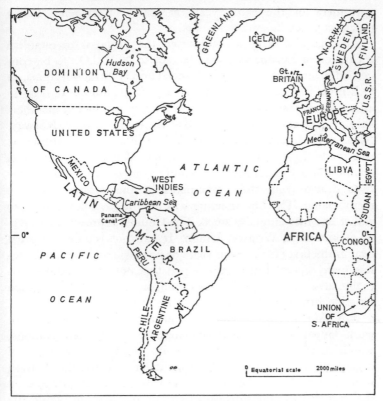

THE ATLANTIC COMMUNITY

American Presidency, and when he was succeeded by another
American, General Ridgway. In that year, too, Greece and
Turkey were admitted to membership of N.A.T.O. Spain hoped
to be admitted, but, in spite of the advocacy of her neighbour,
Portugal, the Western Democracies could not bring themselves
thus to recognise, by implication, Franco's unenlightened
régime. Nevertheless, in 1953 the United States reached an
agreement with Spain, by which, in return for a grant of several
million dollars, Spain permitted the establishment of American
naval and air bases (as already done in Greece by the Athens

301

agreement of the same year) at Cadiz, Cartagena, Palma (Majorca), Seville and Saragossa.

America also strongly supported the proposal to establish a Council of Europe as a supplement to N.A.T.O., to be concerned primarily with political, social and cultural questions, as O.E.E.C. was responsible for economic planning. It was, in effect, an extension of the Brussels Treaty, and had in membership, besides the signatories to that treaty, Eire, Italy, Norway, Sweden, Denmark, Greece and Turkey. The Council of Europe was made up of a Council of Foreign Ministers to direct its affairs and a Consultative Assembly composed of representatives drawn from the Parliaments of the various states in membership. The first meeting was held in Strasbourg in 1949 and it has met annually since. The Council represents a movement known as Western Union. It had not achieved a great deal in the first six or seven years of its existence, but nevertheless many liberal Europeans hoped that out of it might eventually arise a European Federation, such as that for which Aristide Briand had worked between the wars.

N.A.T.O. and the Council of Europe pledged themselves to work loyally within the framework of the United Nations, which, as we have seen, allowed in its constitution for regional organisations. The United Nations itself reflected the division into two worlds, for the delegates of Communist countries used the organisation for purposes of their propaganda, while the representatives of the Western Democracies found their every serious move countered, especially in the Security Council, where the veto could be exercised.

ANTI-COMMUNIST REACTION IN AMERICA

The success of the Berlin Air Lift and the determination of the West to organise itself against the Communist threat undoubtedly had the effect of creating a more balanced situation in Europe. But, meanwhile, the conflict of the two worlds had been transferred to the Far East, where, as we shall see in the following chapter, the Cold War became hot through the outbreak of hostilities in Korea, which intensified anti-Communist feeling in America. In fact, the growing bitterness of the Cold War affected not only American foreign policy but American society itself, and even began to threaten the American way of life. Some Americans, indeed, felt that the destruction of Nazism and Fascism had only opened the way for another form of totalitarianism which threatened their own traditions of liberty. And, as so often happens in such circumstances, the methods used to remedy the evil tended to become like those used to spread it.

As early as 1946 there had been disclosed in Canada the existence of a spy ring working in the interests of Communism by gathering information about Great Britain and the United States which might be useful to a "foreign Power". Several Canadian officials and persons in positions of trust were tried and some imprisoned. In 1947 similar inquiries began into the alleged activities of Communists in the United States. The House of Representatives appointed a Committee to investigate the question, and this led to the arrest and conviction of a Communist agent and later to the dismissal of a number of employees of film companies in Hollywood. Then the President instituted a scrutiny of the civil service, which resulted in the imprisonment of an officer in the State Department and the summary dismissal of several civil servants for suspected disloyalty. Moreover, the political clauses of the Taft-Hartley Act were invoked to require trade unions to submit proof that they were free from the "Communist taint".

From these beginnings grew the anti-Communist feeling which at last became a sort of scare. It was aggravated by the frustrations of the Korean War, in which America was suffering nearly as many casualties as in the Second World War itself, so that many American families were bereaved. In 1951 the Supreme Court confirmed the conviction of the "twelve top Communists". There followed a hunt for Communists in the armed forces, the civil service, the universities and the schools. The leader in this hunt was Joseph McCarthy, a Republican

Senator for the state of Wisconsin, who went round the country alleging that the public service was riddled with Communism. In September 1953 it was announced that, since the beginning of the year, 863 government employees had been dismissed and another 593 had resigned as a result of these investigations.

Under the American political system the Senate carries out most of its work by means of Committees. One such Committee of the Senate is the Committee on Government Operations, with a Permanent Investigating Sub-Committee. It was of this Committee and its Sub-Committee that McCarthy became Chairman. Under his Chairmanship the Sub-Committee investigated hundreds of cases in the Services, both at home and overseas. McCarthy even succeeded in causing the destruction of books by alleged Communist authors in American libraries. The upshot was that in August 1954 President Eisenhower signed a Bill passed by Congress outlawing the Communist Party in the United States. But in the end Senator McCarthy went farther than his own party could allow, and in December 1954 he was formally condemned by the Senate, for "his course in various matters related to Senatorial Committees or to expressions concerning State colleagues". He died in 1957.

McCarthyism, as it is called, is a spirit of repression which can exist whether a man named McCarthy directs it or not. It threatens a development entirely foreign to American traditions of liberty. But its growth in America is a measure of the American fear of the spread of Communism in that continent and a further proof of the division of the world by conflicting ideologies. Yet, despite McCarthyism, the spirit of liberty, which gave birth to the United States, assuredly remains strong in the hearts of the vast majority of the American people.

HARRY S. TRUMAN (born 1884
...ident of the United States (1945–53), who
encouraged Marshall Aid.

GEORGE MARSHALL (1880–1959)
American Secretary of State (1946–9) and author of
the Marshall Plan.

THE NEW HEADQUARTERS OF N.A.T.O.
At the Porte Dauphine, Paris.

THE WAR IN KOREA (1950–3)

Distribution of sugar by United Nations officials to Korean refugees on the outskirts of Pusan.

THE OPENING OF THE FOUR-POWER CONFERENCE AT GENEVA, JULY, 1955

The four delegations are seen round the table as follows: lower left: Britain (leader, Sir Anthony Eden); upper left: U.S.S.R. (Marshal Bulganin); upper right: U.S.A. (President Eisenhower); lower right: France (M. Edgar Faure).

Chapter 26

THE KOREAN WAR AND THE REARMING OF GERMANY

THE TWO WORLDS IN ASIA

BOTH the U.S.A. and the U.S.S.R., as we have seen, had vast commitments in Far Eastern Asia, and it was there at length that the two worlds of Western Democracy and Eastern Communism came into armed conflict, where, in fact, the general Cold War became, at least locally, hot. America's main interest in the Pacific immediately after the war lay in Japan, whereas Russia's chief concern with respect to Japan was to oppose the conclusion of a peace treaty, which nevertheless was signed in 1951. Russia's interest in China, on the other hand, grew with the rising tide of Communist successes there, and when, with Russian sympathy and aid, Mao Tse-tung triumphed, the United States was driven to sustain Chiang Kai-shek on his island fortress of Formosa.

Among the imperial possessions which Japan lost as a result of the war was Korea, a peninsula lying between Japan and China and covering an area of about 85,000 square miles, roughly equal to that of the island of Britain, with a population estimated in 1950 at approximately thirty millions. Korea was deeply impregnated with Chinese culture and had for many centuries been an object of rivalry between China and Japan. In modern times, however, in spite of many vicissitudes, it retained a nominal independence until 1910, when it was annexed to the Japanese Empire, to which it continued to belong until 1945. At the end of the war Korea found itself divided into two zones of military occupation, the north under the Russians and the south under the Americans, with the dividing line along the 38th Parallel. It was an unequal division, for, while South Korea contained nearly three-quarters of the total population of the peninsula, North Korea possessed the larger share of its industrial resources.

The Americans tried to persuade the Russians to agree to the creation of a united Korea so that both occupying forces might retire, and when this proposal failed in 1947 the United States submitted the whole question to the United Nations. With a view to establishing a united government in Korea, the U.N. General Assembly resolved that elections should be held under the supervision of an international Commission. The Russians refused to allow the Commission in their zone, so that its functions were confined to the south, where a general election was duly held in 1948. The first National Assembly, thus elected, met in Seoul, the capital, in 1948, and approved a constitution establishing a republic under the presidency of Dr. Syngman Rhee, who had been pleading to the world the cause of Korean independence for a quarter of a century.

Meanwhile, in the north the Russians fostered a "People's Democracy" under Communist leadership. Consequently, a Supreme People's Soviet was elected and met at Pyongyang. The Soviet state was recognised not only by Russia but also by her Communist associates in Europe and Asia. Having thus secured an acquiescent régime, the Russians, in December 1948, withdrew their troops from North Korea. In June 1949 the Americans followed suit and withdrew their occupying forces from the south. This, then, was the position in Korea at the end of 1949: north of the 38th Parallel was a firmly founded Soviet régime with a powerful army apparently indoctrinated with Communist idealism; south of it was a rather shaky democratic government with comparatively restricted resources and a poorly equipped native army. In the following year Soviet Russia and Communist China signed a treaty by which Russia granted China a financial loan and agreed to the eventual restoration of Port Arthur, a transaction which was not, in fact, completed until 1955.

Thus Communist Russia and Communist China were hand in hand, and together commanded an unbroken territory stretching eastward from Central Europe to the Pacific coast of North Korea. It was a situation full of peril for non-Communist South Korea, occupying a mere peninsular tip of that vast continental area. The peril became a reality when, at dawn on June 25, 1950, North Korean forces crossed the border at the 38th Parallel and invaded South Korea. The republican forces of the south could not withstand this attack and hastily retreated. Within a few days they lost their capital, Seoul, and, when it looked as though their country would be completely overrun, the United States intervened. American troops and munitions were hastily dispatched and General MacArthur was appointed to the command.

Then a crucial test for the United Nations arrived when the United States submitted to it for condemnation this first act of overt aggression since the institution of the Organisation. Would history repeat itself and the United Nations fail to take action in face of this aggression in 1948 as the League of Nations had failed in face of that of Japan against China in 1931? The answer came when, in the absence of the Russian delegate, the Security Council denounced the North Koreans as aggressors, called on them to withdraw to their own territory, and, when they refused to do so, authorised collective action to expel them. Consequently, contingents from various member states of the United Nations joined the American and South Korean forces under MacArthur's command, although these contingents were far outnumbered by the Americans who bore the brunt of the fighting.

The Americans made two landings at opposite ends of South Korea. To escape being trapped between the two, the North Koreans retreated and within a fortnight were driven back

SCENE OF THE WAR IN KOREA,
1950–3

into their own territory with great losses in men and arms. Having thus vindicated their denunciation of the aggressors, the United Nations then had to decide whether they would proceed to execute the plan to unify the two parts of Korea, which meant crossing the 38th Parallel dividing them. After much discussion and with many misgivings, the U.N. General Assembly resolved to follow up the operations, and in October 1950 the South Koreans, followed by the Americans, crossed the border into North Korea. The Chinese then came "unofficially" to the aid of their Korean comrades. Thus stiffened, the North Koreans annihilated a South Korean army, forced MacArthur to retreat, advanced into South Korea, and captured Seoul once more.

This second phase of the Korean war had some peculiar features. War was never declared by the United Nations against China, and still less against Russia in the background. Indeed, in 1950 Great Britain had actually recognised Communist China. Moreover, so anxious were the United Nations to keep the war "localised" that they refused to allow Mac-Arthur to bomb Chinese bases, and, when he complained about these restrictions on his action, President Truman, in April 1951, dismissed him from his command. Nevertheless, the war continued to be fought with great bitterness, and Seoul,

308

which the United Nations troops recaptured in the autumn of 1951, was reduced to rubble. In an effort to stop the slaughter, General Ridgway, MacArthur's successor, acting on behalf of the United Nations, had already made approaches with a view to an armistice. Negotiations were opened, but were prolonged while the inconclusive war went on.

The main difficulty in the negotiations was caused by China's insistence on the unconditional handing over of all prisoners of war taken by the United Nations, even though some of them did not wish to return to a Communist country. At last, in 1953, when Stalin's death momentarily eased the international tension, the Indian Prime Minister, Nehru, acting as mediator over the prisoner-of-war problem, found a formula which the Chinese could accept without "losing face". Syngman Rhee, the South Korean Premier, objected to these proceedings and threatened to "go it alone". Nevertheless, an armistice was signed on July 27, 1953, and the questions which had to be settled before a formal peace could be signed were referred to a Conference of the Powers concerned, which opened in Geneva in April 1954 but failed to reach agreement on measures to re-unify the country. So divided it has since remained.

THE DEATH OF STALIN

It is difficult to speak with any confidence about the internal affairs of Russia during these post-war years, because so little news was allowed to pass through the Iron Curtain. There was a new Five-year Plan for the years 1951–5, but before it had run half its course Joseph Stalin died in March 1953.

Stalin had been a Bolshevik since 1903, when he first joined Lenin, and had been in the saddle since Lenin's death in 1924. During his long period of personal power, lasting nearly thirty years, Stalin had ruthlessly guided the destinies of the Russian people. When his position seemed to be threatened by a rival, he carried out a "purge". When he realised the unlikelihood of an international revolution, he announced a policy of

"Socialism in one country", meanwhile taking every opportunity to spread the seeds of Communism on any promising soil. When Hitler's attack on Poland was imminent, he made a peace pact with the Nazis, and when the Germans invaded Russia, he became the acknowledged war leader. When he needed all possible help from his allies in the war, he let them believe that their purposes were his, but when it was over he showed how little he valued their permanent association.

Stalin's power was personal in Russia, where he held a position of supreme authority. It was natural, therefore, that the leaders and the people should speculate on the consequences of his death. A proclamation was issued giving a list, in order of precedence, of those who were to succeed Stalin. Malenkov was to be Premier, or Chairman of the Council of Ministers, and he was to be assisted by five vice-Premiers, including Beria, Bulganin and Molotov. But in the following July Beria was executed for treason, and in 1955 Malenkov was replaced by Bulganin as Premier. At first sight it appeared that the general effect of Stalin's death was to replace his personal dictatorship by the "collective leadership" of a few principal Communists who shared executive responsibility. But it soon became evident that the autocratic mantle of Stalin had, in fact, fallen on Nikita Krushchev, First Secretary of the Central Committee of the Communist Party, who in 1958 removed Bulganin and took his place as Premier. Meanwhile, Soviet foreign policy remained essentially unchanged, especially with regard to the problem of German reunification.

TWO GERMAN REPUBLICS

The war in Korea had shown how hopelessly divided the world had become between the forces of Communism and Democracy in Asia. Germany was the scene of a similar division in Europe. One of the professed objects of the occupation of Germany by the victorious Powers, as you will recall, was to prepare for the eventual reconstruction of German political life on a democratic basis and for the eventual peaceful co-operation of Germany in international affairs. This objective and the means of achieving it were differently interpreted by the Russians in the east of Germany and the Democratic Powers in the west and south. The Russian Zone was much smaller than the three other zones put together. It covered an area of about 41,000 square miles and had a population, as estimated in 1946, of about 17 millions. The area of the three other zones together was about 97,000 square miles and their population, as estimated in 1953, about 49 millions. This artificial division gave rise to serious economic problems.

Some of the most productive agricultural areas in pre-war Germany had been transferred to Poland after the war. The Soviet Zone contained some of the principal centres of light industry, while Western Germany had most of the heavy industries but was less rich in agricultural resources. Between 1945 and 1948 the Russians took considerable capital equipment from East Germany by way of reparations. After 1948 East Germany continued to pay reparations to the U.S.S.R. from current production, an obligation which, under the reparations settlement, was planned to continue until 1965.

From the beginning of the occupation, in fact, Russia treated East Germany as a satellite. The Russians took over important plants and operated them as state concerns. They centralised economic control, subjected industry to rigid central planning, and replaced private enterprise by state ownership, while they gave priority to basic industries over secondary industries. At the same time, they so strengthened the ties between East Germany and the other Soviet satellites that by the 1950's not less than 80 per cent. of the zone's foreign trade was being done with Eastern Europe. A Five-year Economic Plan, introduced in 1951, aimed at doubling the level of industrial production by 1955. The Russians, having reduced East Germany to the status of an economic satellite, governed the zone accordingly. In 1948 they set up a "People's Council", which was soon converted into a "Provisional People's Chamber". In 1949 this body approved a constitution, on the Soviet model, and thus established what was called the "German Democratic Republic".

By contrast, the three Western Occupying Powers treated the Germans in their zones as liberally as the circumstances allowed, and took very seriously their pledge to reconstruct German political life on a democratic basis. In December 1946 Britain and America agreed to the economic fusion of their zones, and the resulting "Bizone", as it was called, was later joined by the French. This amalgamation facilitated the handling of the acute difficulties caused by the influx of refugees from the East, the shortage of food, and the breakdown of the currency. With the aid of food supplies from America and Britain and by means of a currency reform, the economic recovery of Western Germany seriously began, and this hastened her political rehabilitation.

The first serious step towards the creation of new political institutions in Western Germany was taken in 1947 when local councils were elected, and this was followed by the establishment of an elected Diet in each of the three Western Zones. In 1948 the three Diets elected a Parliamentary Council which drafted a provisional Democratic Federal Constitution. This draft constitution, having been approved by the three Occupying Powers, was finally adopted by a Constituent Assembly at Bonn, in the Rhineland, and in 1949 the Federal Republic was inaugurated at Bonn, which became its capital.

The area immediately covered by the new republic comprises eleven *Länder*, or states, broadly corresponding to eleven former *Länder* of the Weimar Republic. The Federal Republic thus established has a legislature of two Chambers. The Upper House, called the Federal Council (*Bundesrat*), is composed of delegates from the eleven *Länder*. The Lower House, called the Federal Diet (*Bundestag*), is elected for a term of four years, by direct universal suffrage. The head of the republic is the President, elected for a five-year term by absolute majorities of both Houses. He acts through a Prime Minister (Federal Chancellor) and a Cabinet responsible to Parliament. The Constitution left

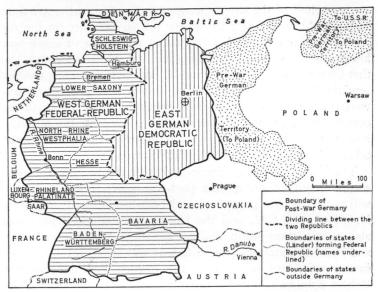

THE TWO GERMAN REPUBLICS AFTER THE SECOND WORLD
WAR

in the hands of the legislature of each *Land* wide powers of
government over its local affairs. Thus the new republic restored the traditional federalism of the German state which
Hitler had destroyed.

The Bonn Constitution was so designed as to be ultimately
applicable to the whole of Germany, when it should be re-
united. Meanwhile, it was confined to Western Germany. Thus
by 1949 there were two republics in Germany: the Federal
Republic, sponsored by the Western Powers, and the People's
Republic, sponsored by Soviet Russia.

WESTERN EUROPEAN UNION AND GERMANY

On the establishment of the Federal Republic of Western
Germany, the Allied Military Governors, who had until then
been responsible for their respective Zones of Occupation, were
replaced by Civilian Commissioners who were to continue to

act on behalf of the three Occupying Powers until such time as it should be felt safe to bestow full sovereignty on the republic. Under Dr. Konrad Adenauer, the leader of a coalition known as the Christian Democratic Union, who became the first Chancellor of the new republic, Western Germany made a remarkable recovery. Gradually, more and more functions were transferred to the German Government until by 1952 the occupation had virtually ceased. There now arose the question how Western Germany was to be brought into the common scheme for the defence of Western Europe.

The idea of a Western European Union went through various stages of growth during the post-war years. Already, as you will recall, several groupings had been established, including N.A.T.O., O.E.E.C., and the Council of Europe. There was also an important group of states known as the European Coal and Steel Community (E.C.S.C.). It was based on a proposal first put forward in 1950 by the French Foreign Minister, Robert Schuman, and was therefore called the Schuman Plan. Its aim was "the removal of all barriers to the free flow of coal and steel and the establishment of a single market in these commodities among the states which agreed to join it". It was backed by the Council of Europe, and in 1952 it was ratified by the Parliaments of France, Italy, Belgium, The Netherlands and Luxemburg. But the most significant fact was that Western Germany was admitted to the Community as an equal member with the other five democratic states.

The next step was to bring Western Germany into a Defence Community. The attempt to establish such a community in the form originally proposed was not successful, but, largely through the efforts of Anthony Eden, then British Foreign Minister and later Prime Minister, an alternative plan was provisionally adopted by a conference in London in October 1954, and shortly afterwards approved at a conference in Paris. Under the Paris agreements a Western European Union with common defence forces was to be set up, and to them Western Germany was to contribute twelve army divisions and twelve reserve divisions. This proposed rearmament of Germany was a serious step, about which grave doubts were entertained. But by the autumn of 1954 all the states concerned had ratified the Paris Agreements. On May 5, 1955, the "instruments of ratification" were deposited at Bonn, and the German Federal Republic thus attained its full sovereign independence, entered the Western European Union, joined N.A.T.O. as its fifteenth member, and became "a free and equal partner of the West".

Meanwhile, in East Germany there was much economic and political unrest. The discontent, which had long been evident in the constant flow of refugees from east to west, reached a climax in June 1953, when there was a spontaneous outbreak of riots and demonstrations by German workers in all the chief towns in the Russian-occupied zone. This working-class revolt was short-lived and easily suppressed, but it had clearly shown that the mass of the East Germans had no love for the so-called Democratic Republic which Russia controlled through a German Communist minority. And if the East Germans could thus show their hatred of a Communist régime, it was not likely that the free Germans of the West would ever tolerate one. Hence the Russians realised that, if the question of the re-unification of Germany were left to the voluntary decision of the whole German people, the result would inevitably be a defeat for Communism. This helps to explain Russia's vehement reaction to the proposal to rearm Western Germany.

Russia employed every device of propaganda to prevent the ratification of the Paris agreements, but when, nevertheless, the proposals seemed likely to mature, she summoned her satellites to a meeting in Moscow. The result, as announced in May 1955, was that the U.S.S.R., in consultation with China, concluded a treaty, signed at Warsaw, with Poland and the other Russian satellite states. The Warsaw Treaty arranged for mutual military aid under a unified command which would come into effect as soon as the Paris agreements should be ratified. The treaty was, in fact, an announcement that Russia

ORGANISATION	MEMBER STATES
Benelux (1948)	Belgium, Netherlands, Luxemburg
Brussels Treaty (1948)	Benelux, France, United Kingdom
Organisation for European Economic Co-operation [O.E.E.C.] (1948)	Austria, Benelux, Denmark, Eire, France, Greece, Iceland, Italy, Norway, Portugal, Sweden, Switzerland, Turkey, U.K.
North Atlantic Treaty Organisation [N.A.T.O.] (1949)	Benelux, Canada, Denmark, France, Greece, Iceland, Italy, Norway, Portugal, Turkey, U.K., U.S.A., Western Germany
Council of Europe (1949)	Benelux, Denmark, Eire, France, Greece, Iceland, Italy, Norway, Sweden, Turkey, U.K., Western Germany
European Coal and Steel Community [E.C.S.C.] (1952)	Benelux, France, Italy, Western Germany
Western European Union [W.E.U.] (1955)	Benelux, France, Italy, U.K., Western Germany
Arab League (1945)	Egypt, Syria and Yemen, Iraq, Jordan, Lebanon, Libya, Morocco, Saudi Arabia, Sudan, Tunisia
Organisation of American States (1948)	Argentine, Bolivia, Brazil, Chile, Colombia, Costa Rica, Cuba, Dominican Republic, Ecuador, Guatemala, Haiti, Honduras, Mexico, Nicaragua, Panama, Paraguay, Peru, Salvador, Uruguay, U.S.A., Venezuela
Colombo Plan (1950)	Australia, British North Borneo, Brunei, Burma, Cambodia, Canada, Ceylon, India, Indonesia, Laos, Malaya, Nepal, New Zealand, Pakistan, Philippines, Sarawak, Siam, Singapore, U.K., U.S.A., Viet-Nam
Warsaw Treaty (1955)	Albania, Bulgaria, Czechoslovakia, East Germany, Hungary, Poland, Rumania, U.S.S.R.

PRINCIPAL INTERNATIONAL ORGANISATIONS (OTHER THAN THE UNITED NATIONS) FORMED SINCE THE END OF THE SECOND WORLD WAR had decided to rearm Eastern Germany in a Communist block as a counterblast to the decision to rearm Western Germany in a Democratic union for defence. Thus in the summer of 1955 the reunification of Germany—an essential condition of world peace—seemed as remote as ever. Indeed, there was every prospect of an arms race between its two parts.

In this situation it was suddenly announced that the four Powers—the U.S.A., the U.S.S.R., Britain and France—had decided to meet at a conference at Geneva. After amicable overtures among the heads of states in July 1955, detailed discussion of four related questions—security, armaments, German unification, and contact between East and West—was left to the four Foreign Ministers, who held their first meeting on October 27. The world watched anxiously for a sign of solid progress towards closing the breach, but none appeared. After three weeks of amiable but ineffectual debate, the conference closed with a recommendation that the future course of the discussion should be "settled through diplomatic channels".

So the year 1955 ended in an international stalemate. Superficially, no doubt, the Geneva Conference had created a more friendly international atmosphere, but fundamentally the situation had not changed. Nor had it materially altered by 1960. In May of that year the heads of the Four Powers arrived in Paris for a so-called "Summit" meeting. But the indirect preliminary exchanges between Premier Krushchev and President Eisenhower were mutually so unsatisfactory that, in fact, the four statesmen never met as a group in conference. So the effort proved entirely abortive and ended without even the pretence of international good will. By then fully fifteen years had passed since the overthrow of Hitlerite Germany and the founding of the United Nations; yet the basic problem of world peace and security remained unsolved.

Chapter 27

SCIENCE AND CIVILISATION

THE PROGRESS OF SCIENCE IN THE TWENTIETH CENTURY

SCIENCE, which made such notable progress in the nine-teenth century, has advanced even more rapidly in the twen-tieth, while its relationship to technology has become still more intimate. The scientific developments of the last half-century could not, of course, have occurred without the pioneer work of earlier scientists, particularly from Newton onwards. But the earlier scientists felt much more certain about the cause and effect of their discoveries than those in the twentieth century and the contemporary world, and they believed that the conse-quences were much more determined than more recent scientists will allow. Thus in physics, while Newton's theory of gravitation has not been overthrown, it has been modified by the theory of relativity. Again, in biology, while the Darwinian theory of evolution stands as the basic explanation of the life-process, there has been a growing doubt about the causes of evolution, and in particular about natural selection as a com-plete explanation of it, a doubt which Darwin himself began to entertain towards the end of his life.

The general theory of relativity was propounded in 1916 by the German physicist, Albert Einstein, probably the greatest scientist of the first half of the twentieth century, who, after the rise of the Nazis, left Germany to live in the United States where, having meanwhile become an American citizen, he died in 1955. The importance of Einstein's theory lay in the fact that it implied a revision of Newton's law of gravitation. Newton had assumed that time and space are absolutes and the

318

same for all observers. But Einstein realised that a signal sent from one place to another takes time in its passage and that this time-factor must be taken into account if a statement of motion is to be equally correct for an observer on the earth and on any other planet or star. Einstein's work stimulated experiment in astronomy and allied sciences. Ultimately it led to the new science of astronautics and to the current competition in the creation of earth satellites and moon rockets.

A no less important development in physics in the twentieth century has been that relating to the atom. The greatest researcher in this field was Ernest (afterwards Lord) Rutherford (1871–1937), a New Zealander, who later settled in England, where he did his most distinguished work at the Cavendish Laboratory in Cambridge. In 1911 Rutherford propounded a new atomic theory which held that each atom is made up of a nucleus charged with positive electricity, and that revolving round this nucleus are particles negatively charged. The nucleus is now believed to consist of clusters of two kinds of particles, called protons and neutrons, and scientists have found ways of splitting the nuclei of the heavier elements, such as uranium, into smaller clusters. In this process of nuclear fission, or splitting the atom, great quantities of energy are released. The Second World War hastened research in nuclear physics, which reached a climax in 1945 when atom bombs were dropped on Japanese cities.

Further research in nuclear physics since the war has opened up even more ghastly prospects of destruction. While stockpiling of atom bombs has proceeded in both America and Russia, scientists have discovered that much greater energy can be released by forcing the nuclei of heavy hydrogen to combine and thus to form nuclei of helium: hence the hydrogen bomb. Such a bomb is reckoned to be capable of devastating an area of a hundred square miles and destroying all life within it. Besides the immediate destruction that such bombs can cause, there is the further danger of the spread of radio-activity far beyond the area attacked, leaving behind a trail of disease which may be transmitted by parents to their children and thus to future generations. Nor is this genetic peril confined to wartime activity, for it may happen in peace-time as a result of the tests which have to be carried out in connection with each new stock of atom and hydrogen bombs.

There is, fortunately, a brighter side to this dark picture. Simultaneous research is going on in the peaceful uses of atomic energy whose potentialities for the progress of mankind are incalculable. In the United States, for example, there is a powerful trend towards industrial development. In 1953 the American Atomic Energy Commission announced a programme to construct a nuclear power reactor capable of producing 60,000 kilowatts of electrical energy, or even more, and it was hoped that the plant would be in operation within three or four years. In Britain, too, in 1953, an experimental "breeder-reactor" was nearing completion at the new town of Harwell, and another was started in Cumberland, capable eventually of producing enough electricity to serve a town of 50,000 inhabitants. In February 1955 plans were announced for the eventual building of twelve nuclear power stations in Britain. In 1954 the Americans launched the first atom-powered submarine and in 1958 actually navigated one under the North Pole ice cap. In 1954 also Russia claimed to possess the first electrical power-station actually to use atomic energy. In 1954 the United Nations General Assembly approved a plan called "Atoms for Peace", and in 1955 a world conference met in Geneva to explore the whole problem. Since then several other nations have made plans to provide the means of generating atomic energy for industrial purposes.

ADVANCES IN TECHNOLOGY

Among the most creative technological developments stimulated by the Second World War, and greatly advanced since, have been those connected with aeronautics and wireless, and particularly in jet propulsion and radiolocation. As we saw earlier, great progress was made in aviation during and after

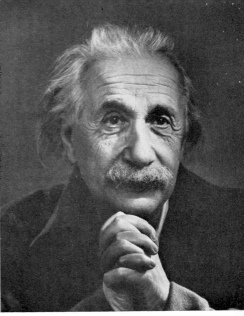

ERNEST (LORD) RUTHERFORD
(1871–1937)
Propounder of a new Atomic Theory which led to
nuclear fission and atomic energy.

ALBERT EINSTEIN
(1879–1955)
Propounder of the theory of Relativity which
revolutionised scientific thought.

BRITAIN'S FIRST ATOMIC POWER STATION
Opened at Calder Hall, Cumberland, by the Queen on October 17, 1956, for the generation of electric power.

ALEXANDER FLEMING (1881-1955)
Physician and bacteriologist and discoverer of penicillin.

MARIE CURIE (1867-1934)
French physicist and discoverer of radium a radio-activity.

FOOD AND HEALTH IN ASIA
A "still" from the United Nations film, *Battle for Bread*, showing young Chinese peasants who have brought their chickens many miles to a government animal health centre (set up under a scheme sponsored by F.A.O.) for free inoculation against the scourge of fowl pest.

the First World War. By the opening of the Second World War the airship had been virtually abandoned in favour of the aeroplane, which had reached a stage hardly foreseen in 1914. The Second World War saw the application of the idea of jet propulsion, which was used by the Germans in their flying-bombs (V1) and rockets (V2), and by the Allies in their anti-aircraft rockets. Jet propulsion, which depends on the principle that "action and reaction are equal and opposite", has greater power, in relation to weight, than the petrol engine, and is more easily maintained. Moreover, as it burns kerosene, there is less risk of fire.

The speed of jet-propelled aircraft leaves the records of petrol-driven planes far behind. By 1948 they reached speeds over short distances of 1,000 miles an hour, thus even passing the speed of sound and achieving what is called super-sonic flight. On August 24, 1955, the English Electric Canberra PR7 twin-jet photo-reconnaissance aircraft flew from London to New York and back in 14 hours 21 minutes 45·4 seconds at an average speed of 481·52 miles an hour. In the same year a Comet III airliner flew from London to Sydney in less than 25 hours. In 1957 three American eight-jet Strato-Fortresses flew non-stop round the world in 45 hours, being refuelled in the air by flying tankers. Such exploits have encouraged an increasing provision of jet air services in various countries, and so helped to spread the habit of flying as a rapid and comfortable means of world travel.

Another interesting post-war aspect of aeronautics was seen in the development of the helicopter, a form of flying with a great future because of the small space required for taking-off and landing. Helicopters were used, for example, by the Americans in the Korean War (1950–3) for carrying stores from rear dumps to the front line, while in 1954 the first helicopter actually to land in London alighted on the South Bank of the Thames at Westminster. Another striking instance of the advance of aeronautics was seen in the inauguration, in November 1954, of the first commercial air service between Europe and North America across the North Polar regions.

Among the most remarkable and beneficial advances in technology during and since the Second World War have been those made in the sphere of wireless. The most important, perhaps, is radiolocation, or radar, as it is more familiarly called from the initials of the phrase, used by the American navy, Radio Detection and Ranging. Radiolocation involves exact calculations based on the time taken by wireless waves to travel between a radio transmitting station and a radar target. By means of the reflection back of wireless waves from solid objects, radar can determine the position, for example, of ships, submarines, buoys and aircraft, as well as coastlines and icebergs. Ships and aircraft can thus find their way through darkness, aeroplanes can be followed through fog and cloud, and warning can be given of their approach. Radar has, therefore, a great part to play in the future in facilitating travel and making it safer. Radar has also a contribution to make to astronomy, meteorology and aerial photography. In fact, it may be said that its potentialities for the service of mankind are as great as those that could arise from the splitting of the atom.

Television is another side of wireless which has advanced enormously since the war. Important though sound broadcasting is, television has more far-reaching possibilities. It is most highly developed in the United States, where, by the middle of 1953, there were no fewer than 397 television stations included in a total of 3,698 broadcasting stations, in operation or under construction. In Britain, while sound broadcasting had been, from its beginnings, the monopoly of the B.B.C., in 1955 an Independent Television Authority was set up to share with the Corporation the service of television. Great developments are expected in television. Already colour television is on the way, and the potentialities of this great medium in helping the education of backward peoples and in improving world intercourse are almost limitless.

Another technological development, but of a different sort, which has moved rapidly in the post-war years, has been in plastics. Plastics are products of chemical reactions which are neither liquid nor crystalline, so called because when heated they are plastic and can be moulded into any desired shape which they retain when cooled. Plastics can be used for the manufacture of innumerable household articles, such as furniture, doors and windows, fibres for clothing, and such things as motor-car bodies. Because of the great variety of uses to which plastics can be put and because they are ideally suited to mass production, they are bound to grow in range and popularity. They are, in fact, being increasingly produced in many countries, but particularly in Germany. The German plastic industry led the world before the war, but in 1947 Western Germany's output of plastics was only 3 per cent. of the world's production. Yet, starting again almost from scratch, by 1955 Western Germany had reached second place among the countries producing plastics.

CHEMISTRY, MEDICINE AND FOOD

The twentieth century has been characterised by a great increase in individual and social health, and this progress has been largely due to the interaction of chemistry and medicine. The field in which the chemist has been of direct help to medicine is in the production of new synthetic drugs. Among these drugs is one called paludrine, which has proved much more effective than quinine in the treatment of malaria. Another is the group called sulphonamide, or sulpha, drugs, the most famous of which is sulpha-pyridine, more familiarly known as M. and B. It was introduced in 1938, and soon all but conquered the disease which had up till then been one of the three major causes of death, namely pneumonia. But sulpha-pyridine has now been largely replaced for the treatment of pneumonia and other diseases by penicillin, the greatest of all modern drugs.

Penicillin was discovered in 1928 by Alexander Fleming while carrying out researches into bacteria culture at St. Mary's Hospital in London. It all arose out of the accidental appearance on a laboratory plate of a common green mould.

From this, after fifteen years of devoted labour, Fleming produced a "substance of unexampled therapeutic power", which was then in urgent demand for controlling sepsis in war wounds. Penicillin was found to be capable of many other uses, particularly in the treatment of anthrax, gangrene, diphtheria and pneumonia. Further researches on moulds led in 1944 to the discovery by an American bacteriologist, named Selman Waksman, of streptomycin, a drug found to be effective in certain infections which had resisted penicillin, and particularly in the treatment of tuberculosis.

One of the most striking examples of the application of science to medicine is the treatment of cancer by radiotherapy, resulting from the discovery of radium in 1898 by the French physicist and chemist Marie Curie and her husband Pierre Curie. Their equally distinguished daughter, Irène, who died in 1956, continued, in association with her husband, Frédéric Joliot, her parents' researches and succeeded in producing artificial radio-activity.

Going with the treatment of disease in its widest sense is the problem of world food production, for under-nourishment and malnutrition are among the major causes of disease. The figures here are frightening. The population of the world increased by about 175 millions between 1937 and 1947. In the first of those years the League of Nations stated that half the world's population suffered from under-nourishment. Apart from the destruction and dislocation caused by the war meanwhile, world population (as we said earlier) is now estimated to be increasing annually by more than 50 millions, so that, as in 1958 it had reached 2,850 millions, by 1980 it is likely to exceed 3,600 millions (as shown in the table on page 22). In 1950 the United Nations Food and Agriculture Organisation prepared a report which showed that less than one-third of the world's food is produced in the Far East, where more than half the population of the world lives. In North America, on the other hand, as the report showed, more than one-fifth of the world's food is grown, although only three-fortieths of the world's population live there.

Here, then, is a highly complicated question. Lord Boyd Orr, a Scottish physician and agricultural scientist, who is the leading expert on the subject, has for some years carried on a vigorous campaign to arouse public opinion to the urgency of the problem set by what he calls "the rising tide of population", on the one hand, and "the falling reservoir of land fertility", on the other hand. It is, he says, the biggest problem facing mankind to-day, because "a civilisation which cannot feed its people is doomed". Some sociologists believe that the problem cannot be solved unless backward peoples learn to limit the size of their families and so to keep the population in check. This becomes increasingly necessary because the spread of Western medical science is progressively lowering the death-rate among the populations of under-developed countries. Many scientists, on the other hand, contend that the problem can be solved by the treatment of the soil with modern fertilisers, the use of up-to-date agricultural implements, and the spread of hygienic methods to cope with disease in human beings, animals and the products of the earth.

Great efforts to help under-developed areas are being made by various agencies under the ægis of the United Nations Social and Economic Council, especially F.A.O., W.H.O. and U.N.E.S.C.O. Further aid is being given by programmes of technical assistance under the Colombo Plan and the American Point Four scheme, as well as by such bodies as the Colonial Development Corporation. But it is not merely a technical question: there are also political and economic aspects of the problem. The various schemes just mentioned are long-term policies, and while they are slowly working themselves out, Communism thrives on the bad social and economic conditions which continue to exist in backward countries. What is needed is a concerted effort on the part of all the better-off communities to assist the worse-off, and this implies an end to political conflict. But, even so, there would still remain the question how those nations with a surplus of implements and foodstuffs are to distribute that surplus to the areas most in need of these goods and services. Ultimately, the answer to that question can be found only through the breaking-down of economic barriers and a new conception of distribution and exchange.

Finally, it is a question of education in backward communities. This is an obvious and immediate need if those communities are to be persuaded to abandon their primitive methods in favour of modern scientific methods of tillage. It is also necessary if hygiene and medicine are to make real progress among backward peoples. But, above all, it demands that there should be a grand attack on the evil of illiteracy, which is most widespread precisely in those regions of the world where the majority live on or below the starvation line, and where there is hence the greatest need for the introduction of modern agricultural techniques.

LITERACY, TRUSTEESHIP AND HUMAN RIGHTS

It is estimated that approximately two-thirds of the people in the world to-day are illiterate. Illiteracy, however, is by no means confined to certain regions. In most countries of Central and Northern Europe—Germany, Switzerland, France, and Britain, the Benelux and Scandinavian states, and Finland—not more than 1 per cent. of the population are totally illiterate. Yet in certain areas of even those countries, the proportion of semi-literates may be as high as 20 per cent. In Southern Europe the proportion of illiterates varies from 25 to 60 per cent., being lowest in Italy and highest in the Balkans. In North America the figures are roughly the same as in Northern Europe. In Latin America the proportion of illiterates varies from 13 per cent. in Argentina to 62 per cent. in Brazil, while the average over all is above 50 per cent.

In Asiatic countries, with the exception of Japan, 80 to 90 per cent. of the population are, on the average, illiterate. In the Pacific Islands illiteracy is not so marked as in most Asiatic countries. After Australia and New Zealand, where the proportion is only about 5 per cent., the most advanced of the islands, from this point of view, is Hawaii with 15 per cent., followed by Guam with 22 per cent. Africa is the most backward continent, if we exclude Egypt, with 10 per cent., and the Union of South Africa, with 12 per cent., the position in the rest of the continent being the exact opposite of that in Northern Europe; that is to say, the average proportion of illiterates is about 99 per cent.

It is only since the Second World War that even the most enlightened nations have begun seriously to tackle the problem of the eradication of illiteracy in colonial territories. In such territories a literacy campaign is a complicated undertaking, involving the careful planning of a long-term policy. Generally the native language exists only as a means of communication by speech. Hence the first task is to reduce it to a written form. Then teachers must be trained and furnished with teaching material, while their students must have reading manuals. In any given locality with a well-organised scheme of instruction and material, it may be possible to make individuals literate in three months. But they can easily lapse from literacy and become illiterate again unless their interest is kept alive by a constant flow of reading matter. In other words, effective literacy campaigns must be highly organised and incessant. Such campaigns have been vigorously pursued in Soviet Russia and Communist China.

The eradication of illiteracy is one of the fundamental problems of our time. While it is important in itself as the means of enlightening unfortunate individual people who have hitherto had no educational opportunities, its social implications are wider and deeper. In 1944 the British Colonial Office issued a memorandum entitled *Mass Education in African Society*, in which illiteracy was described as the primary limiting factor in the development of effective self-governing communities. In other words, here was an acknowledgment of the fact that backward peoples can never learn to govern themselves and to control their economic destiny without the ability to read and write. Since the Second World War the removal of the handicap of illiteracy has become a recognised part of the function of trusteeship for under-developed countries and backward peoples. In fact, the development of literacy is now regarded as an instrument of world peace and prosperity. That it has become an international problem in the widest sense is exemplified in the work of U.N.E.S.C.O., which includes literacy campaigns in its programmes of fundamental education.

The idea that the more advanced nations which still hold colonial territories are trustees for the people living in them was carried much farther after the Second World War than after the First. As we saw, the League of Nations set up a Permanent Mandates Commission, whose business it was to examine the annual reports of those Powers which held a mandate under the League. The Mandatories had no further answerability to the League than to produce such reports. The Charter of the United Nations, however, established the Trusteeship Council as one of its permanent organs. The League's Mandates Commission was a body of experts: the U.N. Trusteeship Council is a body of representatives of member-states. Yet all the political machinery that man can devise will not suffice without a change of attitude towards the backward peoples. It has been proved beyond all question that the so-called coloured people, given educational opportunities, are fully capable of reaching the highest stages of human achievement and are thus potentially the equal of white people. This is the final argument against those who support that form of race prejudice popularly known as the colour bar, which is seen at work, for example, in the social behaviour of some white people in the Southern States of the United States and in the policy of racial segregation (*Apartheid*) pursued by the Government of the Union of South Africa.

In the conviction that all men and women all over the world should have equality of opportunity, the General Assembly of the United Nations in 1948 approved by a large majority the issue of the Declaration of Human Rights. This Declaration contains thirty articles which lay down certain general principles, including the condemnation of slavery and torture, the universal recognition of the right to a fair trial (*Habeas Corpus*), equal pay for equal work, social security, and the freedoms of expression, of religion, of association, and of peaceful assembly. As issued in 1948, the Declaration was in the form of a general draft, and the Assembly appointed a special Commission to work it up into its final shape, a task which was completed in 1951, when it was finally adopted by the Assembly. Each nation signing the Declaration was required to agree "to bring its own laws into line with all its clauses". That, of course, was a distant prospect, but several governments, including the British, have signed the Declaration and in doing so have undertaken to work towards the ideals which it enunciates.

EUROPE, BRITAIN AND THE WORLD

Up to the outbreak of the First World War in 1914 the modern world had been characterised by the growing domination of Europe. From the Age of Discovery at the end of the fifteenth century there had been a gradual process of European expansion. It began with the setting up of trading-stations in the Indies and India in the east, and the colonisation of America in the west. The struggle in the east resulted in the establishment of Britain's Indian Empire. In the west the French power was overthrown; the British colonies achieved their independence and established the United States; the colonies farther north moved towards the creation of the Dominion of Canada; and the Spanish and Portuguese colonies in Central and South America revolted from their European masters and founded the independent republics which now comprise Latin America. But all these areas in America had been peopled mainly by emigrants from Europe, who thus diffused European culture in those lands.

As the outcome of the Industrial Revolution a new wave of European imperialism spread across the world. The nations of Europe, in search of world markets, established control over undeveloped areas in Africa and in Far Eastern Asia. So it remained until 1914. Europe never truly recovered from the First World War. Between the wars there appeared disturbing signs that European expansion had passed its zenith. The new situation thus foreshadowed clearly emerged after the second war. The nations of Western and Central Europe which had carried their trade, capital, military power, technical skill and culture to the ends of the earth now found themselves impoverished, their assets abroad largely liquidated, and their overseas possessions seething with demands for independence.

After the Second World War the European states which had enjoyed this period of world domination themselves became subject to the ascendancy of two super-World Powers: the United States and Soviet Russia, the one transatlantic and the other largely Asiatic. Yet it is hard to believe that the contribution which Europe has made to the progress of the world will not continue to be fruitful, even though Europe's power has permanently declined. The diverse culture of the European nations, their creative experience in politics and law, their scientific and technological genius, and their medical skill—all these have left an indelible mark on the character of contemporary communities in every continent, and not least in America, whose way of life, after all, has its roots in Europe.

And where does Britain stand in this new situation? No nation has given to the peoples of the world more valuable lessons in the art of self-government, in the virtue of social discipline, in the development of justice and the rule of law, in the application of science to technology, and in the shaping of language to the production of great literature. The imperial and material power which Britain for so long enjoyed has gone beyond recall, but the formative influences of her world achievements remain to help to mould the world of the future. Moreover, the quality, above all, which the British people have displayed in the course of their island and imperial story is the ability to adapt themselves to changing circumstances. If they prove themselves capable of continuing to exercise that quality, their moral influence on world affairs can be as great in the future as their material influence has been in the past.

The contemporary world, as we have seen earlier, has built upon the Classical and Christian foundations of Western Civilisation a monstrous technological superstructure. We have now reached a stage where, if a halt is not called to war, science, as the mother of technology, will destroy civilised society. So mankind is presented with the alternatives of blundering to its own extinction or turning the destructive forces let loose for the objects of war to the constructive purposes of peace. The choice is a real one because most scientific advances, although stimulated by war, have immense potentialities for human progress and happiness. Indeed, modern technology, while making war progressively more destructive, creates, by its very universality, the possibility of a world citizenship which, if realised, would end armed international strife.

In the event of a new world war in this atomic age, Britain, for reasons manifestly beyond her control, would inevitably be among the first countries to suffer irreparable disaster. But if, in the confrontation of the two great world Powers, that misfortune can be avoided, Britain and the British Commonwealth have a great part to play in the creation of a true world citizenship which would at length outlaw war for ever. Meanwhile, as the nations move uneasily into the second half of the twentieth century, they find themselves, no less than before, in an epoch of ferment and change. But there is still hope that, although the ferment and change must necessarily continue as the very condition of life itself, reason will prevail and the two parts into which the contemporary world is divided may find the means of "peaceful co-existence".

A. SUMMARY OF PART THREE

Chapter 19. The general framework of the United Nations Organisation having been laid down at Dumbarton Oaks (1944) and approved at Yalta (February 1945), the representatives of 51 nations (including Poland a little later) signed the Charter at San Francisco (June 1945). By 1950 the membership had grown to 60; in 1960 it totalled 99. The basic purposes of the Organisation are "to maintain international peace and security" and "to achieve international co-operation in the treatment of economic, social, cultural and humanitarian questions". It has six organs: the General Assembly, the Security Council, the Economic and Social Council, the Trusteeship Council, the International Court of Justice, and the Secretariat of permanent officers. There are several U.N. Specialised Agencies, including U.N.E.S.C.O., F.A.O. and W.H.O. The early work of the United Nations, whose organisation allowed for regional agreements, was made difficult by the growing differences between the Communist and non-Communist parts of the world and by the Russian exercise of the Veto in the Security Council.

Chapter 20. After the war Germany was divided into four occupation zones (British, American, French and Russian) and Berlin into four sectors; Austria and Vienna being similarly divided. The main purposes of the occupation were to disarm and demilitarise the Germans and prepare them for the reconstruction of their life on a democratic basis. Japan was deprived of all territories gained since 1895 and placed under the control of an eleven-Power Committee, in which the Americans took the lead. War Criminals were tried and punished. Treaties were concluded for Italy, Rumania, Bulgaria, Hungary and Finland, involving redistribution of territory, limitation of armed forces, payment of reparations, and destruction of Fascism and Nazism. The Austrian Treaty, however, was not signed until 1955. In France the Fourth Republic was established (1946); in Italy the Monarchy was replaced by a Republic (1947); in Norway, The Netherlands and Belgium the royal families were restored. Western Europe ceased to be the centre of power in the world, which was now dominated by the U.S.A., controlling the West, and the U.S.S.R., controlling the East through its satellites. The Russians dropped an Iron Curtain, and the Cold War developed between the two parts into which the world was divided.

Chapter 21. In 1945 the Labour Party was returned with an absolute majority and Attlee succeeded Churchill as Prime Minister. Labour's "Five-year Plan" involved a policy of full employment, extension of social security, and nationalisation. Following the main lines of the Beveridge Report (1942), Parliament passed the Children's Allowances Act (1945), the National Insurance Act (1946), and the National Health Service Act (1948). Fuel, power and transport were nationalised : coal (1946), electricity (1947) and gas (1948); civil aviation (1946); railways and most other forms of inland transport (1947). An Act to nationalise iron and steel, and the road haulage sections of the Transport Act, were repealed in 1951 after the Conservatives had returned to power. The Labour Government also nationalised the Bank of England (1946), repealed the Trade Disputes Act of 1927, and amended the Parliament Act of 1911 so as to reduce the period of the Lords' suspensive veto to one year (1949). They also raised the school-leaving age to 15 (1947). Since the war many other states have introduced similar legislation tending towards the creation of the Welfare State.

Chapter 22. After the Second World War there was a colonial revolution which involved the liquidation of most of Europe's imperial enterprises in Asia. The British left India, which, by the Indian Independence Act (1947), was partitioned to form the Self-governing Dominions of India and Pakistan, both of which have since become independent republics, although remaining attached to the British Commonwealth. Ceylon became a Self-governing Dominion, and Burma an independent republic, in 1948. In Malaya the achievement of full self-government was retarded by the spread of Communism. France and The Netherlands have similarly retreated from Asia and recognised independent native governments in Indo-China and Indonesia. Interesting movements of self-government in British territories overseas included the institution of the Federation of Rhodesia and Nyasaland (1954), the Sudanese Republic (1956), the independent state of Ghana (1957), and the Federation of the British West Indies (1958).

333

Several schemes of aid towards the economic and social development of all these peoples were envisaged in the British Colonial Development and Welfare Acts, and in the still wider scope of the Colombo Plan, projected in 1950.

Chapter 23. After the war, anti-British feeling became intense in Egypt and Persia. In 1953 the Egyptians established a republic, and in 1954 the British agreed to evacuate the Suez Canal Zone in twenty months. The decision to use Cyprus as an alternative base led to trouble with Cypriot nationalists. In Persia the government nationalised the oil industry in 1951 and took possession of the installations of the Anglo-Iranian Oil Company. But the consequent economic distress forced a compromise in 1954, when the Company's rights were partially restored. Saudi Arabia, Iraq, Lebanon, Jordan, Egypt, Syria and Yemen, Sudan, Libya, Morocco and Tunisia make up the Arab League, whose main bond is a common hostility to the Jewish State of Israel, founded in 1948. The most stable state in the Middle East after the war was Turkey, where, in 1950, the dictatorship voluntarily surrendered its powers after the electoral defeat of the party founded by Kemal Ataturk.

Chapter 24. The Second World War offered Soviet Russia a new opportunity to extend the Communist influence in both Europe and Asia. The Baltic States, East Prussia, Ruthenia, eastern Poland, and parts of Finland and Rumania were incorporated in the Soviet Union. Also Russia set up, or sponsored, Communist régimes in Poland, Czechoslovakia, Hungary, Rumania, Bulgaria and Albania, as well as in the Russian-occupied Zone of East Germany, and, though in a modified form, in Yugoslavia. In Asia, Russia supported Communist revolutions in North Korea, Outer Mongolia and China. As a result of all these movements, the Communist World to-day covers about a quarter of the area of the globe and comprises about a third of the world's total population. Of the Communist states in Europe, only Yugoslavia, under Tito, has shown any real independence of Moscow dominance. In France and Italy there are Russian-inspired Communist parties of considerable strength in Parliament. The constitution of the People's Republic of China, promulgated by the Communist leader, Mao Tse-tung, in 1949, was largely modelled on that of Soviet Russia.

Chapter 25. In the United States in 1947 President Truman appointed as his Secretary of State George Marshall, who developed the idea of financially helping the economic recovery of European nations. Hence, in 1948, Marshall Aid was granted to sixteen European states, which set up in Paris a permanent Organisation for European Economic Recovery (O.E.E.C.), and, in order to stimulate European exports to America, the pound sterling and other currencies were devalued in relation to the dollar. The Russian reaction to the Marshall Plan was to intensify Communist propaganda everywhere; hence the Communist *coup d'état* in Czechoslovakia in 1948, the conclusion of the Treaty of Brussels between Britain, France and the Benelux countries, and the beginning of American rearmament. At the same time, pursuing its "good neighbour" policy, the United States formed with 20 Latin-American Republics the Organisation of American States (1948).In April 1948 the Russians had declared a Berlin blockade, which, however, they were forced to abandon in May 1949 by the success of the Western Powers' "Air Lift". In 1949, too, the North Atlantic Treaty Organisation (N.A.T.O.) was established by the United States and several Western European states, which were later joined by others. Thus the rearmament of Western Europe seriously began, while Russia's attitude encouraged in the U.S.A. the growth of a strong anti-Communist reaction which led in 1954 to the passing of an Act of Congress outlawing the Communist Party in America.

Chapter 26. In 1945 Korea, taken from Japan, was divided along the 38th Parallel, Russian forces occupying the North and American the South. In 1948 a republican constitution was approved in the South and a People's Soviet in the North, and both the Russians and the Americans withdrew. When the North Koreans invaded the South in 1950, the United Nations denounced them as aggressors, and various contingents, mostly American, expelled them. Communist China sent help to the North Koreans, who reinvaded the South. In 1953 an armistice was finally signed. Stalin's death (1953) did not essentially change Soviet policy. In Germany, where the Russians established a German Democratic Republic on the Soviet model in the east and the Western Powers approved a parliamentary Federal Republic in the west, the division remained acute. In 1955 the Paris Agreements for the rearming of Western Germany, within the scheme of Western European defence, were ratified, and Russia took counter steps for the rearming of Eastern Germany, so that the reunification of the country seemed as far off as ever. Nor did the four-Power Geneva Conference in 1955 fundamentally change the situation.

Chapter 27. The twentieth century has been remarkable for scientific progress. Einstein's theory of Relativity (1916) has profoundly affected scientific thought, and Rutherford's atomic theory (1911) has led to nuclear fission and the development of atomic energy for both war and peace. Technological developments include jet-propelled aircraft, radiolocation (radar), plastics and television. Health has been vastly improved through the interaction of chemistry and medicine and the production of such drugs as penicillin and streptomycin. The spread of Western medical science is progressively lowering the death-rate in under-developed communities, and this makes more acute the problem of world food supply in relation to world population. This problem raises questions of education in the widest sense, involving not only the permanent conquest of illiteracy but growing respect for the dignity of under-developed peoples, as laid down by the United Nations in the Declaration of Human Rights. The triumphs of modern science threaten the existence of civilised society, so that the choice for mankind is between peace and extinction. But, if peace is to be maintained, the two parts into which the contemporary world is divided must find the means of "peaceful co-existence".

B. FURTHER STUDY

1. IMPORTANT WORDS

Amalgamation, bacteria, *bloc*, cadre, centralisation, coercion, commandant, commitment, confiscation, culture, decree, devaluation, distribution, fertility, function, helicopter, hygiene, illiteracy, implication, installation, limbo, metaphysics, meteorology, monopoly, orbit, pamphlet, panacea, plastics, plunder, preamble, prejudice, prerequisite, priority, radioactivity, radiolocation, ratification, recrudescence, relativity, repeal, repression, satellite, scrutiny, sector, sepsis, sociology, sovereignty, sterling, stratagem, supremacy, technique, therapeutics, tillage, trusteeship, usage, vicissitude, visa, zone.

2. IMPORTANT TECHNICAL TERMS

Arab League, atomic energy, "Atoms for Peace", Benelux, Beveridge Report, bi-partisan policy, Bizone, children's allowances, civil aviation, Cold War, Colombo Plan, Commonwealth Relations, Congress Party, Control Commission, Crown Colony, draft treaty, death-rate, Electoral College, Electoral Commission, Fabian Society, Fair Deal, "fellow traveller", full employment, *Habeas Corpus*, Human Rights, Iron Curtain, jet propulsion, *Knesset* Israel, *Kommandatura*, Local Authorities, McCarthyism, *Majlis*, Marketing Board, Marshall Aid, Mau Mau, means test, the "Melting-pot", Moslem League, National Assistance Board, National Health Service, National Insurance, nuclear fission, Occupying Powers, People's Republic, Point Four Programme, Red China, running-mate, Schuman Plan, sphere of influence, spy ring, stock-piling, Suez Canal Zone, synthetic drugs, Taft-Hartley Act, 38th Parallel, Viet Minh, Viet Nam, Welfare State, Western Union.

3. IMPORTANT PERSONS

Adenauer, Attlee, Bao Dai, Baudouin (King of Belgium), Beria, Beveridge, Bulganin, Butler, Curie (Marie, Pierre and Irène), de Gasperi, Dewey, Dimitrov, Einstein, Farouk, Fleming, Gottwald, Inönü, Jinnah, Joliot, Krushchev, Lie (Trygve), Liaquat Ali Khan, MacArthur, McCarthy, Malenkov, Mao Tse-tung, Marshall, Masaryk (Jan), Michael (King of Rumania), Michailovich, Mountbatten (Lord), Mussadiq, Nasser, Neguib, Nehru, Nenni, Orr (Boyd), Perón, Reza Khan, Ridgway, Rutherford, Schuman, Simeon II (of Bulgaria), Syngman Rhee, Tito, Truman, Waksman.

4. IMPORTANT DEVELOPMENTS

Emergence and organisation of the United Nations; occupation of Germany, Austria and Japan, and growth of mistrust, leading to the Cold War; post-war Labour policy and the Welfare State in Britain; educational progress in Britain through the Education Act of 1944; the Colonial Revolution and the retreat from Asia: causes, course and consequences; nationalist movements in Egypt, Persia and the Middle East; rise and importance of the Arab League; extension of Communism in Europe and Asia; Marshall Aid: its inception and results; the formation of N.A.T.O.; the United Nations and the war in Korea; anti-Communist reaction in America: influence of McCarthyism; emergence of the two republics in Germany; rearming of Germany and Western defence; de Gaulle and the Fifth Republic; the Geneva Conference of 1955; scientific and technological progress; food and world population; the Declaration of Human Rights; world citizenship; the prospects of "peaceful co-existence".

3. NOTES ON SPECIAL POINTS

(a) *Commonwealth Relations Office*

In modern Britain there have emerged a number of different Secretaryships of State (e.g. for Home and for Foreign Affairs, and for Air), as the sphere of government activities has enlarged. One such office was that of Secretary of State for the Colonies, created in 1854. In 1858, on the abolition of the East India Company, a Secretary of State for India was appointed. With the growth of the distinction between Self-governing Dominions and Colonies, the functions of the Colonial Secretary were divided in 1925, when a separate Secretary of State for Dominion Affairs was appointed. In 1947 the title of this office was changed to Commonwealth Relations. In the same year, when the Self-governing Dominions of India and Pakistan were created, the office of Secretary of State for India was abolished and any minor functions that remained were transferred to the Commonwealth Relations Office. So now there are two Secretaries of State dealing with these affairs, namely the Secretary for Commonwealth Relations and the Secretary for Colonial Affairs.

(b) *The Comintern as the Third International*

Karl Marx organised an International Labour Association which held its first meeting in London in 1864. This became known as the First International, but it failed to live up to Marx's hope that the workers of the world would unite, and by 1876 it had faded out of existence. In 1889, after Marx's death, the International was revived. But this Second International, as it was called, was nothing more than a series of meetings of delegates of the Socialist parties of various countries who spent their time passing "pious resolutions" without achieving any practical results. So, like its predecessor, the Second International faded away. When the Russians organised the Comintern in 1919, it became known as the Third International. That, too, as shown in the text, ceased (during the Second World War), but was revived, under the name of the Cominform, as a counterblast to the proposed Marshall Plan, in 1947.

(c) *The Atom and Peace*

In the summer of 1955, as stated on page 320, shortly after the political heads of the four Powers had opened the conference at Geneva, meetings of scientists from various countries took place in the same city to discuss the peaceful uses of atomic energy. The discussions covered every conceivable use of atomic power, from technology to medicine, and indicated a determination on the part of scientists to turn this great scientific discovery to the constructive purposes of mankind. Shortly before these meetings began in Geneva, a group of celebrated scientists of various nationalities issued a statement (the signatories including Einstein, who signed it just before his death) urging all governments "to find peaceful means for the settlement of all matters of dispute between them", so that atomic energy may be used for peace instead of war.

6. READING AND REFERENCE

(a) *The Post-War International Situation.*—Cole: *The Intelligent Man's Guide to the Post-War World*; Hampden-Jackson: *The Post-War Decade*; Chester Wilmot: *The Struggle for Europe*; Gunther: *Inside Europe*; Warrener: *Revolution in Eastern Europe*; Seton-Watson: *Eastern European Revolution* and *History of the Cold War*; Lloyd: *Democracy and its Rivals*; Boyd: (i) *United Nations Handbook*, (ii) *What is N.A.T.O.?*, (iii) *An Atlas of World Affairs*; H.M. Stationery Office: *The United Nations at Work*; Besterman: *U.N.E.S.C.O.*; Elspeth Huxley: *What are Trustee Nations?*

(b) *British Society and Politics.*—Newman: *English Social Services*; H.M. Stationery Office: *Britain and The British Way and Purpose Series*; Williams: *Fifty Years' March*; Quintin Hogg (Lord Hailsham): *The Case for Conservatism*; Watkins: *The Cautious Revolution*; Mackenzie: *British Political Parties*.

(c) *America.*—Smellie: *Our Two Democracies at Work*; Whitney: *Who are the Americans?*; Gunther: *Inside U.S.A.* and *Inside Latin America*; Strong: *Story of the American People*.

(d) *The Colonial Revolution.*—Hodson: *Twentieth Century Empire*; Griffiths: *The British Achievement in India*; Nehru: *The Discovery of India*; Mellor: *India since Partition*; Spear: *India, Pakistan and the West*; Walker: *Colonies*; Crocker: *Self-government for the Colonies*; Horrabin: *Atlas of Empire*.

(e) *Asia.*—(i) *The Middle East*: Antonius: *The Arab Awakening*;

Atiyah: *The Arabs* (Pelican); (ii) *The Far East*: Fitzgerald: *China*; Davidson: *Daybreak in China*; Snow: *Red Star over China*; Keeton: *China, the Far East and the Future*; Thompson: *Cry Korea.*

(f) *Africa.*—Davidson: *African Awakening*; Gorer: *Africa Dances*; Gunther: *Inside Africa.*

(g) *Food and Population.*—Boyd Orr: *Food and the People* and *The White Man's Dilemma*; Gray: *The Problem of World Poverty.*

(h) *Science and Technology.*—Sherwood Taylor: *A Century of Science* and *An Illustrated History of Science* (1955); Pringle: *Great Discoveries in Modern Science*; Crowther: *British Scientists of the Twentieth Century* and *Discoveries and Inventions of the Twentieth Century*; Gartmann: *Science as History* (1960); Palmer and Penney: *Aircraft*; Mumford: *Technics and Civilisation.*

(i) *Periodical Literature.*—*The Times Fifty Years*; Guest: *News in our Time* (1896–1946); *The Annual Register* (an account of events year by year in all countries, published in the summer of each year to cover the story of the previous year); *Yearbook of The United Nations*; *The Statesman's Yearbook, Whitaker's Almanack,* and *Keesing's Contemporary Archives* (for current affairs). For recent history the supplementary volumes to *Chambers's Encyclopædia,* now issued annually under the title of *World Survey,* will be found most helpful, while many broadcasts published weekly in *The Listener* throw much light, not otherwise available, on vital contemporary questions.

C. TOPICS FOR ESSAYS AND DISCUSSIONS

1. Describe a meeting of the General Assembly or of the Security Council of the United Nations as if you were one of the delegates.

2. Explain how Germany and Austria were divided for purposes of occupation among the victorious Powers at the end of the war, illustrating your answer with a map.

3. What do you understand by the terms Iron Curtain and Cold War? How far do they help us to comprehend the post-war situation in Europe and the world?

4. Give some account of the measures taken by the Labour Party between 1945 and 1951 to carry out their policy of social security and nationalisation. Do you consider it correct to say that they established the Welfare State?

5. Describe the effects of Europe's retreat from Asia after the Second World War. Do you think the changes that have resulted justify the description Colonial Revolution?

6. Write an account of the nationalisation of the oil industry in Persia in 1951, and of the Suez Canal by Egypt in 1956, as if you were a British member of the staff displaced.

7. Show how Communism has spread since the end of the Second World War. Draw a map marking the boundaries of the countries affected.

8. What is the distinction between Communist and Nationalist China? Describe the steps by which the Communist movement triumphed.

9. What was the Marshall Plan and how did it work?

10. Explain the causes of the Korean War (1950–3) and its world significance.

11. What is N.A.T.O.? Explain the circumstances in which it emerged and the way in which Western Germany has become involved in it. Describe also Russia's reaction to it.

12. Give some account of the advances in science and technology in the first half of the twentieth century.

13. Debate the following propositions:

(a) That the United Nations Organisation marks a great advance on the League of Nations as an instrument of collective security.

(b) That the Welfare State is essential to the growth of a true social democracy.

(c) That the European retreat from Asia was inevitable.

(d) That the Arab League is necessary to the peace of the Middle East.

(e) That the Atlantic Community (of Western Europe and America) is the logical outcome of the history of the last three centuries.

(f) That China can never become a Russian satellite.

(g) That the restoration of German unity is necessary to the peace of the world.

(h) That only the moral force of mankind can save civilised society from destruction by atomic power.

CHRONOLOGICAL TABLE
OF PRINCIPAL EVENTS MENTIONED
IN THE TEXT

(*Note*: The events named against each year are given in the following order: Britain, British Commonwealth and Empire, Continental Europe, America, other parts of the world, and Science and Technology.)

1901   Death of Queen Victoria. Commonwealth of Australia inaugurated. T. Roosevelt President of U.S.A. First transatlantic wireless message.

1902   Education Act. Treaty of Vereeniging. Anglo-Japanese Alliance.

1903   Joseph Chamberlain opens Tariff Reform campaign. Wright Brothers' pioneer aeroplane flights in U.S.A.

1904   *Entente Cordiale*. Outbreak of Russo-Japanese War.

1905   Liberal Cabinet formed. Independence of Norway. First Moroccan Crisis. Treaty of Portsmouth.

1906   Liberal victory at General Election. First *Dreadnought* launched. First Russian *Duma* meets.

1907   Triple Entente. Second Hague Conference.

1908   Old Age Pensions. Young Turk revolt. Austria-Hungary annexes Bosnia-Herzegovina.

1909   Lloyd George's Budget. Poor Law Report. Blériot's cross-Channel flight.

1910   Death of Edward VII and accession of George V. Union of South Africa inaugurated. Japan annexes Korea.

1911   Parliament Act. National Insurance Act. Third Moroccan Crisis. Rutherford's Atomic Theory.

1912   Third Home Rule Bill passes Commons. First Balkan War.

1913   Second Balkan War. Treaty of Bucharest.

1914   Outbreak of First World War. Panama Canal completed.

1915   Asquith's Coalition Cabinet. Italy joins Allies. Germans sink *Lusitania*, with American civilians on board.

1916   Lloyd George Prime Minister. Irish Rebellion. Einstein's General Theory of Relativity propounded.

1917   Report on Government of India. Unrestricted U-boat warfare: U.S.A. declares war on Germany. Bolshevik Revolution.

1918   Women enfranchised. Education Act. Treaty of Brest-Litovsk. German offensives in West. Foch supreme Allied Commander. Armistice.

1919   Sankey Coal Commission. Dyarchy in India: Gandhi's "civil disobedience" campaign. Paris Peace Conference. Treaty of Versailles. Weimar Republic established. Mussolini founds Fascist movement. First transatlantic flight.

1920   Southern Irish reject partition. League of Nations established. Hitler founds Nazi Party. Prohibition and Woman Suffrage in U.S.A.

1921   Truce in Ireland. Washington Naval Conference.

1922   Irish Free State founded. Mussolini's March on Rome.

1923   French occupy Ruhr. Union of Soviet Socialist Republics (U.S.S.R.) constituted. Treaty of Lausanne. Turkish Republic established. Failure of Nazi *Putsch* at Munich.

342

CHRONOLOGICAL TABLE OF PRINCIPAL EVENTS

1924 First Labour Government. Death of Lenin and succession of Stalin. Dawes Plan for Reparations adopted.

1925 Pact of Locarno. Death of Sun Yat-sen and succession of Chiang Kai-shek to leadership of Kuomintang in China. Marconi's Beam Service installed.

1926 General Strike. Imperial Conference declares Dominions "autonomous communities". Germany admitted to League of Nations.

1927 Trade Disputes Act. B.B.C. incorporated. Transatlantic Wireless Telephone Service installed. Lindbergh's solo New York-Paris flight.

1928 Briand-Kellogg Pact. Stalin's first Five-Year Plan launched. Chiang captures Peking. Alexander Fleming discovers Penicillin.

1929 Second Labour Government. Dollfuss Chancellor of Austria. Depression in U.S.A. Admiral Byrd's flight to South Pole.

1930 Simon Report on India published. Last Allied troops withdrawn from Germany. Spread of depression through Europe.

1931 Ramsay MacDonald forms National Government. Statute of Westminster. Spanish Republic proclaimed.

1932 Ottawa Conference: Imperial Preference. Disarmament Conference convened at Geneva. Stalin's second Five-Year Plan announced. F. D. Roosevelt elected President of U.S.A. Japanese dominate Manchuria (Manchukuo).

1933 Hitler becomes Chancellor. Germany and Japan withdraw from League of Nations. New Deal in U.S.A. Wiley Post's solo flight round the world.

1934 Disarmament Conference breaks down. Hitler abolishes federalism and the Presidency (on death of Hindenburg) and "purges" Nazi Party. Murder of Dollfuss. U.S.S.R. admitted to League of Nations.

1935 Government of India Act. Saar restored to Germany. Hitler openly revives conscription. Stresa Front. Italian invasion of Abyssinia. League of Nations applies economic sanctions against Italy.

1936 Death of George V. Accession and abdication of Edward VIII. Accession of George VI. Germans reoccupy Rhineland. Germany and Japan sign Anti-Comintern Pact. Italy annexes Abyssinia. Outbreak of Spanish Civil War. Stalin's new constitution of U.S.S.R. Roosevelt re-elected.

1937 Italy withdraws from League of Nations and signs Anti-Comintern Pact. Renewal of Japanese aggression in China.

1938 Hitler annexes Austria. Munich Agreement: Sudetenland transferred to Germany. Death of Kemal Ataturk.

1939 Dismemberment of Czechoslovakia. Mussolini occupies Albania. End of Spanish Civil War and establishment of Franco's dictatorship throughout Spain. Russo-German Non-aggression Pact. German invasion of Poland. Outbreak of Second World War. Partition of Poland between Germany and Russia. The "Phoney War."

1940 Churchill becomes Prime Minister (May). German invasion of Denmark and Norway. Attack on the West. Italy declares war on Germany's side. Evacuation at Dunkirk. Fall of France. Battle of Britain. North African campaign. American Lend-Lease proposed. Roosevelt elected for third term.

1941 Hitler dominates Balkans. German invasion of Russia. Atlantic Charter. Japanese attack on Pearl Harbour: U.S.A. at war.

1942 Battle of El Alamein. Anglo-American landings in North Africa. Russian counter-offensive begins at Stalingrad. Rapid progress of Japanese conquests in Pacific and South-east Asia.

CHRONOLOGICAL TABLE OF PRINCIPAL EVENTS

1943   Casablanca Conference: Eisenhower made Supreme Commander of Anglo-American forces in the West. Africa cleared. Conquest of Sicily. Fall of Mussolini. Italian armistice with Allies. Allied invasion of Italian mainland.

1944   Rome liberated. Allied landings in France (D day). Liberation of Paris and Allied advance into Belgium and Netherlands. Russian westward advance. Beginnings of British and American success against the Japanese. Roosevelt elected for fourth term. Waksman discovers streptomycin.

1945   Labour win General Election and form Government (July). Yalta Conference (February). Hitler's suicide. German unconditional surrender (May). Potsdam Conference opens (July). Death of Roosevelt: Truman President (April). United Nations Charter signed at San Francisco (June). Atom bombs dropped on Hiroshima and Nagasaki. Japanese unconditional surrender (August).

1946   Cabinet Mission to India. First meetings of U.N. General Assembly and Security Council. Fourth French Republic constituted. People's Republics established in Yugoslavia and Poland.

1947   Indian Independence Act. Italy becomes a Republic. Peace treaties signed for Italy, Hungary, Finland, and the Balkan States. People's Republics established in Rumania and Hungary. Cominform organised. Marshall appointed American Secretary of State.

1948   Ceylon becomes a Self-governing Dominion, and Burma an independent Republic. Federation of Malaya established. Communist *coup d'état* in Czechoslovakia. Treaty of Brussels. State of Israel established. Berlin blockade and "Air lift". Truman wins Presidential election in U.S.A. Marshall Aid approved.

1949   Parliament Act. Republic of Ireland recognised. N.A.T.O. set up. Russians abandon blockade of Berlin. Establishment of West German Federal Republic and East German Democratic Republic. Independence of Viet Nam (Indo-China) and Indonesia recognised. Chinese People's Republic established.

1950   India becomes a Republic. Outbreak of war in Korea.

1951   Conservatives returned to power. Nationalisation of the Persian oil industry. U.N. Assembly adopts Declaration of Human Rights.

1952   Death of George VI and accession of Elizabeth II. Outbreak of Mau Mau terrorism in Kenya. European Coal and Steel Community created. Eisenhower elected President of U.S.A.

1953   A Caribbean Federation proposed. Death of Stalin. Republic replaces monarchy in Egypt. U.S.A. agreement for naval and air bases in Spain. Armistice in Korea.

1954   British agree to evacuate Suez Canal Zone. First Sudanese Parliament opened. Federations formed in Rhodesia and Nigeria. Agreements reached for the rearming of Western Germany. Communist Party banned in U.S.A. Armistice in Viet Nam. "Atoms for Peace" plan approved by U.N. General Assembly.

1955   Eden succeeds Churchill as Premier. Independent Television Authority set up. Austrian sovereignty restored. Paris Agreements ratified: German Federal Republic a member of N.A.T.O. and a sovereign state. Warsaw Treaty of aid between Russia and satellites. Four-Power Conference at Geneva fails to reach agreement. International Conference of scientists discusses atomic energy. First transatlantic telephone laid. Record flights included London–New York and back in 15 hours, and London–Sydney in 24 hours.

CHRONOLOGICAL TABLE OF PRINCIPAL EVENTS

1956 Islamic Republic of Pakistan established. Sudan becomes independent republic. Suez Canal Crisis. Hungarian revolt. Eisenhower re-elected. Atomic Power Station opened at Calder Hall, Cumberland.

1957 Macmillan succeeds Eden as Prime Minister. Ghana (Gold Coast) made independent. Russian space satellite (Sputnik) launched. American jet Strato-Fortresses fly non-stop round world in 45 hours.

1958 First women members (life peeresses) of House of Lords. Federation of British West Indies established. De Gaulle recalled to power in France. United Arab Republic (Egypt, Syria, Yemen) formed. American atom-powered submarine navigated under North Pole ice cap.

1959 General Election: Conservatives returned with large majority. Great St. Lawrence Seaway (linking Atlantic and Great Lakes) opened. De Gaulle installed as first President of Fifth French Republic. Admission of Alaska as 49th, and of Hawaii as 50th, State of U.S.A. Mao Tse-tung resigns as Chairman of Chinese People's Republic, but retains chairmanship of Communist Party. First atom-powered passenger ship, the *Savannah*, launched in U.S.A. Soviet rocket reaches the Moon.

1960 British Somaliland declared independent: joins with Somalia to form Somali Republic. Independent Republic of Cyprus established. Publication of Monkton Report on working of Central African Federation, followed by London Conference of representatives of parties involved. Independence of Federation of Nigeria proclaimed. Referendum held in South Africa shows majority in favour of Republic. Abortive attempt at "Summit" meeting in Paris. Belgian Congo becomes independent: entry of United Nations force to prevent further civil disorder. John F. Kennedy, the Democratic candidate, elected President of the United States to succeed President Eisenhower. Britain's first nuclear-powered submarine, *Dreadnought*, launched.

INDEX

Note: The attention of the reader is again called, as on page 9, to the fact that, in the following Index, whenever a subject is illustrated, the number of the page facing which the picture appears is printed in heavy type. When a picture facing a page is referred to, the letter f. in brackets follows the number of the page; e.g. Roosevelt, F. D., **176** (f.).